Publications

of

The Colonial Society of Massachusetts

VOLUME LXX

New England
Silver & Silversmithing
1620–1815

EDITED BY

Jeannine Falino & Gerald W. R. Ward

BOSTON

The Colonial Society of Massachusetts

Distributed by the University Press of Virginia

2001

The Riddell family coat of arms illustrated on the title page is engraved on a silver punch bowl (see page xiii) made by John Coney (1655/56–1722) of Boston, Massachusetts, ca. 1708–9 (Museum of Fine Arts, Boston, Theodora Wilbour Fund in memory of Charlotte Beebe Wilbour; 1972.913).

Contents

Regional Topics

Foreword

OVER A DECADE AGO the idea of a conference on New England silver, to be cosponsored by the Colonial Society of Massachusetts and the Museum of Fine Arts, Boston, was a mere gleam in the eye of the Society's treasurer, Frederick D. Ballou, an avid collector of silver in a variety of senses. Many qualities combine to make Ballou the ideal treasurer for a Boston non-profit institution: a paragon of Yankee thrift, as his battered briefcase (held together by odd bits of string and bailing wire) attests, Ballou is genial and open-handed when it comes to spending money for the Society's stated purposes. Amiable and good-humored, he might be, but Ballou is also persistent, and not many a meeting of the Colonial Society's Council would pass without Ballou sideling up next to me and asking about the possibilities for a conference on colonial New England silver.

The laws of physics as applied to human relations dictate that those who persevere long enough eventually succeed in transmitting their preoccupations to someone else. Thus, I began to ask the same question of Jonathan Fairbanks, at that time head of American Decorative Arts and Sculpture at the Museum of Fine Arts, Boston. These requests became so frequent that I began to imagine that Fairbanks was actually sprinting away from me each time he saw me across a crowded gathering. Whenever I would succeed in catching hold of Jonathan's coattails, he would kindly promise to consult the Museum's Higher Authorities, and each time the message would return that the auguries were not yet right for such an event. Sometime around 1994, Fairbanks, worn down by all my pleading, surrendered and observed that since the Museum would be exhibiting the recently acquired Firestone Collection of pre-Revolutionary French silver in the spring of 1996, perhaps that would be a good time for a conference!

Now it only remained to find suitable editors for the volume of conference proceedings that would eventually transpire. Fairbanks himself had edited a similar volume for the Colonial Society on Boston furniture, and although it remains the Society's all-time best seller, he well knew the headaches involved. We could not have been more fortunate in the two members of the Department of American Decorative Arts who then stepped forward to assume the task: Jeannine Falino and Gerald W. R. Ward. Falino combined great tact and organizational ability with tenacity and the necessary attention to detail, and Ward was well known for the style and wit of his essays on similar subjects and for editing many books, catalogues, and conference reports.

William M. Fowler, Jr., and Linda Smith Rhoads, at that time the Colonial Society's President and Chair of the Publications Committee respectively, stepped in to help with the delicate negotiations that are inevitable when two non-profit organizations cooperate and each is equally convinced that it ought not to spend more than a fair share of its precious resources for their joint endeavors. Falino, ably assisted by Jane Port and the dedicated American Decorative Arts staff, saw to it that the conference progressed smoothly and elegantly. April 19 and 20, 1996, were also red letter days in the history of the Colonial Society, because although we had sponsored many scholarly conferences before, this one, thanks to the generous support of the Lowell Institute, was the first ever to be open to the public at large.

Those attending the conference heard fourteen papers over the course of two days (including several essays not represented in this volume). The hardest work of all in any volume of conference proceedings is extracting completed manuscripts from careful authors who are understandably anxious to make a variety of emendations before they commit themselves to print. The process takes long enough for a single author, but when so many people are involved it can (and did!) take years. Here Falino's diplomacy and patient application served us well. As it arrived, each essay was read first by Linda Smith Rhoads and benefited from her long experience as co-editor of the *New England Quarterly*. Rhoads's observations were eventually incorporated by Falino and Ward with their own more specialized substantive comments, and authors had another chance to reconsider before the essays were turned over to Ondine LeBlanc of the Massachusetts Historical Society, the skilled copy editor of the volume. Further negotiations with authors took place by email before disks were eventually turned over to Avanda Peters and Roderick Stinehour of The Stinehour Press, the volume's talented designers and printers responsible for the handsome result you see today. Jane Port once again stepped to the fore to take on the mammoth task of assembling all the photographs needed to illustrate the various essays.

Thus each Colonial Society volume is the work of many hands and much uncompensated labor all dedicated to the Society's stated purposes of "propagating knowledge" and "encouraging individual research" into the lives, deeds, and material culture of New England's early history. We can only be grateful to those who gave their time so generously.

Groton, Massachusetts
February, 2001

J OHN W. TYLER
Editor of Publications

Introduction

OR MORE THAN a century, the Museum of Fine Arts, Boston, has been a leader in the field of early New England silver. Starting with acquisitions of silver and gold in the 1880s and 1890s and the "American Silver" exhibition of 1906 (the first museum exhibition of American decorative arts of any kind), the Museum's curators have compiled an impressive record of acquisitions, exhibitions, and publications that have enhanced our knowledge and understanding of the work of American silversmiths — the first true artists in America. Generations of scholars and curators have played essential roles in this effort, from Francis Hill Bigelow to Jonathan L. Fairbanks, and including Florence V. Paull (later Mrs. Henri Leon Berger), Edwin J. Hipkiss, Wendy A. Cooper, Robert F. Trent, Michael K. Brown, and many others. No one, however, was more important than Kathryn C. Buhler, whose association with the collection began in the late 1920s and continued until her death in 1986. Her two-volume catalogue of the MFA's collection, published in 1972 and containing detailed information on more than six hundred objects, remains a cornerstone of any library on American silver, but it is only one of her many publications that add a wealth of information to our knowledge of the early silversmith and his patrons. Today, although the Museum's interests in American silver and gold extend from Pre-Columbian times to the present, the cherished objects from colonial and federal New England are still a major focus of scholarly attention and collecting activity.

This volume of essays, produced through the good and patient auspices of the Colonial Society of Massachusetts, is a direct outgrowth of this longstanding dedication to the lives and works of New England's first generations of silversmiths, from Hull and Sanderson through Paul Revere, by the Museum's curators. It is the permanent record of a conference held at the Museum in April 1996. While each essay that follows can stand alone, they are grouped here around four broad themes, in roughly the same order as they were presented at the symposium. Naturally, there is much overlapping and interconnectedness. As a whole, the papers reflect a general trend away from traditional issues of connoisseurship, such as the identification of marks and the compilation of dry biographies, and toward a more integrated understanding of silver objects as part of the material world and as reflective of the attitudes and values of their makers and users.

Professor Richard Bushman of Columbia University opened the conference with his sweeping, insightful overview that examines "The Complexity of Silver." His essay focuses on the power of silver in the colonial world, a status derived from its use as money, its beauty when fashioned into stylish objects, its significant use in a religious context, and its priority in a hierarchical world of men and materials. These attributes made silver, in Bushman's view, a powerful tool used by the colonial gentry to solidify their own position (a theme reiterated by many of the essays in this volume). But, as he reminds us, silver also had a "darker existence." Its value naturally led to its theft by criminals and its replication by counterfeiters, both destabilizing factors in society. Even more importantly, silver ore mined in Mexico and South America with the use of slave labor was the ultimate source for the coins and teapots of early America. Shiny objects, Bushman observes, were thus tarnished by their shady past.

Four papers comprised the Style, Form, and Function section of the conference. Robert Barker, an independent scholar located in London, began this portion of the proceedings with a richly detailed study, largely based on primary sources in England, of "Exports of English Silver: A Factor Affecting the Transmission of Style to Colonial Silversmiths, 1730–1769." His remarks will be incorporated into his doctoral dissertation, and thus are not repeated here.

In a subtle and sophisticated iconographical analysis, Patricia E. Kane of the Yale University Art Gallery examines images of the chase on the small (and apparently unique) group of eight pieces of Boston rococo-style silver made in the 1740s and 1750s. Her analysis of the narrative scenes on these pieces—images of the military conflicts of the day, of aristocratic hunting scenes and pastoral landscapes, and also of tales of courtship and sexual pursuit — draws upon popular songs, poetry, and other texts to tease out their meaning to people of the eighteenth century. As with Edward Nygren's analysis of the iconography of Edward Winslow's sugar boxes, published in 1971, Kane's look at silver (and related textiles) casts Bostonians in a somewhat surprising light. As she notes in reference to a teapot by William Simpkins, its narrative scenes suggest "a close association between the sports of the day and the sports of the night." Chased decoration, apparently, is not necessarily chaste.

The next two papers focus largely on both the manifest and latent functions of early objects. Madeline Siefke Estill discusses one of the smallest forms of hollowware — colonial silver tobacco, snuff, and patch boxes. A refinement of her master's thesis in the Winterthur Program in Early American Culture at the University of Delaware, this essay examines the specific forms of etiquette, social interaction, and even posture associated with these small precious objects. Using essays, sermons, poems, diaries, and other written sources, as well as the engraved decoration on the boxes themselves, Estill, like Kane, places her objects firmly within the genteel world of the eighteenth century and helps us understand, in context, such customs as patching, snuff-taking, and smoking. Some boxes were intended as love tokens and, like the teapots and creampots with narrative scenes, were an important part of courtship rituals.

In the concluding paper of this section, Gerald W. R. Ward inventories and examines the small group of silver chocolate pots made in Boston in the early eighteenth century by John Coney, Edward Winslow, Peter Oliver, and Edward Webb, as well as two later examples by Zachariah Brigden. The drinking of chocolate — an exotic beverage at the time, served hot — is often regarded as a somewhat "corrupt" practice associated with Spain, Italy, and other Catholic countries. Again, these silver vessels — like those examined by Kane and Estill — open a window on life in provincial and colonial Boston that reveals more of an interest in luxury and frippery than one might expect in the world of Samuel Sewall and his immediate descendants.

Much early American silver is associated with the Congregational churches of New England, and this material has fascinated and concerned scholars since the exhibition and catalogue of *American Church Silver* at the MFA in 1911 and the publication of E. Alfred Jones's monumental *Old Silver of American Churches* two years later. At the conference, Jayne Stokes of the Museum of Art, Rhode Island School of Design, presented a thorough report on her ongoing work (to be published elsewhere) in updating the Rhode Island section of Jones. Mark A. Peterson, then teaching at Harvard and now at the University of Iowa, also looked at communion silver, Puritanism, and gentility in early New England. His presentation, not repeated here, is published in expanded form in the *William and Mary Quarterly* in April 2001.

In her essay, Karen Parsons looks at church silver in a specific context — examining the motivations and meanings behind the gift by Elizabeth Porter Phelps of silver to her church in Northampton, Massachusetts, in the 1810s. While the gift may have been meant to reaffirm Phelps's status in the community, Parsons argues convincingly that her action also reflected a much more complex theological situation involving religious principles, the specific life of the congregation at the time of the gift (including the recent death of their minister), and other factors. Her paper is thus a strong reminder that individual acts of presentation need to be understood with the full circumstances of their time and place, including both public life and the more difficult to discern, but no less essential, world of private and spiritual beliefs and behaviors.

Barbara McLean Ward, author of "'In a Feasting Posture': Communion Vessels and Community Values in Seventeenth- and Eighteenth-Century New England," published in *Winterthur Portfolio* in 1988, continues her analysis of the forms and functions of church silver by expanding her investigation into the federal period. In particular, she seeks to understand why communion vessels — so diverse prior to 1800 — become more uniform in the early decades of the nineteenth century. She shows how, after the Revolution, many New England Congregational churches traded in their assemblages of communion vessels for sets of cups similar to those in use in Anglican and Episcopal churches. While older cups, tankards, caudle cups, and beakers may have remained on view to remind congregations of their past, these new cups of uniform size and shape signaled a more egalitarian relationship between congregants, and emphasized the dominant churches' desire — even as they faced disestablishment — to portray the church and community as one entity by adopting an inclusive model for the practice of communion.

While all the papers in this volume are concerned with issues of social context to some degree, the next three essays are primarily devoted to the world of craftsman and patron. The section begins with an essay by Jonathan L. Fairbanks, the Katharine Lane Weems Curator of American Decorative Arts and Sculpture Emeritus at the Museum of Fine Arts. In this essay, based on a spirited presentation given at a meeting of the Colonial Society on the eve of the public conference, Fairbanks provides a "thick description" of two key objects created in the pivotal year 1768 — John Singleton Copley's famous portrait of Paul Revere and Revere's own Sons of Liberty bowl. In so doing, he uncovers previously unnoticed political symbolism and sheds new light on the meaning of these two icons of Americana, proving how even the most familiar works can reveal new meaning when examined afresh.

Revere is also the central figure in Jeannine Falino's statistical study of his patrons. Using Revere's daybooks as well as the list of surviving objects recently compiled for the Yale-based study of colonial Massachusetts silversmiths and jewelers, Falino looks at issues of class and consumption in the acquisition of objects by the more than 750 people who patronized New England's most prolific silversmith. The results reveal much about the day-to-day activities of a working craftsman and also place silversmithing and the use of silver objects firmly within the "consumer revolution" of the eighteenth century.

Janine E. Skerry of Colonial Williamsburg concludes this section with a look at the silver given to and used at Harvard College in the colonial period, placing them within the context, to a degree, of collegiate plate used in England and on the Continent. She looks at corporate plate, the archaic and often misunderstood custom of "fellow commoner" plate, and tutorial plate (silver given by grateful students to their teachers), and compiles the written record of these pieces utilizing Harvard's extensive archives. The result is an in-depth study of well-documented pieces that tell us a great deal about New England silversmithing as well as college life in the seventeenth and eighteenth centuries.

Fig. 1. Kathryn C. Buhler and Jonathan L. Fairbanks examine a John Coney punch bowl in 1972.

This section of the conference also included a fine presentation by Martha Wilson Hamilton on "New England Silversmiths in the Fur Trade." Her excellent work on this little understood subject had just been published in greater depth in her book, *Silver in the Fur Trade, 1680–1820* (1995) and thus is not repeated here.

Two very different essays conclude the volume. In the first, Edwin A. Churchill of the Maine State Museum provides an extensive and thorough look at silver on the Maine frontier. Although we usually think of silver objects as urban luxury goods, Churchill has found surprisingly abundant evidence of their use and importance in Maine, both economically and socially.

The last paper here is a detailed biographical sketch of Samuel Bartlett by David F. Wood of the Concord Museum. Bartlett was a Concord silversmith — but he was more than that, as Wood deftly shows in this study that illuminates much about Bartlett the man as well as changes in the worlds of craft and citizenship that were taking place in the early years of the new republic. Bartlett's decision to leave his silversmith's bench in favor of becoming a clerk is a strong reminder that we should not over-romanticize the lives of early artisans.

Silversmithing in New England changed a great deal in the decades after Samuel Bartlett's death in 1821. Mechanization, the introduction and popularization of electroplating, and the concomitant growth of large companies such as the Gorham Manufacturing Company and the Meriden Britannia Company, changed silvermaking from a craft to an industry. Arthur Stone and members of the Boston Society of Arts and Crafts revived the small shop tradition at the end of the nineteenth century, and today's metalsmiths, often centered in academia, continue to produce silver and gold jewelry and, occasionally, hollowware. In recent years, these more modern products of the Victorian, arts and crafts, and contemporary world have attracted an increasing amount of attention, as indeed they should. Yet, as the eleven essays contained herein demonstrate, seventeenth- and eighteenth-century New England silver is a fertile field of scholarly endeavor, and we are certain that it will remain so in the future.

Art of the Americas
Museum of Fine Arts, Boston

JEANNINE FALINO
Carolyn and Peter Lynch Curator of
Decorative Arts and Sculpture

GERALD W. R. WARD
Katharine Lane Weems Curator of
Decorative Arts and Sculpture

The Complexity of Silver

RICHARD LYMAN BUSHMAN

BEFORE THEIR MARRIAGE in 1727, minister Jonathan Edwards had written of his wife, Sarah Pierpont Edwards, that "she hardly cares for any thing, except to meditate on him," "the Great Being, who made and rules the world. . . . If you present all the world before her, with the richest of its treasures, she disregards it and cares not for it."[1] Nonetheless, Sarah held among her possessions a small silver patch box with "S Pierpont" inscribed on the bottom (illustrated here on p. 53). It was a noteworthy possession of a notable woman. She valued it so much that she took it with her to Northampton, Jonathan's pulpit, held on to it when the parish criticized her for dressing too stylishly, and, after his dismissal from Northampton, carried it to Stockbridge, the frontier town where Edwards preached to a small congregation of white settlers and Mahican Indians. The devout, modest, discreet Sarah Pierpont Edwards would not let go of this tiny silver symbol of refinement and dignity.[2]

Wherein lay the power of her silver patch box over the imagination of this pious woman? Her attachment demonstrates, in a small example, the hold of silver over colonial culture in general. Silver was brandished by virtually all of the contestants in the cultural contests of the eighteenth century. Everywhere, silver was used to command assent, to assert authority, or to claim respect. Why was silver such a powerful material for establishing identity and configuring hierarchical relationships?

In attempting an answer, I have three themes in mind: silver as bullion and money (fig. 1); silver's association with divinity, through its beauty; and silver's high position in a world of ranked materials. My belief is that these three — money, beauty, and rank — converged to make silver uniquely effective in sustaining the authority of the eighteenth-century gentry. The three imparted a radiance to a silver spoon, making it a telling gift from a mother to her child, and invested value beyond monetary worth in a silver patch box.

The Measure of All Things

Although the least awe-inspiring of its eighteenth-century meanings, silver's incarnation as bullion is in some ways its most fundamental. In this respect, silver was distinguished from other materials used for luxury commodities.

Fig 1. Five Massachusetts silver coins minted by John Hull (1624–1683) and Robert Sanderson, Sr. (1608–1693), Boston, Massachusetts, working together beginning in 1652. Silver; various dimensions. Museum of Fine Arts, Boston, gift of Dr. Samuel A. Green (17.292, 17.298, 17.300), gift of Henry B. Thomas (29.52), bequest of Miss Rebecca Salisbury (92.1534).

Mahogany had no life in the colonies other than as furniture, nor silk except as clothing. Only silver led a double life, its use as money equaling its importance in the decorative arts. The two forms of silver – coin and *objet d'art* – were seemingly separate: one lived in the marketplace in people's purses and pockets; the other sat still most of the time on shelves or tabletops. The life of money was busy and crass, the life of plate serene and refined. Yet in the colonial mind the two merged. The owners of silver plate knew that silver was also bullion and potentially money. In estate inventories silver was often listed and valued only by weight: the value of the metal overshadowed any supposed value imparted by its form. At the end of the seventeenth century, silver became the standard for measuring value across the British empire.

The seventeenth-century debate over silver money, culminating in the great recoinage of 1696, affected silver's cultural functions for the next century. For a century and a half, the British empire agonized over the fluctuations in the value of silver coins. Henry VIII had debased the coinage to make it stretch as far as possible, using the gain to pay for the fortifications he was building. At the other end of the social scale, sharpers clipped coins to steal a little silver from each one, slowly reducing the coin's value. Despite efforts by Charles I and Charles II to issue stable coinage, bad money continued to drive out good. By the end of the century, the coinage had lost on the average a full quarter of its value. At last the government saw it must call in the depreciated coins and replace them with new money milled on the edges to stop clipping.

As plans were laid for the great recoinage, officials had to decide on the silver content of the new coins, which meant specifying exactly what constituted their monetary worth. Since the old coins had lost such a large portion of their sterling value, the authorities faced a difficult choice. To restore the silver content to the stated value on the coin's face would entail a huge expenditure; all the metal lost through clipping would have to be replaced. Alternatively, the silver content of the coins could be maintained at the current, depreciated levels, but with milled edges that would prevent further clipping. Old coins would be exchanged for stabilized new coins with the same amount of silver. John Locke argued that the coins had to contain full weight or they would not function as coins. People would discount them from their face value, and they would be worth no more than the price of their silver content on the international market. Even the stamp of the king on a coin declaring its worth as a full shilling would not sustain its value. Only the worth of the silver on the bullion market was intractable and irresistible.[3]

Locke won the argument. Despite the cost of recoinage, English coins after 1696 contained the full market value of silver. Isaac Newton, warden of the mint, disagreed with Locke, but nonetheless presided over the last stages of the great recoinage completed in 1699. These two luminaries of the English Enlightenment converged at this significant moment in the history of English money to disagree over the uses of silver. Out of the encounter, silver emerged as the single measure of value in the empire. Every exchange of wheat, tobacco, fabric, every purchase of labor and land, every levy of taxes, the value of an estate, the payment of fees and salaries, all rested ultimately on the worth of silver.[4]

In the eighteenth century, silver in any of its forms always meant money. Silver's value on the world market overshadowed any value added by the silversmith's art. Silver was not just money, but fixed and certain money, unaffected by the vacillations that troubled ephemeral paper currencies. In the colonies, paper money lost value continually and sometimes in terrifying falls, as between 1740 and 1750 when Massachusetts currency dropped by half against sterling. In such an economy, no material had more compelling recommendations than silver or offered better credentials to an insecure gentry.[5] Wherever silver traveled, in whatever guise, it carried with it the authority of British sterling and behind that the intractable worth of bullion. That was the wordless message of the tea services, snuffboxes, and Sarah Edwards's patch box.

Divine Beauty

As fundamental as was silver's monetary worth to the role it played in eighteenth-century culture, crass economics alone certainly cannot sufficiently explain that role. The awe in which both the English and the colonials held silver derived from a source that they did not associate with money: the conjunction of aesthetics and divinity. Inquiries into the nature of beauty were pursued everywhere in eighteenth-century discourse. The intellectual historian Paul Kristeller has called the period the "classical century of modern aesthetics," the time when philosophers set down fundamental notions of beauty — most of which we still take for granted today.[6] All across Western Europe, it was believed possible to define beauty through precise and objective laws, some of them pointing toward the divine.

This search for an understanding of beauty was a widely diffused effort, involving, along with the theorists, the artisans who produced house furnishings and decorative objects. Seeking to please their customers and enhance their profits, artisans turned out objects in conformity to the standards of the theorists, as if they had embarked on the same project in unison. In his *Philosophical Enquiry into the Origin of Our Ideas of the Sublime and Beautiful* (1756), for example, Edmund Burke, perhaps the leading eighteenth-century English aesthetician, listed the "sensible qualities" that were in his view "the real cause of Beauty." Prominent among them was smoothness, which he found "so essential to beauty, that I do not now recollect any thing beautiful that is not smooth" — smooth leaves on trees, smooth slopes of earth, smooth streams in landscapes, smooth skins on fine women.[7] By some means of cultural communication, artisans who had never heard Burke's name produced objects as if working by his philosophical principles. Moved by their own sensibilities and the desires of their patrons, they took great pains to smooth silver forms (fig. 2) just as Burke specified.

Making silver smooth was no small task for the smiths. After the object was shaped in the raising process, the smith used planishing hammers to remove any residual marks. Because the faces of those hammers had to be perfect, they were covered with tallow when not in use to prevent deterioration. Then the silver was buffed, polished with a fine abrasive such as rottenstone and oil, and minute roughnesses flattened with jeweller's rouge[8] — all to produce that silky smoothness that makes silver so sensuously appealing to the eye and touch. The effort the smiths expended suggests a widely diffused sense of the beautiful, an awareness shared by smiths, patrons, and philosophers.

The value of beauty in the eighteenth century may have gone beyond the mundane. One thinker, Jonathan Edwards, America's leading theologian and Sarah Pierpont Edwards's husband, articulated a connection between beauty and divinity. He used the word *beauty* to describe the disposition of God. Edwards propounded a deeply aesthetic theology. God, he wrote, is the "foundation and fountain of all being and all beauty." He is distinguished from all other beings "chiefly by his divine beauty." Roland Delattre, in his *Beauty and Sensibility*, argues that in Edwards's thought beauty was "the first principle of being, the inner, structural principle of being-itself." God was not only the most gloriously beautiful of all beings, "the Beauty of the world is a communication of God's beauty."[9] We do not have to comprehend the intricacies of Edwards's theology to be impressed with the height and reach of the word "beauty" in his discourse. Simply by association, some of the transcendence of beauty and

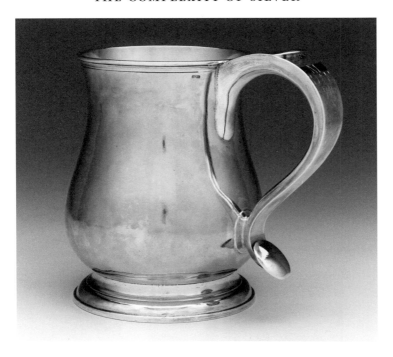

Fig. 2. Jacob Hurd (1702/03–1758), cann, Boston, Massachusetts, 1746.
Silver; h. 5 ½ in. Museum of Fine Arts, Boston, Gift of the First Church
in Malden, Congregational (1991.499).

therefore of God was transferred to everything beautiful. A beautiful teapot
trailed clouds of glory as it performed its duties.

It did so in part because silver was the preferred material for communion vessels; in Catholic churches, traditionally only gold and silver were used in the
Eucharist. Among Protestants, including New England Protestants, plate was
also considered best suited to bear the emblems of Christ's flesh and blood.
Silver was the right material for one of the few Puritan rituals where divinity
was embodied in external forms. Silver mediated between the high holiness of
Christ's atoning body and the bodies of the communicants who accepted the
tokens of his death into their mouths. Gleaming on the communion table, or
raised to the lips, silver was the preferred material for approaching God. If the
streets of heaven were paved with gold, silver was the earthly avenue to heaven's
gates. In New England, no material was more sanctified, more dedicated, or
more intimate with divinity (fig. 3). Contact with the emblems of Christ's body
in the sight of all churchgoers could only add to the numinous patina formed
on silver. Such associations were an ineluctable part of silver's power, and perhaps a partial explanation of a pious woman's attachment to a silver patch box.

Fig. 3. Silver from the First Church, Boston. Jacob Hurd (1702/03–1758), baptismal basin, Boston, Massachusetts, 1733. Silver; h. 2 13/16 in., diam. 13 5/16 in. John Hull (1624–1683) and Robert Sanderson, Sr. (1609–1693), tunn, Boston, Massachusetts, ca. 1659. Silver; h. 3 7/8 in. John Hull and Robert Sanderson, Sr., wine cup, Boston, Massachusetts, 1660–80. Silver; h. 8 in. John Edwards (1671/72–1746), flagon, Boston, Massachusetts, 1726. H. 13 3/16 in. Museum of Fine Arts, Anonymous Gift (1999.89–92).

High and Mighty

An essay in the *New-York Weekly Journal* in 1835 suggests how silver figured in the cultural power structure of that century. The essayist intended to rebuke consumers for desiring unnecessary luxuries, such as silver, but in so doing he inadvertently attested to the cultural power of all such beautiful and haughty materials:

> A Cottage may keep a Man as warm as a Palace; and there is no absolute Necessity of covering our Bodies with Silk. Is there no quenching of our Thirst, but in Chrystal? No cutting of our Bread, unless the Knife has an Agate Handle? We may wash as clean in an Earthen Vessel as in a Silver, and see as well by a Candle in a Pewter-socket, as in a Plate.

The purpose of the comment was to puncture the superficiality of high living. Why reach for the elegant when cottages shelter people as well as palaces, homespun covers bodies as well as silk, earthenware holds water as effectively as silver? The author writes in the tradition of eighteenth-century anti-luxury rhetoric, condemning the unnecessary expense and the sinful vanity of elegant furnishings.

For the historian reading this argument as a piece of documentary evidence, of course, the article has a meaning different from the one intended: it attests to how much consumers desired the very signs of status the author condemned. His words conjure up a world where materials, along with people, were divided into high and low along a social spectrum. Practical value alone had little or nothing to do with social value, as the essayist points out. Beginning with a comparison of palaces and cottages, the essayist suggests that high materials belonged in the residences of kings and aristocrats, while lowly objects furnished cottages. Silver and silk went with wealth, might, and eminence. Pewter and earthenware were low and weak.

In the common understanding of the world in the seventeenth and eighteenth centuries, precise hierarchies structured relations among people and among their belongings. Seventeenth-century French courtesy manuals specified ranks for chairs according to their size and to the presence or absence of arms. Places in a room were ranked according to nearness to a bed or distance from a door. There was a right way to knock on doors. You could pound on the doors of lowly people, but only scratch lightly the doors of the mighty.

The English scoffed at French niceties but had plenty of their own. In America, George Washington's *Rules of Civility*, maxims copied from an English courtesy manual when Washington was a boy, told young men which was the side of honor when walking with a superior, how far to walk behind him, and when to doff one's hat. The general principle was "Let thy ceremonies in Courtesie be proper to the Dignity of his place with whom thou conversest for it is absurd to act the same with a Clown and a Prince."[10] To be polite, a person had to identify the rank of everyone in the room and act accordingly, just as military officers today are immediately ranked by their insignia or Washington protocol demands that government rank be observed on social occasions. The ranking of materials followed naturally from the social ranks indelibly traced in society itself.

Silver's high rank made it particularly useful in eighteenth-century colonial society. Silver proclaimed taste, refinement, and civilization. Its testament to the owner's superior culture gave support where it was badly needed. A shaky ruling class, the colonial gentry lacked the stable designations of social rank that anchored the English aristocracy — traditional recognition based on ancient estates, titles, and established family names. In colonial locales, conversely, the gentry's standing rested almost wholly on wealth, and wealth was notoriously precarious, especially in the North where so much capital was invested in trade. Not only could a merchant lose a fortune quickly, but people with new money were forever arriving on the scene, claiming a place among the gentry and displacing older families. In this fluid society the visible marks of cultural superiority were especially useful. Manners, a grand house, fashionable dress, and elegant furnishings supported claims to social and political authority. Silver, shining upon American sideboards and tea tables, reflected the precious glory that the American gentry craved. On the premise that a culturally superior person merited a superior position in society and government, silver became an instrument of cultural politics, a passive but powerful marker in the colonials' ongoing struggle for power.

Silver served its social purpose well because it could play such an intimate role in its owners' personal lives. Like most of the arts in the colonies, the decorative arts were mainly associated with persons. Nearly all of the painting was portraiture. The greatest artistic expenditure was for houses and furnishings. The fundamental connection of art and society was through the magnates who constructed mansions and lavishly furnished them to enhance their families' standings and cultural authority.

The gentry wished to draw into themselves whatever powers their possessions held — the refinement, beauty, and rank of the objects in their houses. Among the decorative arts in their possession, few were so accessible, so close to their owners' bodies as silver for ready appropriation. As buttons and buckles, silver touched the body like the fabric in clothing, joining the beauty of the object to the person wearing it. But silver surpassed fabric in its access, through the mouth, to the body's interior. The majority of all silver objects produced was tableware and, by far, the most common individual items were spoons and drinking vessels.[11] Spoons, forks, mugs, canns, and tankards all entered the mouth. It was a notable intrusion, for eighteenth-century people were self-conscious about mouths. The conduct books instructed readers not to leave their mouths open as they walked or to smile so widely as to show the teeth. "Do not puff up the cheeks, loll not out the tongue, rub the hands, or beard, thrust out the lips or bite them, or keep the lips too open or too close," instructed Washington's rules of civility.[12] Washington's mouth posture in the famous portrait was the proper one for the time: a pleasant line firmly closed. Silver, nonetheless, breached that aperture with perfect decorum and propriety.

We can only imagine the complicated symbolic exchange that went on as a silver cup entered an elitist mouth. In a sense the drinker was ingesting all the values that silver brought to their relationship, the powers of its beauty, its aura of godly service, and its high rank among the preferred materials of palaces and mansions. To be born with a silver spoon in one's mouth became an emblem of

Fig. 4. John Burt (1692/93–1745/46), tankard, Boston, Massachusetts, ca. 1724–30. Silver; h. 7 13/16 in. Museum of Fine Arts, Boston, Gift of Abby S. Niss, in memory of Ruth Morison Sharples (1981.504).

aristocratic breeding, as if silver could infuse its powers into a privileged child at the instant of birth. On the other hand, silver in turn benefited from the intimate association with the mighty families of colonial society. It enhanced silver's powers to be so honored by the elite. The admission to the intimacy of the bedroom had long been a mark of favor in European society. The privilege of attending while the king dressed or undressed was reserved for the privileged. Access to the body was more than sexual or friendly; it was socially elevating. If silver secured the cultural foundations of the colonial gentry's social authority, intimate association with the gentry in their dining rooms added to silver's luster.

Beneath the Surface

The faint aura of silver's association with divinity entered into the room with a tea service, the fragrance of familiarity with the elite came too, and above all sounded the ring of money. All of these together made silver perhaps the surest way to assert cultural authority and superiority in colonial society, but silver led another life, a darker existence, in the colonial underground. The ties to divinity, rank, and money also made silver of value to thieves and counterfeiters. Because it had monetary value as well as social prestige, silver became a primary target for theft. Unlike portraiture and fine furniture, stolen pieces could be melted down and converted into money. A counterculture of fraud and theft tested the hierarchical structure that silver was meant to support. Criminals, as much as gentlemen, wanted to enjoy the benefits of silver, and so fraudulently appropriated silver's powers to themselves. The colonial gentry were always in danger of being tricked by silver or losing it entirely to a clever thief. A set of underground characters preying upon silver subverted the social order the authorities worked so hard to sustain.

Counterfeiters debased coins by increasing the percentage of copper in the silver alloy, passing the new coins as the real thing. A silver wash over a largely copper coin would give a temporary bright appearance. Silversmiths, otherwise the most honored of craftsmen, were sometimes the counterfeiters. In 1720 Edward Hunt, a Philadelphia silversmith, was hanged; in 1742 the goldsmith Obadiah Mors suffered an hour in the Newport pillory, had his ear cropped, and was sold into service. Charles Hamilton, the first known silversmith in Poughkeepsie, made debased Spanish cobs, which he coated with quicksilver. After he was apprehended and imprisoned, Hamilton hanged himself with his handkerchief.[13]

After the middle of the eighteenth century, counterfeiting became a widespread problem in New England. The counterfeiters formed into gangs situated at various sites in New Hampshire, Rhode Island, and Connecticut. Samuel Casey, for example, worked in league with his brother — also a silversmith — and two other silversmiths. Besides the silversmiths who made the coins, a circle of confederates passed them. Nine men were implicated with Gilbert Belcher, a Great Barrington silversmith who made Spanish dollars. Some prosecutors felt the whole community conspired with the counterfeiters, presumably because many benefited from circulating debased money. When Samuel Casey was tried, the jury refused to convict and the judge had to send them back to reconsider. When finally convicted and imprisoned, he was released in the dead of night by a mob and never punished. The various gangs may also have been loosely tied to one another. One newspaper account estimated that 500 people were involved from North Carolina to New Hampshire.[14]

The size and nature of these counterfeiting clubs was never fully discovered, but their existence nonetheless cast a shadow over all silver money. Although the exact volume of counterfeit coins in circulation could not be determined, concern about their existence disconcerted everyone. When a coin was laid on a tavern table, no one knew for sure if it was real. Silver, the measure of all value, was constantly in question. What generally appeared to be the rock of a fundamental social hierarchy, what seemed to be insurance for a prestigious family's sense of status, in fact could turn out at any moment to be loose sand, ready to give way.

Thieves as well as counterfeiters trafficked in silver. Judging from the newspaper ads, thieves often broke into houses and shops and made off with valuable loot. Not just professional thieves, but deserting soldiers, servants, and many among the mobile population that thronged the port towns threatened possessors of silver. In August 1750, the *Boston Gazette* ran an advertisement typical of such notices in the city: "Taken out of a House in Cambridge, a silver Can, which holds a full Ale pint, mark'd at the Bottom ESL and the maker's Name Austin."[15] In April 1763, Jacob Jennings of Norwalk advertised in Boston for silver worth £100, offering a £20 reward.[16] The frequency of theft involving silver objects created an environment in which silver offered for sale aroused suspicion. Joseph Moulton of Newbury advertised a large silver spoon that someone brought into his shop. Suspecting theft, Moulton went to the Justice of the Peace who "stopped" the spoon until the purveyor could provide a better account of his source.

With thieves on the prowl for silver, the plate in the great houses rested uneasily on the shelves. Silver was precarious, forever at risk. Its owners had to guard against the predations of criminals with no scruples about invading mansions and shops to rob their stores of silver. The stolen pieces could then disappear into an underworld to reemerge as counterfeit coins or as fenced objects. Silver's high value in respectable society was the very reason it was counterfeited and stolen; that traffic necessarily caused the gentry to look upon individual pieces with some doubt or worry. Because their own sense of social worth depended on silver, among other luxuries, the colonial elite then had to view their own position as similarly precarious.

The gentry probably thought less about the disreputable path that silver took from its origins as ore, buried in the earth, to their tabletops and tea trays, but the production of silver cast another shadow over this glorious metal. Although colonials had an imperfect knowledge of silver's origins, they vaguely understood that silver began in mines, in which oppressive and exploitative conditions reigned. Some of that past lingered on in silver's cultural associations. Most of the silver objects made in the American colonies began with older plate or with silver coins that were melted down and refabricated; little bullion was actually imported. But the plate and coins were at one time ingots, before that ore, and before that rocks buried in a mountain.

The larger part of eighteenth-century silver came from Mexico and Peru, where large deposits had been located in the sixteenth century. Potosi (fig. 5), for example, in what was then Peru and is now Bolivia, was a mountain of rich silver ore. The owners used forced Indian labor, as many as 13,000 men a year, conscripted from the villages in the surrounding area under the traditional *mita*, the villagers' labor obligation. The *mitayos*, as the conscripted Indians were called, were paid sixty-five pesos for twenty-six weeks of work, while the cost of supporting themselves for that period came to three times as much. Of necessity, they had to work for another six months as "volunteer" workers, or *mingas*, to pay off their debts.

The miners lived in very simple conditions and performed arduous tasks. They pursued the veins of silver deep into the mountain, whence narrow shafts, averaging 650 feet in height, led to the surface. Many of the Indians were employed in carrying up the ore in woolen blankets (which they had to provide for themselves) slung over their shoulders. In places they crawled with the ore-filled bags through narrow tunnels two feet square, dragging the bags with their feet. At the end they climbed up the shafts on ladders of hide strung with wooden crosspieces. They labored up in groups of three, with a single candle (also supplied by themselves) tied to the finger or the forehead of the lead climber. At the top, sweating and exhausted, they were commonly rebuked for bringing up light loads and sent back for more. If they failed to meet their quotas, they were whipped. According to regulations meant to protect the Indians, the routine was supposed to go on from an hour and a half after sunrise to sunset, but the shifts lasted for twelve hours in much of the operation.[17] In their six months as mingas, many worked in the refining process involving mercury amalgams, exposing the Indians to mercury through skin contact or inhalation. The poisoning brought on loss of teeth, shaking, paralysis, and sometimes death.[18]

American colonists knew that silver came from Mexico and Peru and probably understood that forced Indian labor produced it. In a 1797 *Poem on the Industry of the United States of America*, the Connecticut Wit David Humphreys made the Potosi laborers a foil for highlighting the happiness of New England's free farmers. The oppressed miners worked the mountain, Humphreys wrote,

> Where, shut from day, in central caverns deep,
> Hopeless for freedom, wretches watch and weep;
> Compell'd for gold to rip the womb of earth,
> And drag the precious mischief into birth.[19]

Fig. 5. Unknown artist, probably Portuguese, untitled view of Potosí, showing the water-powered operation for extracting silver, ca. 1585. From *Atlas of Sea Charts* (Peru?, ca. 1585). The Hispanic Society of America, New York.

Happy with the well-being of Connecticut people, Humphreys said nothing about what this suffering meant for the plate on the tables of the New England gentry. The gentry's efforts to attain or maintain authority and place left little room for the contemplation of social injustice. Silver's origins, of course, were not unique. They were no worse than the estates built on slave labor in the Caribbean and the South. Most forms of eighteenth-century wealth had a shady past.

○

Thus silver bravely carried on its work on behalf of the colonial gentry. Silver provided the monetary bedrock on which the economy rested. Silver gleamed upon shelves and tables, emanating beauty and refinement. Silver silently attested to taste and civilization, sustaining the gentry's claims to social and political leadership. But these duties were carried out under a cloud of ambiguities. The most splendid, the best connected, and the most noble — next to gold — of all decorative materials was vulnerable to capture and misuse by a criminal counterculture; at least in modern eyes, its sheen is also tarnished by its origins in forced labor. Like much of genteel existence, silver was a show, a beautiful surface, a magnificent pretense concealing many flaws. Rather than playing a part in a simple story of art and beauty, eighteenth-century New England silver figured in a complex and ambiguous narrative of power.

Notes

1. "Sarah Pierrepoint," in *Jonathan Edwards: Representative Selections*, ed. Clarence H. Faust and Thomas H. Johnson (New York: Hill and Wang, 1962), 56.

2. Gerald W. R. Ward and William N. Hosley, Jr., eds., *The Great River: Art and Society of the Connecticut Valley, 1635–1820* (Hartford: Wadsworth Atheneum, 1986), 282–83.

3. Joyce Oldham Appleby, "Locke, Liberalism, and the Natural Law of Money," *Past and Present* 17 (1976): 43–69; Glyn Davies, *A History of Money: From Ancient Times to the Present Day* (Cardiff: University of Wales Press, 1994), 245–46; Karen Iversen Vaughan, *John Locke: Economist and Social Scientist* (Chicago: University of Chicago Press, 1980).

4. Vaughan, *John Locke*, 35.

5. John J. McCusker, *Money and Exchange in Europe and America, 1600–1775: A Handbook* (Chapel Hill: University of North Carolina Press, 1978), 141.

6. Paul Oskar Kristeller, "The Modern System of the Arts: A Study in the History of Aesthetics," in *Essays on the History of Aesthetics*, ed. Peter Kivy (Rochester, N.Y.: University of Rochester Press, 1992), 3. Originally published in *Journal of the History of Ideas* 12, no. 4 (October 1951).

7. Edmund Burke, *A Philosophical Enquiry into the Origin of Our Ideas of the Sublime and Beautiful*, ed. Adam Phillips (Oxford: Oxford University Press, 1990), 102–4.

8. Henry J. Kauffman, *The Colonial Silversmith: His Techniques and His Products* (Camden, N.J.: Thomas Nelson, 1969), 42; Gerald Taylor, *Silver* (Harmondsworth: Penguin Books, 1956), 15.

9. Quotations from Jonathan Edwards are found in Sang Hyun Lee, *The Philosophical Theology of Jonathan Edwards* (Princeton: Princeton University Press, 1988), 83, 179, 260; Roland DeLattre, *Beauty and Sensibility in the Thought of Jonathan Edwards: An Essay in Aesthetics and Theological Ethics* (New Haven: Yale University Press, 1968).

10. Richard L. Bushman, *The Refinement of America: Persons, Houses, Cities* (New York: Alfred A. Knopf, 1992), 38–39; Charles Moore, ed., *George Washington's Rules of Civility and Decent Behaviour in Company and Conversation* (Boston and New York, 1926), 7, 9, 13, 17, 21.

11. Kauffman, *Colonial Silversmith*, 50; Hermann Frederick Clarke, *John Coney, Silversmith, 1655–1722* (Boston: Houghton Mifflin, 1932).

12. *Washington's Rules of Civility*, rule 16.

13. Kenneth Scott, *Counterfeiting in Colonial America* (New York: Oxford University Press, 1957), 210, 212.

14. Scott, *Counterfeiting in Colonial America*, 4, 211, 218, 222, 230, 232, 233, 235.

15. *Boston Gazette*, August 14, 1750, in George Francis Dow, comp., *The Arts and Crafts in New England, 1704–1775: Gleanings from Boston Newspapers* (Topsfield, Mass.: Wayside Press, 1927), 41.

16. *Boston Gazette*, April 18, 1763, in Dow, *Arts and Crafts in New England*, 48.

17. Peter Bakewell, *Miners of the Red Mountain: Indian Labor in Potosi, 1545–1650* (Albuquerque: University of New Mexico Press, 1984), 23, 105, 142–44, 150–57, 162.

18. Bakewell, *Miners of the Red Mountain*, 21, 150–51.

19. David Humphreys, *The Miscellaneous Works* (Gainesville, Fla.: Scholars' Facsimiles and Reprints, 1968), 98. Half a century later, Emily Dickinson, in a poem on dangerous speech, said "Talk with prudence to a beggar of 'Potosi' and the mines!" *Selected Poems of Emily Dickinson*, ed. Conrad Aiken (New York, 1924), 34.

Style, Form, and Function

Chasers, the Chase, and Other Scenes on Boston Rococo-Style Silver

PATRICIA E. KANE

IN THE MID-EIGHTEENTH century, silversmiths in London, Dublin, and Jamaica were making rococo-style silver ornamented with narrative scenes. On the mainland of British North America, however, the practice apparently went on only among Boston silversmiths; according to the evidence, silversmiths in New York, Philadelphia, and Baltimore did not ornament silver in this way.[1] The narrative scenes chased on the pieces explored here, eight pieces of rococo-style silver made in Boston between 1745 and 1760, correspond to themes represented in other art forms, such as embroidery, made in that colonial center at the same time. While the themes depicted at times overlap in meaning and at other times diverge, they nonetheless provide us with a moment frozen in time — a moment that captures the stories this class of colonial New England consumers told themselves, the stories that reflect their concerns and interests.

As other papers in this volume demonstrate, those colonials who could afford to buy silver needed to articulate, establish, and/or consolidate their status within their culture. It will be no surprise, then, that the narratives depicted on most of these pieces express some aspect of that same socioeconomic concern, as we will see with hunt scenes, equestrian motifs, and pastoral landscapes. Less obvious might be the timeliness of scenes about courtship and sexual pursuit; while these concerns have a certain timelessness as well, their particular expression on these pieces depends on motifs particular to eighteenth-century Anglo culture and therefore relate to the social aspirations and anxieties of their users. Finally, the most specific to these colonials are pieces that actually refer relatively explicitly to the military conflicts of the 1740s.

Today, there are only eight known pieces of Boston-made rococo-style silver with narrative chasing.[2] Four are creampots made by Jacob Hurd between about 1745 and his retirement from silversmithing in roughly 1755. Thomas Edwards produced a creampot with narrative chasing between 1744, when he returned to Boston after a fourteen-year sojourn in New York, and his death in 1755. A snuffbox by Thomas Dane dates from 1752, and the other two pieces considered here, a creampot and a teapot circa 1750, come from the shop of William Simpkins.[3]

Chasing is a specialization within the silversmiths' trade, and the silversmiths who marked these eight pieces may not have executed the chasing on them. In this decorative technique the smith distends the silver by striking it on the inside with a snarling iron, a long iron rod with either a goose-necked or angular short stem. Once the metal has been pushed out, the smith fills the object with or embeds it in pitch (a mixture of resins, plaster of Paris, and tallow). Working from the exterior the craftsman then hammers the surface of the metal with chasing tools — three- to five-inch long iron rods with decorative ends — to give definition to the distended areas. The process, which is time-consuming and therefore adds to the cost of an object, requires excellent drawing skills.

Status

For eighteenth-century American colonials, the desire to establish or express status generally led them to the trappings of gentility most enjoyed by their counterparts in England; those trappings appear prominently on the teapots and creampots that these New Englanders would have set on their tea tables. Several of the pieces here capture images of the manor life associated with England's landed gentry: the hunt, horsemanship in general, and most broadly, the "tamed nature" of the country estate.

Two pieces, the creampot by Edwards and the teapot by Simpkins, display scenes of the chase. On the Edwards creampot, a male figure astride a horse at full gallop and a running hound chase a leaping stag (figs. 1 and 2). The horse's lunging front legs are bent and its rear legs are splayed backward; only its right rear hoof touches the ground. The horse's head and ears stand erect and his full tail streams behind. The rider, wearing a long coat and a brimmed hat, sits in the saddle with his knees bent and his arms pressed close to his body as he clasps the reins. The Simpkins teapot (fig. 3), on the pourer's side, is also illustrated with a stag hunt (fig. 4). An archer, wearing a buttoned knee-length coat with a large pocket and a button below the dropped waist, is shooting at a stag. Two hounds pursue the stag through a wooded countryside; one bird flies overhead and another bird perches on a tree branch.

The identification of hunting as an aristocratic sport has a long history. As early as the sixteenth century, publications espousing the importance of hunting were available to English readers. Young men aspiring to a higher social status read hunting treatises in order to master this aristocratic pursuit, which each hoped would further his acceptance as a gentleman. Publications recommending the wholesomeness and overall value of outdoor recreation, and especially the hunt, abounded in England and certainly made their way to colonial read-

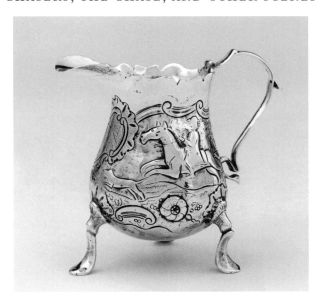

Fig. 1. Thomas Edwards (1702–1755), creampot (left side), Boston, Massachusetts, ca. 1750–60. Silver; h. 3⁵⁄₁₆ in. The Cleveland Museum of Art, Gift of Hollis French (40.393). © Cleveland Museum of Art, 2000.

Fig. 2. Right side of Thomas Edwards creampot illustrated in fig. 1.

Fig. 3. William Simpkins (1704–1780), teapot, Boston, Massachusetts, ca. 1750. Silver; h. 5¼ in. The Burrows Collection, on loan to the Sterling and Francine Clark Art Institute (1984.149).

ers as well. Both Richard Blome and Nicholas Cox published books called *The Gentleman's Recreation* in the late seventeenth century.[4] More modest publications included *An Essay on Hunting by a Country Squire*, published by Thomas Gosden (London, 1733), and *The Sportsman's Dictionary, or, The Country Gentlemen's Companion* (London, 1735). These volumes covered hawking, hunting, fowling, fishing, racing, and riding. The chaser of the Simpkins teapot might have had access to the *Sportsman's Dictionary*, which included an illustration of

Fig. 4. Detail of William Simpkins teapot shown in fig. 3.

Fig. 5. "Hunting." From
The Sportsman's Dictionary
(London, 1735), vol. 1,
plate 14. The Beinecke
Rare Book and Manu-
script Library, Yale Uni-
versity.

Fig. 6. Plate from George Bickham, Jr. (1706?–1771), *General Rures* [sic] *for painting in oil and watercolors; washing prints, maps, and mezzotintoes. With the art of japanning, etching* (London, 1747). Yale Center for British Art, Paul Mellon Collection.

hunting (fig. 5). The chaser of the horseman on the Edwards creampot may have had access to a sheet of designs from a set of japanning prints published by George Bickham in 1747 (fig. 6).

Although riding to the hounds was less popular in New England than else-where, the popularity of the chase scenes in Massachusetts, which turned up in embroideries as well as silver, was due to the status suggested by the association with the prescribed activities of Old World gentry. The contextual evidence for the meaning of the hunt to New England's elite and aspiring elite is easy enough to find, not just in the silver itself and the embroidery, discussed below, but in the prints we know Bostonians owned. Merchant John Simpson, for example, who owned embroidered pictures described as "1 large work picture & 7 small ditto," also owned "4 Hunting pieces" when he died in 1764. The like-lihood that a larger market existed is suggested by a notice in a Boston news-paper offering hunting prints for sale at auction in 1758.[5]

Many of these prints or publications could have served as sources for the sil-ver engraver. Or, if not directly for the chaser, then for the tent-stitched needle-work pictures Massachusetts women made during this same era.[6] As Betty Ring has written, pictorial canvas work appeared in Boston by the early 1730s, but with the exception of Norwich, Connecticut, needlework of this type failed to become popular in the other colonies.[7] Needlework was one among an array of genteel accomplishments expected of young ladies; consequently, as part of their education, well-to-do young women worked these pictures from patterns drawn by their instructors. Dated examples of pictures made in Massachusetts survive from 1746 and 1748.[8]

Nancy Graves Cabot established that many of the figures and scenes in these embroideries derived from print sources; the scenes on the silver may well have derived from print sources as well. Some of the horsemen and hounds — for example, those on a picture embroidered by Sarah Warren in 1748 (fig. 7) — mirror those in the lower left corner of *The Chace* (1726), engraved by Bernard Baron after John Wootton (fig. 8).[9] The later objects and the earlier image differ significantly only in the prey: the stag depicted on the silver and in the embroidered pictures replaces a hare in the engraving. In historical context, the change makes sense: stag hunting had the most prestige for English hunters, since deer were in shorter supply than any other type of game. On the Simpkins teapot, only the figure with the bow and arrow lacks a direct coun-terpart in the embroidered pictures.[10]

Horsemanship in general also suggested traditional status to colonials, as in a creampot (fig. 9) made by Jacob Hurd for the Providence, Rhode Island, merchant William Corey and his wife Mary (Aiken) Corey. On the front panel, a man wearing boots, trousers, a short jacket, and a hat holds a whip in his left

Fig. 7. Sarah Warren (1730–1797), needlework picture, Boston, Massachusetts, 1748. Silk, wool, linen; h. 10 in., w. 20 ⅝. Winterthur Museum (1962.69A).

Fig. 8. Bernard Baron (after John Wootton) (ca. 1683–1764), *The Chace*, 1726. Line engraving; h. 21 ¾ in., w. 31 in. National Trust, Clandon Park, England.

hand and the bridle of the horse he is facing in his right hand (fig. 10). The saddled horse with cropped tail stands in profile with his head and ears erect and his right front leg raised. Like the scenes of the chase, the image on this cream-pot associates the owner with the activities of a gentleman. The posture of the man echos a figure common in the hunting prints, which often feature a groom

Fig. 9. Jacob Hurd (1702/03–1758), creampot, Boston, Massachusetts, ca. 1750. Silver; h. 4 1/16 in. Museum of Fine Arts, Houston, Bayou Bend Collection, Gift of Miss Ima Hogg (B.69.112).

Fig. 10. Detail of Jacob Hurd creampot shown in fig. 9.

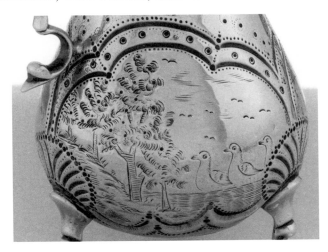

Fig. 11. Detail of Jacob Hurd creampot shown in fig. 9.

holding a horse on a lead.[11] Other precedents for this kind of equestrian imagery, also not necessarily about hunting, turn up in the colonies earlier in the century, such as prints of race horses. When Mrs. Sarah Dolbear died in Boston in 1745, for example, her estate included "a picture of Duke Bolton's Horse," possibly a print of Fear-Nought, a horse owned by the duke of Bolton and the winner of famous matches in 1732 and 1733.[12] At least one explicit example of the colonial desire to acquire prestige through riding appeared later in the century, in a 1773 Boston advertisement, when a Frenchman named Regnier offered to teach, among other things, "HORSEMANSHIP; — An Art justly admired and counted Part of polite Education."[13]

Another chased panel on the Corey family creampot depicts waterfowl swimming in a small body of water (fig. 11). Similarly, on another Hurd creampot, two swans swim along, one preening its neck feathers. A panel on the same pot shows a landscape that suggests a traditional manor estate: a large building looms on a hill below which is a gate and a fence. Like the hunt, this kind of landscape, particularly with the manor in evidence, suggests the traditional wealth and stability of the English gentry. The popularity of such allusions among New Englanders is also attested to in the embroidered needlework, where birds swimming in small bodies of water were stock imagery.[14] These generalized allusions to the pastoral, to the delights of tamed nature, enjoyed wide appeal in the mid-eighteenth century when they were fundamental to rococo taste.

Sexual Pursuit and Courtship

The depiction of noble pursuits on the side of a silver teapot has a solid and

27

Fig. 12. Detail of William Simpkins teapot shown in fig. 3.

fairly obvious class association: the hunt, horsemanship, ownership of a country estate all supposedly demonstrated one's gentility, as did the possession of a silver tea set. The meaning of other narratives chased on the silver might seem less self-evident today, but their importance to the class of people using the tea sets would have been no less vital.

One piece under consideration here actually pulls together the hunt image discussed above and another prominent narrative theme, that of courtship or sexual pursuit, by virtue of a metaphorical connection that would have been immediate to its contemporary viewers. The Simpkins teapot, described above, demonstrates the depth of meaning of what appears to be a fairly simple image quite well. On the other side of the teapot, one might say the flipside of the stag hunt, is a courtship scene.

This panel shows a woman seated in what appears to be an orchard (fig. 12). Her left hand is raised toward her face and her right hand, extended in front of her, holds what is probably a bird. A standing male figure faces the woman and in his left hand holds toward her a round object, perhaps a piece of fruit from one of the trees that surround the couple. The man is hatless and wears a knee-length coat with cuffed sleeves and a large button at the back of the waist. A dog in profile is seated behind him and birds perch in the trees to the left and right.

Below, I will go over the elements that identify this as a courtship scene, but not before addressing how the pairing of the two scenes, the stag hunt and the seated couple, creates a shared meaning — the hunt as sexual pursuit, courtship as a hunt. While the association is certainly not foreign to us today, it was an association that eighteenth-century viewers would have found in many kinds of texts all around them. Music published at this time, for example, typically drew on the rococo flair for double entendre. *The Musical Entertainer*, first published by George Bickham, Jr., in 1737, contains the song "The Return from the Chace," in which a parallel develops between the pleasures of pursuing the stag and those of pursuing the opposite sex:

> The Stag rouz'd before us
> Away seems to fly,
> And pants to the Chorus,
> Of Hounds in full Cry;
> Then follow follow follow follow
> The Musical Chace,
> Where Pleasure and vig'rous
> Health you embrace
> The Day's Sport when over;
> Makes Blood circle right,
> And gives the brisk lover,
> Fresh Charms for the Night.
> Then let us now enjoy
> All we can while we may
> Let love crown the Night,
> As our Sports crown ye Day.[15]

The Simpkins teapot, as does this verse, suggests a close association between the sports of the day and the sports of the night. And once the association is recognized, the stag hunt on the Simpkins teapot becomes intriguing in other details as well: the archer about to shoot at the deer sharpens the double meaning of the scene by virtue of the possible allusion to Eros, the god of love.

The function of these numinous hunt scenes on objects that were destined for domestic use and display may also have lent their meanings to social activities. As Rodris Roth has written, the tea ceremony was the very core of family life, bringing together as it did the whole family once a day, and it was also a time at which the home welcomed friends, acquaintances, and even strangers. Therefore, the decoration on a teapot, such as converse panels describing a stag hunt and a courting couple, would have had a prominent place in the family's social life. Furthermore, young women acquired silver objects in anticipation of marriage and largely took responsibility for serving at the tea table, a fertile setting for growing acquaintances between marriageable men and women.[16]

The Simpkins teapot and Edwards creampot may well have been made for young unmarried women who would have used the objects during a period of

Fig. 13. Unknown member of Chandler family, needlework picture, Boston, Massachusetts, 1758. Wool and silk on linen; h. 15 in., w. 23 in. Private collection. From Betty Ring, *Girlhood Embroidery: American Samplers and Pictorial Needlework, 1650–1850* (New York: Alfred A. Knopf, 1993), fig. 50.

courtship. Although research has failed to turn up a history of ownership for either piece, certain details point to this possibility. Only one set of initials, MS, appears on the teapot, suggesting ownership by an individual rather than by a married couple. The Speakman coat of arms on the creampot could belong to either a couple or a single person, but it was in fact the custom for women to have their silver ornamented with their arms before or at the time of marriage. Combined with the narrative scenes chased on the panels of the teapot, the likelihood that all referred to a single woman preparing for marriage appears quite high.

Although we cannot know for certain that the man and woman engraved on the Simpkins teapot were intended as a courting couple, examples of Massachusetts needlework once again bolster the reading. Several representations of courtship in embroidered pictures closely resemble the image used here, such as a 1758 embroidery by an unknown member of the Chandler family (fig. 13).[17] The embroidery shows two couples seated in the landscape. A youthful couple seated in separate chairs is at the right. The woman holds a bird in her raised and extended hand while her eyes are directed at the aloof and preoccupied man seated next to her; he is also the imminent target of cupid's arrow. To the left, and more prominent, appears another seated couple accompanied by a bird. This pair is clearly amorous — they sit close together on a sofa and hold hands.[18]

30

While one may with good confidence surmise the individuals in these images to be amorous couples, other details act as icons of sexuality — specifically, the birds and the fruit. An arbor of fruit-bearing trees frames the couple on the Simpkins teapot, and in the embroidery a bird eats fruit from a fruit-laden tree on the horizon above the woman holding a bird. Fruit as a metaphor for fertility, and therefore sexuality, is so well established in Western culture in general that it hardly needs elaboration. Less apparent to us today, however, may be the meaning of the birds in these images, but the bird as a metaphor for awakening sexuality would have been very familiar to the eighteenth-century viewer. The same icon appeared frequently in popular poetry and songs.[19] In "The Request to the Nightingale," a song composed by George Frederick Handel to words by John Lockman, the nightingale is the means for arousing passion.[20] The tradition also has roots in the classical tradition in the myth of Leda and the swan, which we see retold for an eighteenth-century audience in the poem "To a Lady on Her Parrot," included in a collection of poems published in York, England, in 1738:

> When Nymphs were coy, and Love could not prevail,
> The Gods, disguis'd, were seldom known to fail:
> Leda was chaste, but yet a feather'd Jove
> Surpris'd the Fair, and taught her how to Love;
> There's no Celestial but his Heav'n would quit,
> For any Form which might to thee admit.
> See how the wanton Bird, at every Glance,
> Swells his glad Plumes, and feels an amorous Trance
> The Queen of Beauty has forsook the Dove,
> Henceforth Parrot be the Bird of Love.[21]

Interestingly at odds with the courtship scenes is the chasing on the lid of the Dane snuffbox. Inscribed to "Mary Loring / 1752" (fig. 14), the box portrays a standing woman in a wooded landscape; behind her, a leaping dog chases birds. A comparison of the scene on the box with another song from Bickham's *Musical Entertainer*, "The Ladies Case" (fig. 15), suggests a play on words that may be relevant here: *case* as receptacle, *case* as situation, and *case* as argument. The illustrations on both the box and the song show a solitary woman silhouetted against the horizon. The song laments that propriety, which subjugated a woman to her parents and husband, detained her from pursuing her own feelings and desires. Two lines are particularly poignant: "The Parent controuls us untill we are Wives, yᵉ Husband enslaves us yᵉ rest of our lives." The box's owner, Mary Loring, is probably the Mary Loring (nee Giles) whose intentions to marry Nathaniel Loring were recorded in Boston in 1747.[22] That Mary Loring is most likely the same woman whose father John Giles presented her with the gift of a teapot with the Giles arms and a sugar bowl in 1748, the year

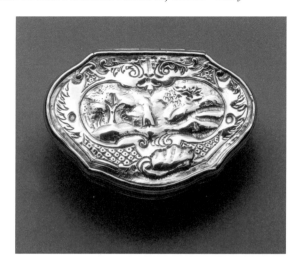

Fig. 14. Thomas Dane (1726–ca. 1795), snuffbox, Boston, Massachusetts, ca. 1752. Silver; h. ⅞ in., w. 2¾, d. 2⅛ in. The Art Institute of Chicago, Laura S. Matthews Fund (1982.996). © 2000, The Art Institute of Chicago. All Rights Reserved.

after her marriage.[23] Both are engraved "Mary Loring / The Gift of her Father / John Gyles Esq. 1748." The inscriptions are unusual in Boston silver for the explicit identification of the relationship of the donor to the donee. Drawing on these other connections and details, one could read the image on the box as a reference to an isolated, possibly even lonely, existence. The inscriptions could suggest that, like the woman in the song, Mary Loring had a controlling parent. In the absence of any evidence about the quality of Mary's marriage to Nathaniel Loring, her husband of five years at that date, one is free to speculate that it was not a happy one.

Conflict

Of these three primary categories of motifs chased on this Boston silver, the first two make no specific reference to the concrete circumstances in which mid-eighteenth-century New Englanders lived: the imagery typical to sport and courtship scenes generally draws on a picturesque countryside borrowed from English ideals rather than any real landscape. Our third category here, military conflict, breaks from this "generic" style to refer, at times with considerable detail, to the real world of the colonial owners of this silver. In general, the martial theme became more prominent for New Englanders during the mid-eighteenth century, when fortifications in the region were enhanced considerably. Of course, King George's War provided the specific context for that enhancement.

That war and its outcome for colonials emerges as an allusion on a Simpkins creampot held today at the Cleveland Museum. With imagery borrowed from John Gay's popular fables, the chasing on the creampot fulfilled a number of needs for its Boston owners: it alluded to the colonies' military endeavors and it drew on English literature such that it demonstrated its owners' refinement

Fig. 15. George Bickham, Jr. (1706?–1771), "The Ladies Case." From *The Musical Entertainer* (London, 1737–39), 69. The Beinecke Rare Book and Manuscript Library, Yale University.

and erudition.[24] Gay's *Fables*, first published in 1727, were second in popularity among his works only to *The Beggar's Opera*, which he released in 1728. Gay, a poet and dramatist, was a friend of Alexander Pope, Jonathan Swift, and Richard Steele. New Englanders admired the work of this literary circle, even to the point of imitating them. The Boston ministers Benjamin Colman and Mather Byles, the merchant Joseph Green, and the almanac publisher Nathaniel Ames were among those who adulated the new English verse.[25]

Nearly every verse in the 1727 publication is original and gives a contemporary twist to the traditional moral emblem. Each of the fifty-one fables is illustrated with an engraving; the chased images on the creampot are taken from the emblem "The Shepherd's Dog and the Wolf" (fig. 16). The verse tells us that the dog, who had long sought the wolf for preying on his master's flock, stumbles by accident on the wolf's den. The dog exhorts the wolf, "Let us awhile the war suspend, And reason as from friend to friend." Replies the wolf, "A truce! 'Tis done." The dog begins the parley by imploring the wolf to give up preying on defenseless sheep. The wolf retorts that the dog should make that speech to his master, who devours far more sheep than he. The fable closes with this thought:

> An open foe may prove a curse
> But a pretended friend is worse.

Fig. 16. Bernard Baron, after John Wootton (ca. 1683–1764), "The Shepherd's Dog and the Wolf." From John Gay, *Fables* (London, 1727). The Beinecke Rare Book and Manuscript Library, Yale University.

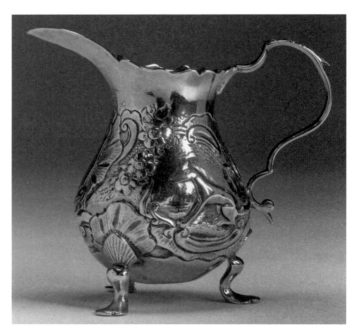

Fig. 17. William Simpkins (1704–1780), creampot (left side), Boston, Massachusetts, ca. 1750. Silver; h. 3 13/16 in. The Cleveland Museum of Art, Gift from the J. H. Wade Fund (21.955). © Cleveland Museum of Art, 2000.

Fig. 18. Right side of William Simpkins creampot shown in fig. 17.

On the creampot, the wolf that appears on one side mirrors exactly the wolf in the book (fig. 17). With head erect and ears perked, he sits with his front legs stretched a little before him and with his large bushy tail extending behind. On the opposite side of the creampot the shepherd's dog sits in a similar pose, but with his nose tilted upward and one of his ears flat against his head (fig. 18).

The creampot is engraved with the monogram G/DS and is said to have been made for a member of the Gray family of Boston. Why would this fable have been thought suitable for the Gray's tea table in roughly 1750? At the ritual of teatime, the illustrations of the fable would have provided a conversation piece to add to the sociability of the occasion. As suggested above, the creampot linked its owners to a large book with lavish illustrations – an object then accessible only to people with money, education, and they would want to think, taste. Moreover, the tenor of the exchange between the dog and wolf would have had implications for New Englanders specific to the ramifications of King George's War.

The creampot was made soon after the resolution of the war, which was part of the ongoing conflict between England and France for the control of North America. New Englanders contributed to that struggle in 1745 with their suc-

35

Fig. 19. Jacob Hurd (1702/03–1758), creampot, Boston, Massachusetts, ca. 1750. Silver; h. 3⅞ in. The Cleveland Museum of Art, Gift of Hollis French (40.219). © Cleveland Museum of Art, 2000.

cessful siege of the French fortress of Louisbourg, a fortification that guarded the entrance to the St. Lawrence River and sheltered French privateers who preyed on the shipping of New England merchants. The colonists took great pride in the capture of Louisbourg. In the treaty made at Aix-la-Chapelle that concluded the war in 1748, however, the English gave Louisbourg back to the French in exchange for Madras, which the French had captured. The colonists felt betrayed by this action. The fable as depicted on the creampot parallels these events: France, the open foe, certainly was a curse for New Englanders, but by returning Louisbourg to France, England, the pretended friend, reveals itself to be the worse enemy.

The pride in their shipping that played a part in these events, and as such became a motivation for colonial self-defense, also appears on several of the creampots. Scenes on two Hurd pieces certainly expressed pride on the part of owners who derived their wealth from the sea. One Hurd creampot depicts a ship tethered to a steep, tree-covered bank, several of which frame the body of water (fig. 19). This creampot, which bears the Vassall arms, probably belonged

Fig. 20. Detail of Jacob Hurd creampot shown in fig. 9.

to John Vassall, a Harvard-educated merchant who lived in Cambridge and had ties to the sugar trade in Jamaica. A chased scene on another Hurd creampot (not illustrated) shows another ship, this one from the rear, moored to the shore; in this illustration, a figure near a house peers at the ship with a spyglass.[26]

The remaining images are more explicit descriptions of conflict, weaponry, and military fortifications, and in several cases they refer almost directly to New England geography. Two more Hurd creampots depict scenes of maritime warfare; on one, two ships confront one another (fig. 20); on the other, a ship tows a small boat from which cannon smoke billows (fig. 21). Such images would have been familiar to New Englanders. In William Burgis's *South East View of ye Great Town of Boston*, first published in 1725, a ship in the left foreground tows a small boat; the billowing puffs of smoke from the ship's cannon seems a likely source for the chasing on the latter creampot.[27] A comparison of the original Burgis view of 1725 and the revised version published in 1743 offers evidence of the enhanced emphasis on militarism and fortifications in Boston in the 1740s. The later version shows an expanded South Battery with the notation "A New Battery 35 guns," the addition of Fort George on Bird Island at the lower left, and of Fort Charles at the middle of the right edge. In the intervening twenty years fortifications had assumed increased importance, including strengthening the Boston Harbor defenses beginning in 1739.[28]

A more elaborate scene chased on another Hurd creampot shows a fortification with ships nearby (fig. 22). A sentinel patrols the fortification, which has masonry walls, cannon, and a watchtower that flies the British flag. Below the fortification a figure stands on a wharf that projects into the water, where a small two-masted vessel is moored. To the right a large ship flying the flag of the East India Company rides with sails furled. The scene has been inter-

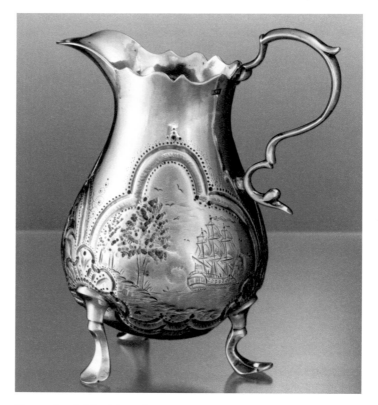

Fig. 21. Jacob Hurd (1702/03–1758), creampot, Boston, Massachusetts, ca. 1750. Silver; h. 4½ in. Yale University Art Gallery, Mabel Brady Garvan Collection (1930.1371).

preted as Castle William, the fortified entrance to Boston Harbor, which was also the subject of an unascribed view done in the early eighteenth century (fig. 23). Or the panel could portray the South Battery, which also flew the British flag from its sentinel tower and was outfitted with gunnery fortifications, as shown in the engraving of it made by Thomas Johnston about 1765 (fig. 24). Of course, the chaser could also have improvised a scene that combined elements from both of these engravings.

⁙

Although this is only a small group of items, its iconography encompasses a broad range of beliefs and social concerns of New Englanders in the years around 1750. The ornament on these pieces might just be viewed as the crafts-man's aping of rococo-style narrative imagery, with a dash of period wit thrown in as the chasers depict the chase. Comparisons with other texts, however, such as popular songs and poetry, show the profound meanings these objects had for

Fig. 22. Jacob Hurd (1702/03–1758), creampot, Boston, Massachusetts, ca. 1750. Silver; h. 4 ½ in. Yale University Art Gallery, Mabel Brady Garvan Collection (1934.348).

Fig. 23. Anonymous, *A View of Castle William By Boston in New England*, ca. 1730. Line engraving; h. 11 ½ in., w. 12 ½ in. The Metropolitan Museum of Art, bequest of Charles Allen Munn, 1924 (24.90.41).

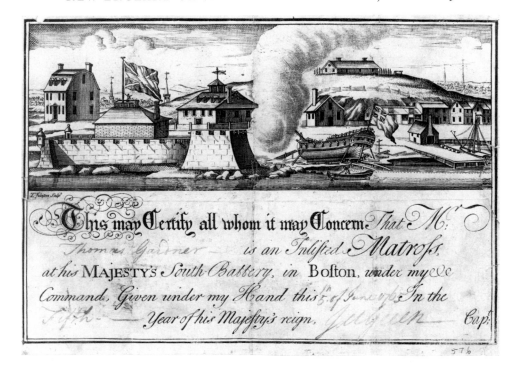

Fig. 24. Thomas Johnston (ca. 1708–1767), *South Battery, Boston*, Boston, Massachusetts, ca. 1765. Line engraving; h. 2 ¹¹⁄₁₆ in., w. 7 ⅜ in. Boston Athenaeum (A/B64B6/For.s. [no. 1]).

the people who owned and used them. While the ideas captured in these narratives transcend their geographical region, and possibly even their historical moment, the objects themselves are remarkable as representatives of a phenomenon apparently unique in the colonies: only mid-eighteenth-century Boston had this rich tradition of expressing these human feelings in pictorial form on their silver.

Notes

1. Craftsmen working in other media in British North America did use narrative scenes to ornament objects. Narrative carving is occasionally found on Philadelphia furniture. Many cast-iron stove plates made in Pennsylvania and New Jersey have scenes based on Aesop's fables. See Morrison H. Heckscher and Leslie Greene Bowman, *American Rococo, 1750–1775: Elegance in Ornament* (New York: The Metropolitan Museum of Art and Los Angeles County Museum of Art, 1992), 202; and Henry C. Mercer, *The Bible in Iron*, 3d ed. (Doylestown, Pa.: Bucks County Historical Society, 1961), 231–32, 236, 248; nos. 291–93, no. 316, no. 381.

2. For a discussion of the introduction of the rococo style in America, see Heckscher and Bowman, *American Rococo, 1750–1775*.

3. The age of the chasing on the creampots by Simpkins and Edwards has been questioned; see Phillip M. Johnston, *Catalogue of American Silver: The Cleveland Museum of Art* (Cleveland: Cleveland Museum of Art in cooperation with Indiana University Press, 1994), 46, 144. A comparison of the chasing on the creampots, however, to the Simpkins teapot and the Dane box suggests it is all by the same hand. In addition, the imagery on the silver is consistent with other forms of artistic expression in Boston at the time these pieces would have been made.

4. Cox's work appeared in many editions throughout the eighteenth and into the nineteenth century. Richard Blome's more elaborate publication appeared in 1686 and was reissued in the early eighteenth century.

5. George Francis Dow, comp., *The Arts and Crafts in New England: Gleanings from Boston Newspapers, 1704–1775* (Topsfield: Wayside Press, 1927), 24. Abbott Lowell Cummings, ed., *Rural Household Inventories: Establishing the Names, Uses, and Furnishings of Rooms in the Colonial New England Home, 1675–1775* (Boston: Society for the Preservation of New England Antiquities, 1964), xxxvi. These prints might have been hunting scenes by John Boydell, as for example, *A North View of Denbigh Castle, in North Wales*; Nancy Graves Cabot, "The Fishing Lady and Boston Common," *Antiques* 40, no. 1 (July 1941): 30; Dudley Snelgrove, *British Sporting and Animal Prints, 1658–1874* (London: Tate Gallery for the Yale Center for British Art, 1981). In Snelgrove, see p. 210 for the set of seven, *Fox-Hunting* engraved by L. Truchy and C. Canot after John Wootton in 1735; see p. 211 for the set of four, *Stag Hunting* engraved by R. Sheppard after Jan Wyck; see p. 155 for a set of twelve hunting prints after James Seymour and others.

6. For the embroideries that include horsemen, hounds, and stags see an anonymous embroidery in Betty Ring, *Girlhood Embroidery: American Samplers and Pictorial Needlework, 1650–1850*, 2 vols. (New York: Alfred A. Knopf, 1993), 1:47, fig. 45, no. 6; a picture attributed to Jane Tyler (b. ca. 1732 or 1733) that descended in the Gilman family of Exeter, N.H. (Nancy Graves Cabot, "Another Needlework Picture, Adam and Eve," *Antiques* 45, no. 6 [June 1944]: 300–301); and a picture by Mary Pickering, ca. 1748 (Ring, *Girlhood Embroidery*, 1:47, fig. 44). The pictures that simply show hounds chasing a stag include an example by Johanna Ball, b. 1732 (Cabot, "The Fishing Lady and Boston Common," fig. 4); a chimneypiece attributed to Eunice Bourne, ca. 1748 (Ring, *Girlhood Embroidery*, 1:44, fig. 40); a chimneypiece that descended in the Lowell family (Helen Bowen, "The Fishing Lady and Boston Common," *Antiques* 4, no. 2 [August 1923]: 72, fig. 5); a picture that descended in the Hill family of Boston (Bowen, "The Fishing Lady and Boston Common," 73, fig. 6); and a picture attributed to Mary (Polly) Burns (1753–1794) (Ring, *Girlhood Embroidery*, 50, fig. 48).

7. Ring, *Girlhood Embroidery*, 1:45.

8. For the example from 1746, see Ring, *Girlhood Embroidery*, fig. 43. For the example from 1748, see Susan Burroughs Swan, *A Winterthur Guide to American Needlework* (New York: Crown Publishers, Inc., 1976), 36, pl. IV.

9. In addition to the picture by Sarah Warren, see the 1748 picture at Winterthur (Nancy Graves Cabot, "Engravings and Embroideries," *Antiques* 40, no. 6 [December 1941]: 367, fig. 1), a picture worked by Miss Derby of Salem (Bowen, "The Fishing Lady and Boston Common," 73, fig. 7), and a picture embroidered by Mary Avery (Bowen, "The Fishing Lady and Boston Common," 73, fig. 8).

10. Only the embroidered picture by Hannah Otis at the Museum of Fine Arts, Boston, ca. 1750, shows a figure practicing archery.

11. See, for example, the engraving by L. Truchy and C. Canot after John Wootton (Yale Center for British Art, B1985.36.1280), although this and other images do not correspond exactly to the pose on the Hurd creampot.

12. See E. McSherry Fowble, *Two Centuries of Prints in America, 1680–1880: A Selective Catalogue of the Winterthur Museum Collection* (Charlottesville: University Press of Virginia for the Henry Francis du Pont Winterthur Museum, 1987), no. 125.

13. Cited in Robert Francis Seybolt, *The Private Schools of Colonial Boston* (Cambridge, Mass.: Harvard University Press, 1935), 70.

14. For the Jacob Hurd creampot (see fig. 22), see Kathryn C. Buhler and Graham Hood, *American Silver: Garvan and Other Collections in the Yale University Art Gallery*, 2 vols. (New Haven: Yale University Press for the Yale University Art Gallery, 1970), 1:128–29, no. 150. Ring, *Girlhood Embroidery*, notes needlework examples of this kind of image; see, for instance, the piece by Eunice Bourne, 44, fig. 40.

15. George Bickham, Jr., *The Musical Entertainer* (1740; New York: Broude Bros., 1965), 7.

16. Rodris Roth, *Tea Drinking in Eighteenth-Century America: Its Etiquette and Equipage* (Washington, D.C.: Smithsonian Institution, 1961), 66–70.

17. Another picture completed by an unknown woman about 1760 has as its central focus a man and a woman standing side by side; the woman holds a bird in her hand (Ring, *Girlhood Embroidery*, 47, fig. 45).

18. This couple bears comparison to another pair pictured on the sheet music for "The Apology," also from Bickham. The theme of the song is male repentance for having shown affection to another woman. However, that does not appear to be the subject of the needlework due to the presence of cupid.

19. In *Masters of Seventeenth-Century Dutch Genre Painting* (Philadelphia: Philadelphia Museum of Art, 1984), Peter C. Sutton, citing E. de Jongh, "Double Entendre in Some Seventeenth-Century Genre Subjects," has written "numerous seventeenth-century texts indicate that in Dutch and German *vogel* (bird) was often synonymous with the phallus; *vogelen* (to bird) was a euphemism for sexual intercourse; and *vogelaar* (bird catcher) could refer to a procurer or a lover." The sexual connotations of birds were expressed in many forms in seventeenth-century Dutch paintings and prints; see pp. 250–51. Thomas Michie brought this information to my attention. Deborah Diemente also supplied a reference to an eighteenth-century French song in which a maiden loses her virginity to a nightingale; see *Bergerettes: Twenty Romances and Songs of the Eighteenth Century*, comp. J. B. Weckerlin (New York: G. Schirmer, Inc., 1941). English songs and popular poetry of the eighteenth century suggest that these connotations prevailed in English culture as well.

20. Bickham, *Musical Entertainer*, 17. See also in the same volume "The Persuasive Lover," 48.

21. Joseph Yarrow, comp., *A Choice Collection of Poetry by the most Ingenious Men of the Age* (York, Eng.: A. Staples, 1738).

22. *A Report of the Record Commissioners of the City of Boston, Containing the Boston Marriages from 1700 to 1751* (Boston: Municipal Printing Office, 1898), 286.

23. For the teapot by John Burt, see Francis J. Puig et al., *English and American Silver in the Collection of The Minneapolis Institute of Arts* (Minneapolis: Minneapolis Institute of Arts, 1989), 236–37. For the sugar bowl by Thomas Dane, see John Marshall Phillips, *Masterpieces of New England Silver, 1650–1800* (New Haven: Yale University Art Gallery, 1939), 35.

24. See L. Stephen, *English Literature and Society in the Eighteenth Century* (New York, 1904).

25. Moses Coit Tyler, *A History of American Literature, 1607–1765* (New York: Collier Books, 1962), 301–14, 363–72.

26. See Buhler and Hood, *American Silver*, 127–28, no. 149. This creampot tentatively has been identified as bearing the Johnson arms and also has the initials "BI" and "I / IS."

27. For illustrations of the different issues of the Burgis view of Boston, see John W. Reps, "Boston by Bostonians: The Printed Plans and Views of the Colonial City by its Artists, Cartographers, Engravers, and Publishers," in *Boston Prints and Printmakers, 1670–1775* (Boston: Colonial Society of Massachusetts, 1973), 36–41.

28. A committee was established in Boston in 1739–40 to improve the deteriorated conditions of the South and North Batteries. In 1744 a vessel arrived from England with twenty forty-two-pound cannon and two mortars for Castle William. Col. Richard Gridley of Boston, who at the siege of Louisbourg erected a battery near the north cape of the harbor, was hired in 1746 by Gov. William Shirley to fortify Governor's Island and to strengthen the Castle. In 1751 Gridley was paid £45 for his services and expenses. See Justin Winsor, ed., *The Memorial History of Boston* (Boston: James R. Osgood and Company, 1881), 2:116, n. 3.

Colonial New England Silver Snuff, Tobacco, and Patch Boxes: Indices of Gentility

MADELINE SIEFKE ESTILL

IN A PORTRAIT by Thomas Gainsborough from the early 1770s, Englishman Ralph Bell embodies an ideal of stylish grace as he takes a pinch of snuff with a negligent air, holding his silver snuffbox lightly in his elegantly crooked fingers (fig. 1). Together with his fine clothes, walking stick, and attitude of leisured assurance, the box is one of the attributes that establishes him as a gentleman.[1] Snuffboxes and their near siblings, tobacco and patch boxes, counted among the "ornaments of life" needed to complete a genteel appearance.[2] Their graceful use demonstrated their owners' knowledge of courtly behavior and promoted a cultural continuity within the Anglo-American world of the seventeenth and eighteenth centuries; a gentleman could be recognized by his behavior and his possessions whether he lived in the Old World or in the New. The boxes both marked social distinctions between classes and affirmed social bonds within a class. This essay illustrates the complex world in which these objects moved by considering them in the rich cultural context of contemporary English and American literary sources such as essays, sermons, poems, and diaries.

Most colonial silver tobacco, snuff, and patch boxes are round or oval in shape, with flat, conforming lids. As a rule, a silversmith fashioned a box from a flat piece of metal onto which he soldered straight, seamed sides; only rarely does a box have sides raised from its base. Lids, whether friction-fit or hinged, generally displayed the same seamed and soldered construction. A craftsman sometimes finished a box with decorative moldings applied to the edge of the base and lid. Although the group of boxes on which this study is based bear the marks of colonial New England silversmiths, the transatlantic scope of this essay reflects an ambiguity in the boxes themselves: although many American craftsmen manufactured boxes, they also imported pieces ready-made from England, to which they could apply their own marks, making it difficult to judge the origin of a given object.[3]

Similarly, the precise intended use of any box can be hard to ascertain. Colonial craftsmen and owners clearly made distinctions among the various

Fig. 1. Thomas Gainsborough (1727–1788), *Ralph Bell (1720–1801)*, 1772–74. Oil on canvas; h. 92 ¼ in., w. 61 ⅛ in. North Carolina Museum of Art, Purchased with funds from the State of North Carolina and the North Carolina Art Society (Robert F. Phifer Funds) (52.9.70).

boxes, as evidenced by silversmiths' advertisements from the period.[4] Today, however, it is exceedingly difficult to sort out the features that distinguished one category of box from another. At best, one sometimes may conjecture a box's planned use, based on its history and decoration, as well as on its general size and type of lid. As a rule, larger boxes with friction-fit lids are catalogued as tobacco boxes, while smaller containers with friction-fit lids are called patch boxes. In turn, boxes made for the purpose of holding snuff would be unlikely to have a removable lid, for it was considered a mark of gentility to be able to gracefully hold a snuffbox in one hand while taking a pinch of snuff with the other.[5] A separate lid would defeat the elegant snuffer. By the mid-eighteenth century, however, some silversmiths made patch boxes with hinged lids, as well; neither size nor type of lid alone can point reliably to a box's intended purpose.[6] Furthermore, one must remember that colonial owners used their boxes for purposes other than the one for which they were made: a notice in the *Boston Gazette* on December 19, 1757, announced: "Taken up in the Street last Thursday, a Silver Snuff Box, with a Mourning Ring in it. The owner may have them again by telling the Marks and paying for this advertisement."[7] Such

45

announcements of lost boxes speak of Americans carrying their boxes with them and using their contents about town.

Despite their usually diminutive size, boxes functioned in seventeenth- and eighteenth-century Anglo-American culture as potent indices of gentility and today can tell us about patterns of colonial social interaction. Like clothing, jewelry, and cosmetics, the silver boxes acted as sign-vehicles in colonial New England, giving clues about their owners' general socioeconomic status, conception of self, and attitudes toward others.[8] Fine objects were the attributes of the genteel, and owning them was the right of the elite. Thus, in *The Complete Gentleman* (1634), Englishman Henry Peacham argued that "among the prerogatives of the gentleman class is the right to have the best material things."[9] By carrying and using the luxurious silver boxes, colonial men and women set themselves apart from the general population who carried objects associated with their trade or craft. Just as tools were sign-vehicles for craftsmen, so too were the boxes sign-vehicles for men who possessed leisure: one could not work and manipulate a box at the same time.

Patches

Made from a wide range of materials — black silk, velvet, paper, or red leather — and cut into a variety of shapes and sizes, patches were applied to the face or bosom with mastic.[10] As understood in their time, they helped to create an impression of formal distinction and enhanced one's beauty and desirability. Some people who decorated themselves with patches believed the spots made them appear younger and more fashionable, while others used patches to hide blemishes.

In England patches became hugely popular among both men and women in stylish circles by the mid-seventeenth century and continued in vogue through the late 1700s. Advertisements for both patch boxes and patches scattered through colonial newspapers indicate that Americans, well aware of prevailing London fashions, soon followed the British lead. English government officials in colonial America contributed to the spread of such courtly fashions, helping to set the standards of tasteful dress and decorum. Members of the Penn family, for example, were noted for their stylishness; in 1655 Samuel Pepys of London wrote in his famed diary that he had seen Sir William Penn's daughter Pegg, then only thirteen years old, wearing patches for the first time.[11] One may suppose that the Penn family brought their refined taste in dress with them to the colonies. Indeed, American colonists admired leaders who lent a sense of polish and dignity to their offices. In the Massachusetts Bay Colony, the pamphlet *Further Quaeries Upon the Present State of New-English Affairs* (ca. 1690) advised voters to elect officials "of good Fashion and Quality, and such as maintain the due Grandure of a Government."[12]

Fig. 2. William Hogarth (1697–1764), *Morning*, 1738. Engraving; h. 19 3/16 in., w. 15 11/16. Museum of Fine Arts, Boston,
Harvey D. Parker Collection (P12008).

Nonetheless, the practice of patching still met with mockery and criticism in
both England and America. Critics condemned patches for contributing to
myriad vices, including lust, vanity, and extravagance. Men who used patches
were ridiculed as effeminate fops, young women who wore spots were accused
of denigrating God's handiwork, and older women were mocked for foolishly
borrowing the trappings of youth. "Morning," an engraving published by the
English artist William Hogarth in 1738, shows a gaunt old maid making her way
through Covent Garden (fig. 2). When seen beside the fresh, young beauty to
her right, she seems even older, and the patch high on her cheek becomes sadly
out of place. During the Interregnum, Parliament took steps to forbid patching all together. When official disapproval proved ineffectual, it fell to clergymen, moralists, and satirists to contain the fashion.

Ministers charged women who wore patches with deliberately kindling lust
in men. In his fiery treatise *The Loathsomnesse of Long Haire* (1654), Englishman
Thomas Hall railed against such wickedness, adding that those who patch bear

responsibility not only for their own damnation but for that of the men aroused by their immodest costume as well. He dismissed patches as the badges of harlots and denounced the spots for the irreverence they show for God's creation.[13] In 1647 Nathaniel Ward, the minister of Ipswich, Massachusetts, reprimanded colonial women for following the vagaries of courtly fashion and for dressing above their station. As members of a church-state intended to be a model for all Christian communities, Massachusetts women should not fritter away their colony's material and spiritual resources by indulging in luxurious fashions.[14]

Visiting Boston in 1740, preacher George Whitefield measured the residents' purity of faith by their costume. He sadly noted in his journal that

> *Boston* is a large populous Place, very wealthy. . . . Ministers and People are obliged to confess, that Love of many is waxed cold. Both, for the Generality, seem'd too much conform'd to the World. There's much of the Pride of Life to be seen in their Assemblies. Jewels, Patches, and Gay Apparel, are commonly worn by the female sex; and even the common People, I observed dress'd up in the Pride of Life.[15]

Patches figured specifically in Whitefield's assessment of colonial failings. Like other moralists, he condemned extravagant dress overall, but found it particularly offensive when worn by the lower classes. It was conceited and disrespectful to dress above one's own station.[16]

Tobacco

A vignette of three figures, engraved on the lid of an English brass tobacco box dated 1772 (fig. 3), suggests the social stereotypes associated with the three prevalent means of tobacco consumption. A richly dressed gentleman wearing a sword offers a snuffbox to his companions and asks, "Voule Vous de Rappe?" (Would you like some snuff?), while the more plainly clad figure in the center holds a pipe and replies in accented tones, "No dis been better." A coarse, rural character at his side offers his own choice of tobacco and asks, "Will you have a quid?" Beneath runs the motto "Thes three unite in the Same Cause / This Snuffs that Smoaks the other Chaws." The box illustrates the broad social appeal of tobacco at the same time that it describes a hierarchy of use.

By the eighteenth century, fashionable Englishmen took their tobacco as snuff. Smoking was associated with soldiers, seamen, country squires, and foreigners; the Dutch were known to be great smokers, which might account for the accent of the brass box's figure with the pipe. None but rude yokels indulged in the messy habit of chewing tobacco. In America, class distinctions regarding the different uses of tobacco were far less rigid, and colonists were not restricted by their station to choosing one method over another; for example, President John Adams is known to have enjoyed using tobacco in all three forms at various stages in his life.[17] Nonetheless, snuffing was largely the urban

Fig. 3. Unknown maker, tobacco box, probably London, England, 1772. Brass; h. 1 in., l. 4 ⅛ in., w. 2 ¹¹⁄₁₆ in. Courtesy, Winterthur Museum (1961.1755).

habit of English and Dutch government officials and merchants, and other colonial leaders, and only slowly spread through society and into the country-side. Throughout the colonial period, smoking remained the most popular means of enjoying tobacco. Tobacco consumption had also played an important role in American life from the very first years of settlement. In his *Wonder-Working Providence*, Edward Johnson described the homesickness suffered by many of the first settlers to Massachusetts and recounted how they lived through their first bleak winter in the New World, enjoying what familiar comforts that they could: "[making] shift to rub out the Winters cold by the Fire-side, having fuell enough growing at their very doores, turning down many a drop of the Bottell, and burning Tobacco with all the Ease they could."[18]

Pleasure and support in times of trial, tobacco also was lauded as a medicinal wonder and source of inspiration. English essayist Sir Richard Steele expressed his fierce devotion to tobacco in a tribute to the tobacco box:

> Whoever in a mean Abode presumes
> To lodge that sacred Herb, whose curling Fumes
> (More grateful than *Sabaean* Odours far)
> Play around the Nose, and wanton in the Air;
> May Aesculapius let him always want
> The Virtues of the Health-restoring plant . . .
> How the defect of Talk it can supply,
> If we this way our Breath employ;
> How it collects the Thoughts, and serves instead
> Of biting Nails, or harrowing up the Head . . .[19]

For Steele, tobacco was a gift from the gods themselves and deserved to be honored as such; silver containers lent tremendous dignity to the tobacco within. Many shared Steele's belief in the medicinal powers of tobacco. The plant was extolled as a panacea and credited with curing such diverse ills as indigestion, paralysis, apoplexy, and toothache.[20] Nor was Steele alone in his appreciation of tobacco's stimulating effect on conversation. Avid users of both tobacco and snuff declared that regular consumption cleared their minds and lifted their thoughts. In "Snuff: A Poem," first published in Edinburgh in 1719, James Arbuckle lauded snuff as a muse and praised snuffboxes as well. He described how holding and using the box skillfully could enhance a man's talents in conversation: he could command an audience's attention by pausing, making his listeners wait while he opened his box and took a pinch of snuff. His speech following the pinch then took on greater emphasis. Arbuckle also argued that snuffboxes were necessary tools for ladies intent on showing themselves to best advantage and winning new suitors:

> Ten Thousand Killing Airs not yet explor'd,
> Does not the Snuff-Box to the Sex afford?
> Her Taper Fingers tap the gay *Machine*.
> How many Charms are in that instant seen?[21]

A lady who could manipulate a snuffbox with elegance drew attention to her beauty and grace.

An aid in courtship and conversation, tobacco became an important feature of social gatherings. In particular, the offer of tobacco functioned as a gesture of friendship. In a 1710 article for the English journal *The Tatler*, the editor related one visit to his club at which an acquaintance "show[ed] his good-will" by giving him a pipe of tobacco. Feeling indebted by such a friendly gesture, the writer then was obliged to prove his own amiability by listening to his companion's tedious stories.[22]

The role of tobacco in colonial taverns mirrored its social functions in genteel London clubs: taverns provided a place to meet with friends and they served liquor — drinking and smoking went hand in hand. *Sea Captains Carousing in*

Fig. 4. John Greenwood (1727–1792), *Sea Captains Carousing in Surinam*, 1758. Oil on bed ticking; h. 37 ¼ in; w. 75 ¼ in. Purchase, St. Louis Art Museum (256.1948).

Surinam, a painting by John Greenwood, illustrates this link (fig. 4) with its view of a group of merchants from Newport, Rhode Island, enjoying a riotous evening in a tavern; the men are drinking punch by the bowl-full, knocking chairs to the floor, and playing tricks on one another. One man staggers about drunkenly, as another vomits, and pipes and tobacco are everywhere.

The part smoking played in the debauched revelry of the eighteenth century was not lost on the critics of tobacco. Even John Adams, himself a smoker, was alarmed at the idle dissipation of the young men of Worcester, Massachusetts, who did not study but embraced sensual pleasures, spending every evening "playing Cards, drinking Punch and Wine, Smoaking Tobacco, swearing &c. while one hundred of the best Books lie on the shelves, Desks, and Chairs, in the same room."[23] If one was smoking, one was not working; colonial moralists sought to prevent their neighbors from falling into lives of idleness and excess.

Critics also recognized the possibility of addiction to tobacco. In a pamphlet addressed to prospective ministers, Cotton Mather expressed his wish that there were more controls on the purchase of tobacco and warned of the hold tobacco could gain on intemperate smokers, reducing them to "*Slave[s]* to the Pipe."[24] He only reluctantly accepted the careful, medicinal use of smoking tobacco, and he vehemently opposed any use of snuff at all, which he believed to lead to ill-health and dissolute craving for sensual pleasure. He thundered

How *shameful* a thing it is, for *People of Reason* to confess that they can't live easily half an Hour together, without a *Delight* so sensual, so Trivial, so very Contemptible, as that of *Tickling their Olfactory Nerves* a little? And even *bury* themselves alive, in *pungent Grains of titillating Dust*. . . . A very just Motto for the

Snuff-box might be, A LEADER TO THE COFFIN. If it be offer'd you, *Away with it*! I say again, *Away with it*![25]

For Mather, snuff serviced man's basest desires and endangered his soul. Unlike smoking tobacco, it had no redeeming qualities whatsoever.

It should be noted, however, that Mather's criticism of tobacco was not echoed by all church leaders. Indeed, a number of preachers enjoyed tobacco; the Yale collections include silver tobacco and snuffboxes owned by such prominent clergymen as Isaac Stiles, Joseph Burbeen, and William Welsteed. These New England clergymen and their families enjoyed considerable status in their communities and displayed that status through their fine dress, silver, and household furnishings. Another box, also in the Yale collections, belonged to Sarah Pierpont Edwards, wife of Jonathan Edwards and daughter of a celebrated New Haven minister (fig. 5). The box was found at the site of the Stockbridge farm occupied by the Edwardses following their dismissal by the Northampton church. In the wilds of western Massachusetts, surrounded only by the few settlers and Indians to whom her husband ministered, Sarah Edwards continued to use and display silver that made manifest her family's stature in its community and that set her family apart from its neighbors.

The decoration, as well as the material, of silver snuff, tobacco, and patch boxes bespoke their owners' genteel aspirations. The possession of a silver box and the knowledge to interpret correctly its decoration were gauges for measuring social standing. Despite living in a society that was not armigerous, socially ambitious New Englanders sometimes borrowed English coats of arms to aggrandize their silver. On the box engraved by John Coney for the Jeffries family (fig. 6), the decoration draws attention to the prestige and power of its owner, his social self-assurance, and his desire to link himself with noble fashion.

Other boxes reflect their owners' genteel erudition, since the engravings often invoked a knowledge of ancient literature that was the hallmark of the liberal education then reserved for the elite. Box lids frequently bore stylized flowers and foliage, many representing plants that carried symbolic meanings. For example, the sunflower engraved on a box marked by the Boston silversmith William Rouse refers, via classical mythology, to abiding love (fig. 7). In *Metamorphosis* Ovid tells the story of the lovers Apollo and Clytie, in which the ignored, jealous Clytie sits so long on the ground, watching the sun god pass above her, that she takes root and turns into a flower; nonetheless, she continues turning her head toward the sun she loves.[26] Most likely the sunflower decoration marked the Rouse box as a love token, but it would have failed in that purpose if its recipient were unable to interpret the engraving. Therefore, the box may well speak both of the affection of the colonial couple who exchanged it and of their refined taste and education.

Fig. 5. John Dixwell (1680/81–1725), patch box, Boston, Massachusetts, ca. 1720–25. Silver; w. 1⅞ in. Yale University Art Gallery, Gift of M. C. Edwards (1980.22).

Fig. 6. Unidentified London silversmith, tobacco box, ca. 1681. Engraved by John Coney (1655/56–1722), Boston, Massachusetts, ca. 1701. Silver; l. 3¹³⁄₁₆ in. Yale University Art Gallery, Mabel Brady Garvan Collection (1935.235).

The possession of a silver box, the knowledge to correctly interpret its decoration, and the ability to skillfully manipulate it in public all commanded considerable cachet. In this, the box became a sign-vehicle in a much larger discourse of the importance of bearing and manners. Gentlemen and social aspirants alike placed great value in knowing the proper, fashionable way to go about small, daily ceremonies, such as using a snuffbox. Dancing classes that taught modish posture and walking, as well as dancing itself, flourished on both sides of the Atlantic, and Americans intent on gentility had a wealth of instructive books to consult in order to polish their bearing. F. Nivelon's *The Rudiments of Genteel Behavior*, published in Britain in 1734, gives step-by-step instructions for walking, standing, dancing, and going through other daily motions in a refined fashion, "thereby distinguish[ing] the polite Gentleman

Fig. 7. William Rouse (1639–1705), patch box, Boston, Massachusetts, ca. 1680–90. Silver; h. 11/16 in., diam. 1 15/16 in. Yale University Art Gallery, John Marshall Phillips Collection, Gift of his nephews Donald and Marshall Phillips (1955.10.2).

from the rude Rustick."[27] One of the engravings in Nivelon's manual illustrates the proper stance a gentleman should take when giving or receiving an object (fig. 8). The accompanying text describes in daunting detail just how each part of the body should move:

> The head and the body to the waist must incline forwards in a circular, easy motion, and the body must rest on the left leg, that knee bending, the right knee straight, and the ball of the foot lightly touching the ground; the right arm must bend at the wrist and elbow to appear a little circular. . . . But at the time of offering or receiving, the arm must be extended, and the look directed to the hand offer'd to, or receiving from, then draw the hand back, and a little circular, as above described, and from that attitude let it fall gently into its proper place.[28]

Status could be defined by the elegance with which one moved as well as the objects that one owned.

Relying on such complex advice, a gentleman sought to exhibit his gracefulness when offering or receiving snuff, and he would look for similar refinement in those with whom he shared the tobacco. A genteel snuffer strove to handle his box with easy grace, usually holding it in his left hand, while taking a dainty pinch of snuff with the forefinger and thumb of the right hand, as illustrated by the portrait of Ralph Bell (see fig. 1). So powerful a tool was the snuffbox in displaying and defining gentility that in the English comedy *The Gentleman Dancing-Master* (1672), by William Wycherley, a character is dismissed with the observation "for being well-bred you shall judge . . . to say no more, he ne'er carries a snuff box about with him."[29] In 1711, the satiric London journal *The Spectator* announced that

> *The Exercise of the Snuff-Box, according to the most fashionable Airs and Motions . . . will be Taught with the best plain or perfum'd Snuff*, at Charles Lillie's, *Perfumer . . . There will be likewise Taught* The Ceremony of the Snuff-Box, *or Rules for offering Snuff to a Stranger, a Friend, or a Mistress, according to the Degrees of Familiarity or*

54

Fig. 8. From F. Nivelon, *The Rudiments of Genteel Behavior* (1734), plate 5. The Beinecke Rare Book and Manuscript Library, Yale University.

Distance; with an Explanation of the Careless, the Scornful, the Politick, and the Surly Pinch, and the Gestures proper to each of them.[30]

Albeit tongue-in-cheek, this advertisement reinforced the idea that there were stylish ways to use snuffboxes. Gentility could be acquired through the study of elegant movement and the rules of social hierarchy. Gentlemen strove for the ideal of graceful, unaffected ease.

In all classes, the sharing of tobacco created a sense of communion and reaffirmed feelings of affiliation, much as sharing food and drink would. A print after Thomas Rowlandson's watercolor "The French Coffee-House" shows one gentleman offering his snuffbox to another (fig. 9). The posture of the recipient echoes that of the donor, strengthening the link between the two as they engage in a common activity. Through the exchange of boxes and their contents Anglo-Americans helped to define their social circles.

Boxes themselves frequently acted as gifts. For example, in his will of 1777,

Fig. 9. Photomechanical reproduction, after Thomas Rowlandson's drawing, "The French Coffee-House." From George Paston, *Social Caricature in the Eighteenth Century* (London: Methuen, 1905), frontispiece. Yale Center for British Art, Paul Mellon Collection.

Boston silversmith Nathaniel Hurd bequeathed his tobacco box bearing his name to his brother-in-law John Furness.[31] Even after death, Hurd and Furness would be linked by the box, and their familial bonds would be acknowledged. Similarly, the diarist John Smith wrote in 1747 of presenting a Philadelphia lady with a tobacco box in the explicit hope of being remembered whenever she smoked a pipe.[32] Thus, a box could transcend its use for storage and act as an "icon of continuity," inducing memories of events or feelings.[33]

Some boxes, like the one engraved with the sunflower by William Rouse, reflect in their design or decoration that they were intended as love tokens. For example, a box attributed to Benjamin Brenton of Newport shows a phoenix, symbol of the undying, perching over a putto's head (fig. 10). The two images together speak of eternal love. A heart-shaped box by the Portsmouth silversmith William Whittemore carries the inscription "A K, This is Thine and Thou art Mine 1734" (fig. 11); its motto is reinforced by its form.

Contemporary literature further substantiates the role silver boxes played in the courtship rituals of the seventeenth and eighteenth centuries. In the poem "Mundus Muliebris," subtitled "A Voyage to Marryland," the Englishwoman

Fig. 10. Attributed to Benjamin Brenton (1710–1766), snuffbox, Newport, Rhode Island, 1730–40. Silver; l. 2 ⅝ in. Courtesy, Winterthur Museum, Gift of H. F. du Pont (1952.290).

a   b

Fig. 11 a (*top*) and b (*bottom*). William Whittemore (1709/10–ca. 1770), box, Portsmouth, New Hampshire, ca. 1734. Silver; w. 1 ⅝ in. Museum of Art, Rhode Island School of Design (63.015).

Mary Evelyn listed patch boxes in her catalogue of the gifts a young man must give to his love; she suggested that a relationship cannot succeed without such presents.[34] Furthermore, a suitor might receive a box as proof of a lady's affection. Popular beaus could accumulate considerable collections of such trophies. Alexander Hamilton noted that Dr. Keith of Newport, a great favorite with the ladies, kept a "cabinet of curiosities" in which he displayed all the objects given him by admiring women, including fans, torn gloves, and snuffboxes.[35]

Thus, colonial silver tobacco, snuff, and patch boxes transcended their manifest function as containers to embrace latent functions as indices of gentility and tools for social interaction. They were used both to create social distance and to create and affirm social bonds. Their graceful use demonstrated their owners' knowledge of courtly behavior. Their very material transformed the boxes, lending them increased importance; they represented tangible wealth.

Furthermore, the polished, reflective silver was inherently beautiful and pleasurable to hold. That pleasure was echoed by the sensual nature of the tobacco and luxurious finery that the boxes held. As manifestations of gentility, and as gifts exchanged within select circles, colonial silver tobacco, snuff, and patch boxes are powerful documents of seventeenth- and eighteenth-century social hierarchy and patterns of interaction. The boxes' layers of meaning were potent during the colonial era, and these continue to be powerful for modern students of early American material culture and social history.

Notes

1. A longer version of this essay may be found in Madeline M. Siefke, "Indices of Gentility and Gifts of Convention: Colonial Silver Tobacco, Snuff, and Patch Boxes" (M.A. thesis, University of Delaware, 1991).

2. *The Tatler*, no. 103 (December 6, 1709), reprinted in *Select British Classics* (Philadelphia: Samuel F. Bradford, 1803), 24: 308.

3. Few English boxes were hallmarked; completely unmarked boxes as well as ones just bearing makers' marks were produced both in Britain and America. Either native-made or imported boxes could be decorated by American craftsmen to the specifications of their local customers. The challenge of unraveling just who made, decorated, and sold a particular box is illustrated by a container engraved with the arms of the Jeffries family (fig. 6). The box bears two sets of marks, one belonging to the Boston silversmith John Coney, who probably engraved it, the other set belonging to an unidentified London smith, who made the box ca. 1681. Coney was prepared to make similar boxes himself; his estate inventory lists a tobacco box anvil. See Barbara McLean Ward and Gerald W. R. Ward, eds., *Silver in American Life: Selections from the Mabel Brady Garvan and Other Collections at Yale University* (New York: American Federation of Arts, 1979), 71.

4. For example, in a series of advertisements in *The South Carolina Gazette* in the 1730s and 1740s, Charleston goldsmith Lewis Janvier announced that he made and repaired snuffboxes, tobacco boxes, and patch boxes. See Alfred Coxe Prime, comp., *The Arts and Crafts in Philadelphia, Maryland, and South Carolina 1721–1785* (New York: The Walpole Society, 1929), 75–76.

5. Making snuff was a long and complex process of cutting, fermenting, drying, grinding, and blending tobacco. Most snuff used in America was imported. Colonial manufacturers advertised the similarity of their product to British snuff and appealed to their customers' loyalty to local craftsmen. See the *Boston Gazette* of August 16, 1756, quoted in George Francis Dow, comp., *The Arts and Crafts in New England: Gleanings from Boston Newspapers, 1704–1775* (Topsfield, Mass.: Wayside Press, 1927), 280–81.

6. A mid-eighteenth-century engraving by Charles-Antoine Coypel, "Folly Adorns Withered Old Age with the Charms of Youth," shows an elderly lady clutching a palm-sized, hinged box filled with patches. See Richard Corson, *Fashions in Make-up: From Ancient to Modern Times* (New York: Universe Books, 1972), 193.

7. *Boston Gazette*, December 19, 1757, quoted in Dow, *Arts and Crafts in New England*, 61.

8. In *The Presentation of Self in Everyday Life* (Garden City, N.Y.: Doubleday Anchor Books, 1959), Erving Goffman defines sign-vehicles as objects that carry information about an individual.

9. Henry Peacham, *The Complete Gentleman* (1634), quoted in Edward J. Nygren, "Edward Winslow's Sugar Boxes: Colonial Echoes of Courtly Love," *Yale University Art Gallery Bulletin* 33, no. 2 (Autumn 1971): 46–48. *The Complete Gentleman* was known to the colonial American elite, having been listed in *A Catalogue of Curious and Valuable Books*, which was published in Boston in 1719.

10. Neville Williams, *Powder and Paint: A History of the Englishwoman's Toilet, Elizabeth I– Elizabeth II* (London: Longmans, Green and Company, 1957), 19.

11. Samuel Pepys, January 13, 1665, *The Diary of Samuel Pepys*, 11 vols., ed. Robert Latham and William Matthews (Berkeley: University of California Press, 1983), 6:9.

12. *Further Quaeries Upon the Present State of New-English Affairs*, quoted in T. H. Breen, *The Character of the Good Ruler: A Study of Puritan Political Ideas in New England, 1630–1730* (New Haven: Yale University Press, 1970), 176.

13. Thomas Hall, *The Loathsomnesse of Long Haire . . . With an Appendix against Painting, Spots, Naked Breasts, &c.* (London: J. G. for Nathanael Webb and William Grantham, 1654), 99–103.

14. Nathaniel Ward, *The Simple Cobler of Aggawam in America* (Boston: Printed for Daniel Henchman, 1713), 30.

15. George Whitefield, *A Continuation of the Rev. Mr. Whitefield's Journal, from A Few Days after his Arrival at Savannah, June the Fourth to his leaving Stamford, the last Town in New-England, October 29, 1740* (Philadelphia: B. Franklin, 1741), 98.

16. For related criticism, see John Barnard, *A Present for an Apprentice: or, a Sure Guide to Gain both Esteem and Estate*, 4th ed. (Philadelphia: B. Franklin and D. Hall, 1749), 15.

17. John Adams, *Diary and Autobiography of John Adams*, ed. L. H. Butterfield (Cambridge, Mass.: The Belknap Press, 1961), 1:12–13.

18. Edward Johnson, *Johnson's Wonder-Working Providence, 1628–51*, ed. J. Franklin Jameson (New York: Barnes and Noble, 1910), 45.

19. Sir Richard Steele, "On a Tobacco Box," in *Poetical Miscellanies, Consisting of Original Poems and Translations* (London: Mr. Steele, 1714), 208–10.

20. Thomas Short, *Discourses on Tea, Sugar, Milk, Made-Wines, Spirits, Punch, Tobacco, etc., with Plain and Useful Rules for Gouty People*, in *Tobacco, its History Illustrated by the Books, Manuscripts, and Engravings in the Library of George Arents, Jr.*, ed. Jerome E. Brooks (New York: Rosenbach Company, 1937–52), 3: 333. Brooks's compendium of the Arents collection is an invaluable and exhaustive source for primary materials relating to the history of the European discovery of tobacco in the New World and its subsequent reception and use in Britain.

21. James Arbuckle, "Snuff: A Poem" (London: Printed for F. Cogan, 1732), 3–18.

22. *The Tatler*, no. 132 (February 11, 1710), in *Select British Classics*, 25:93.

23. Adams, *Diary*, 1:76–77.

24. Cotton Mather, *Manuductio ad Ministerium. Directions for a Candidate of the Ministry* (Boston: Printed for Thomas Hancock, 1726), 133.

25. Mather, *Manuductio*, 135.

26. Ovid, *Metamorphosis*, trans. Mary M. Innes (London: Penguin Group, 1955), 99–101.

27. F. Nivelon, *The Rudiments of Genteel Behavior* (1737), unpaginated.

28. Nivelon, *Rudiments*, unpaginated.

29. William Wycherley, *The Gentleman Dancing-Master*, in *The Plays of William Wycherley*, ed. Peter Holland (Cambridge: Cambridge University Press, 1981), 125.

30. *The Spectator*, vol. 138 (August 8, 1711), unpaginated. *The Spectator* was read avidly in the colonies; Benjamin Franklin, Jonathan Edwards, and Cotton Mather are all known to have owned copies, and as early as 1721, Harvard students were publishing their own periodical, *The Telltale*, based on the English model.

31. Hollis French, *Jacob Hurd and His Sons Nathaniel and Benjamin Silversmiths, 1702–1781* (Cambridge, Mass.: Riverside Press for the Walpole Society, 1939), 60.

32. Diary of John Smith, quoted in Kathryn C. Buhler and Graham Hood, *American Silver, Garvan and Other Collections in the Yale University Art Gallery,* 2 vols. (New Haven: Yale University Press for the Yale University Art Gallery, 1970), 1:141–42.

33. For a discussion of the associative power of objects, see Mihaly Csikszentmihalyi and Eugene Rochberg-Halton, *The Meaning of Things: Domestic Symbols and the Self* (Cambridge: Cambridge University Press, 1981).

34. Mary Evelyn, "Mundus Muliebris: or, The Ladies Dressing Room Unlock'd, and her Toilette Spread," in *The Miscellaneous Writings of John Evelyn*, ed. William Upcott (London: Henry Colburn, 1825), 707–11.

35. Alexander Hamilton, *Hamilton's Itinerarium*, ed. Albert Bushnell Hart (St. Louis: William K. Bixby, 1907), 123–24.

The Silver Chocolate Pots of Colonial Boston

GERALD W. R. WARD

TEA, COFFEE, AND CHOCOLATE — three drinks we now take for granted — were introduced to England and North America in the seventeenth century. Initially considered exotic beverages, each arrived in the Anglo-American world from a remote part of the globe. Tea came from the Orient, coffee from North Africa and the Middle East. Chocolate was the gift of Mexico, Central America, and South America; it first arrived in Spain in the sixteenth century and then migrated to France, England, and the rest of Europe, before making the trip to North America and to our area of concern here, New England, through the West Indies trade. Flavorful, rich, and nutritious, chocolate was indeed a boon to the seventeenth- and eighteenth-century diet. Usually consumed as a beverage in those days, chocolate was "of a dusky colour, soft, and oily; usually drank hot, and esteemed not only an excellent food, as being very nourishing, but also a good medicine; at least a diet, for keeping up the warmth of the stomach, and assisting digestion." Wealthy consumers and silversmiths responded to this expensive novelty in the Anglo-American world by demanding and creating a specialized form — the chocolate pot — to be used for serving this luxurious new drink.[1]

Most scholars give 1657 as the date of the first documented instance of chocolate's appearance in London.[2] By the 1660s, Samuel Pepys took chocolate frequently there, often at breakfast, as on May 3, 1664, when he "went to Mr. Blands and there drinking my morning draught in good chocolatte, and slabbering my band sent home for another."[3] It seems likely that chocolate appeared in Boston not long after it arrived in England. In the winter of 1667–68, the merchant and goldsmith John Hull was trading in cocoa and tobacco, and in 1670, chocolate was common enough in town that the Boston selectmen approved the separate petitions of two women, Dorothy Jones and Jane Barnard, "to keepe a house of publique Entertainment for the sellinge of Coffee and Chucalettoe." These women and other individuals were granted similar licenses in the years following, as chocolate became a more standard item on the bill of fare in public establishments.[4]

In typical New England fashion, chocolate was too enjoyable to be considered entirely respectable. In 1676, Benjamin Tompson (1642–1714), a largely forgotten New England poet, wrote a lengthy poem entitled "New-Englands Crisis," published right in the middle of the bloody conflict known to the English colonists as King Philip's War. Tompson laments that the "golden times" of New England have passed — that the strength of the Puritan forebears had been "quickly sin'd away for love of gold." Citizens once noted for their strong character and religious piety have been corrupted by licentiousness and idle pleasures. Chocolate figures into his elegy. Remembering the past, he recalled the days before outside influences worked their evil ways. This age, he recalled,

> Twas ere the Islands sent their Presents in,
> Which but to use was counted next to sin.
> Twas ere a *Barge* had made so rich a fraight
> as *Chocholatte*, dust-gold and bitts of eight.

He further blames "fruits and dilicacies" from "western Isles" that "Did rot maids teeth and spoil their hansome faces." Despite such concerns, chocolate soon became accepted, even among the Puritan elite.[5]

Samuel Sewall (1652–1730) of Boston (fig. 1) mentions chocolate several times in his famous diary and in so doing gives us our first glimpses of chocolate drinking as a form of social interaction in New England. On October 20, 1697, he visited Lieutenant Governor William Stoughton (fig. 2) in Dorchester, and they had "breakfast together on Venison and Chockalatte." Sewall observed that "Massachusetts and Mexico met at his Honour's Table."[6] On October 1, 1709, Sewall went to Mr. Belcher's in Dedham, where in the morning he drank "warm chockelat, and no Beer; find my self much refresh'd by it after great Sweating to day, and yesterday."[7] On other occasions, as revealed by entries in his diary and letter-book, Sewall gave gifts of chocolate to friends. In April 1687, for example, he bought "21 balls [of] chokolatto," probably to be shipped in linen bags in chunks known as balls, rowls, lumps, cakes, or tablets in the contemporary literature.[8] These balls may have resembled the irregular pieces of chocolate depicted in the lower right side of a still-life painting of 1770 by the Spanish artist Luis Melendez (fig. 3). In 1707, for example, he "gave Mr. Solomon Stoddard two half pounds of Chockalat, instead of Commencement Cake," and on another occasion in 1723 he presented a new mother with a gift of "two pounds of Chockalet." Sewall also gave silver objects as gifts, and his use of chocolate for similar presentation purposes suggests its high social status.[9]

Other Bostonians no doubt shared Sewall's enjoyment of chocolate. The Reverend Thomas Prince (1687–1758), minister of Old South Church and historian of early New England, made it part of his daily routine. Following graduation from Harvard, Prince spent a decade abroad before returning to Boston in 1717 and assuming his position at Old South the next year. After his marriage,

Fig. 1. John Smibert (1688–1751), *Judge Samuel Sewall*, 1729. Oil on canvas; h. 30 in., w. 25 in. Museum of Fine Arts, Boston, bequest of William L. Barnard (by exchange), and Emily L. Ainsley Fund (58.358).

he drew up his plans in 1719 for carrying out each day. His "proposed order" called for rising at 5 a.m. and spending an hour in prayer and reading the Bible in his study, after which he would wake up the rest of the family. At 6:30, they would have family prayers, and then "only the Porringer of Chocolat for Breakfast," before setting out on an arduous day.[10]

Prince's porringer of "Chocolat" and the "warm chockelat" Sewall enjoyed were probably prepared with equipment and utensils of the type depicted in the Melendez painting (see fig. 3), following directions of the kind described in an English publication of 1675 by John Worlidge. Some people "boil [the chocolate] in water and sugar; others mix half water and half milk and boil it, then add powdered chocolate to it and boil them together; others add wine and water." "Be sure," the author continues, "whilst it is boiling to keep it stirring, and when it is off the fire, whir it with your hand mill [the mill being a stick, sometimes of silver or another material but usually wooden, with a flange on one end, used for stirring the thick chocolate mixture; sometimes referred to as

Fig. 2. Unknown artist, *William Stoughton (1631/32–1701)*, ca. 1700. Oil on canvas; h. 49 ⅜ in., w. 45 ¼ in. Courtesy of the Harvard University Portrait Collection. Gift of John Cooper to Harvard College, 1810 (H037). © President and Fellows of Harvard College, Harvard University.

Fig. 3. Luis Melendez (1716–1780), *Still Life of Chocolate Service*, ca. 1760. Oil on canvas; h. 18 ⅞ in., w. 14 ³⁄₁₆ in. Museo del Prado, Madrid.

a *molinet*]. That is, it must be mixed in a deep pot of Tin, copper [as in the Melendez painting] or stone [stoneware], with a cover with a hole in the middle of it, for the handle of the mill to come out at, or without a cover. The mill is only a knop at the end of slender handle or stick, turned in a turner's lathe, and cut in notches, or rough at the end. They are sold at turners for that purpose. This being whirled between your hands, whilst the pot is over the fire, and the rough end in the liquor causes an equal mixture of the liquor with the chocolate and raises a head of froth over it. Then pour it out for use in small dishes for that purpose. You must add a convenient quantity of sugar to the mixture."[11]

In this passage the author has identified the distinguishing characteristic of a chocolate pot — the opening in the lid which allows for the insertion of the essential stirring rod. The opening can be achieved in a variety of ways — by a removable cap or finial, or the presence of a small hole accessed by a sliding cover — but it must be present in order to consider an object a chocolate (as opposed to a coffee or tea) pot. The sediment in hot chocolate — unlike that in tea and coffee — is desirable, and thus the mixture needs to be stirred continually. Otherwise, chocolate pots and coffee pots — both usually taller and generally larger than teapots — are virtually indistinguishable. For example, each form was made with the spout in line with the handle, or occasionally with the spout at a right angle to the handle.

The basic recipe outlined by Worlidge changed little for more than a century, although many methods of preparation must have been used by individuals. Although chocolate was probably prepared in a copper or brass pot in large quantities and perhaps served in a ceramic or base-metal pouring vessel, in a few of the most fashionable New England homes chocolate was served in a silver chocolate pot. The earliest reference to such an object in Boston comes in 1690, when William Pleay owned a "jocolato pot."[12] Only eight examples made in colonial Boston are known to have survived; a potential ninth example, unknown today, has been published as both a chocolate and a coffeepot. Their rarity is underlined by the fact that chocolate pots represent only an infinitesimal percentage of the more than six thousand pieces of extant silver made by colonial Massachusetts silversmiths.[13]

Despite their low numbers, the Boston silver chocolate pots — especially the six made before 1720 by John Coney, Edward Winslow, Edward Webb, and Peter Oliver — provide a glimpse of life in Boston during a period of florescence in the decorative arts. Extraordinarily stylish and costly, the pots were faddish in their response to a new custom. Used in the process of consuming a luxurious beverage in a custom that migrated from Catholic Spain and southern Europe, silver chocolate pots seem almost antithetical in Protestant Boston, yet

Fig. 4. John Coney (1655/56–1722), chocolate pot, Boston, Massachusetts, 1701. Silver; h. 8 1/16 in., diam. (base) 3 5/8 in. Museum of Fine Arts, Boston, Gift of Edwin Jackson Holmes (29.1091).

their existence — when taken into account with other stylish forms of silver, furniture, and architecture — is a small slice of material evidence of the changes, ultimately dramatic in their extent, that were moving Boston from its origins as a Puritan enclave in the seventeenth century to its place as a cosmopolitan, sophisticated, commercial colonial city in the very earliest years of the eighteenth century.

The Boston Chocolate Pots

Of this group of eight, the earliest example is probably the one made by John Coney about 1701 (fig. 4). It is engraved on the bottom "The gift of Wm Stoughton Esquire / to Mrs. Sarah Tailer : 701," presumably in error for 1701. In his will, executed on July 6, 1701, Lt. Gov. Stoughton left his niece, Mrs. Sarah Byfield Tailer, twelve pounds to buy a piece of plate as a "particular remembrance" of him, and presumably this vessel is the result of that bequest. It may have been a fitting choice, for Stoughton (see fig. 2) is known to have enjoyed a cup of chocolate at breakfast with Samuel Sewall, and he may have

Fig. 5. Isaac Dighton (w. 1697–99), chocolate pot,
London, 1697. Silver; h. 7¾ in. Metropolitan Museum of
Art, New York, Gift of George O. May, 1943 (43.108).

had a fondness for the drink. In form, this Coney pot resembles an Oriental
vase, and it would have been virtually at the height of fashion in London and
smaller English towns when it was made. It has its handles at right angles to the
spout, as many (but not all) examples do, perhaps to facilitate stirring while
pouring. The turned-ball finial covers the hole necessary for insertion of the
stirring rod. The curved spout originally had a hinged lid at the end, now lost,
that perhaps helped to keep the contents warm. The Coney pot is further distinguished by its cut-card ornament around the base.[14]

Sarah Tailer was the wife of Lieutenant Governor William Tailer (1677–1732).
Their household included many stylish goods, including two English cane
chairs that have survived (one in the Massachusetts Historical Society and the
other in the Bostonian Society); these were probably among eighteen such
chairs in the fashionable Tailer household.[15]

An English example (fig. 5), made by Isaac Dighton of London in 1697, provides a high-style analogue to the Coney pot, with its more elaborate gadroon-
ing and other ornament and its gilt surface. A London pot made by George

Fig. 6. George Garthorne (d. 1730), chocolate pot, London, 1686. Silver; h. 7 ¾ in. Private collection. Photo, courtesy David B. Nicolay, New Orleans Auction Galleries, Inc.

Garthorne (fig. 6) in 1686 is more similar to the Coney example, and some provincial English examples, like one made by R. Williamson of Leeds about 1695, are also close in feeling. In other words, Coney's work, while not at the highest level of court silver, was nevertheless stylish and up-to-date in the Anglo-American community.[16]

Coney, who was probably apprenticed to Jeremiah Dummer, was the leading Boston goldsmith of his day. His work included rare forms such as sugar boxes, punch bowls, and monteith bowls, as well as the earliest known American silver teapot, and thus it is not surprising that a second chocolate pot by him is known (fig. 7). This example was probably made between 1715 and 1720, as indicated by its curvilinear pear-shaped body in the incipient late baroque taste. Its most decorative feature is its serpent-headed spout. This pot originally had a sliding or pivoted finial for the insertion of the stirring rod, and the underside of its base shows a circular pattern of wear that suggests the pot was often placed on a small brazier or chafing dish to keep it warm. The original owners of this pot, unfortunately, are not known — their initials have been erased and replaced with those of William Downes and his wife, Elizabeth Edwards Cheever, who were not married until 1749. This Coney example also has its counterparts in English work.[17]

Fig. 7. John Coney (1655/56–1722), chocolate pot, ca. 1710–22. Silver; h. 9⁷⁄₁₆ in., diam. (base) 4⁷⁄₁₆ in., Museum of Fine Arts, Boston. Partial gift of Dr. Lamar Soutter, Theodora Wilbour Fund in memory of Charlotte Beebe Wilbour, and the Marion E. Davis Fund (1976.771).

Perhaps the most beautiful American chocolate pot was made by Edward Winslow of Boston between 1700 and 1710 (fig. 8). It is richly decorated with gadrooned ornament that is played off of plain areas, creating what the silver scholar John Marshall Phillips of Yale University called the beautiful counterpoise of baroque silver. This pot, now in the Metropolitan Museum of Art, has an acorn finial that unscrews and is then held in place by a chain. It was owned originally by Thomas Hutchinson (1675–1739), a wealthy merchant and husband of Sarah Foster, the daughter of Colonel John Foster. They were the parents of the notorious Tory Governor Thomas Hutchinson.[18]

Another Winslow pot, very similar to the one in the Metropolitan Museum, is now in the collection of the Yale University Art Gallery (fig. 9). Also made in the first decade of the eighteenth century, the Yale Winslow pot has had its spout moved to a higher location on the body, perhaps as early as 1740 — the hole where the original spout was located was patched with a decorative

Fig. 8. Edward Winslow (1669–1753), chocolate pot, Boston, Massachusetts, ca. 1705. Silver; h. 9½ in. Metropolitan Museum of Art, New York, bequest of Judge A. T. Clearwater, 1933 (33.120.221).

Fig. 9. Edward Winslow (1669–1753), chocolate pot, Boston, Massachusetts, ca. 1705. Silver; h. 9%16 in. Yale University Art Gallery, Mabel Brady Garvan Collection (1944.71).

Fig. 10. Peter Oliver (ca. 1682–1712), chocolate pot, Boston, Massachusetts, ca. 1705. Silver; h. 10 ⅜ in. From B. K. McLanathan, ed., *Colonial Silversmiths, Masters and Apprentices* (Boston: Museum of Fine Arts, Boston, 1956), cat. no. III, fig. 45. Photo, courtesy Museum of Fine Arts, Boston.

plaque. This alteration probably had its origins in the function of the object. A higher location for the spout allowed for sediment to settle more easily in the pot, and thus the change may have allowed the chocolate to flow more smoothly. The Yale Winslow pot is engraved with what are thought to be the Auchmuty family arms; if such is the case, the pot's original owner may have been lawyer Robert Auchmuty (1687–1750) of Roxbury.[19]

A fifth Boston silver chocolate pot was made by Peter Oliver, who died at the young age of thirty and left only about seven examples of his work behind (fig. 10). Oliver was probably apprenticed to Coney, "his trusty friend." His chocolate pot must have been made in the short period of time between the completion of Oliver's training in about 1703 and his death in 1712. Visually, Oliver's pot is similar to the Winslow examples, sharing the use of gadrooned ornament, and the finial, originally removable, has been soldered in place. The pot was probably made for Beulah Jacquett, who married Thomas Coates, and then it subsequently descended in their family in the female line through many generations.[20]

Edward Webb was the maker of a sixth Boston silver chocolate pot (fig. 11). While it bears an overall resemblance to the Winslow and Oliver examples, it has some significant differences. It has an unusual finial assembly, consisting essentially of a screw-on cap, and it has fluted, rather than gadrooned, ornament

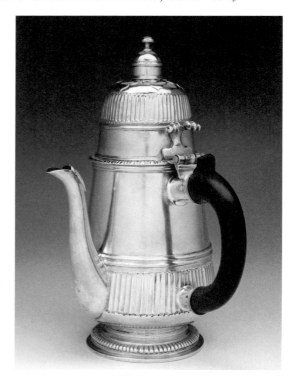

Fig. 11. Edward Webb (ca. 1666–1718), chocolate pot, Boston, Massachusetts, ca. 1710. Silver; h. 10 in. Museum of Fine Arts, Boston, Gift of a Friend of the Department of American Decorative Arts and Sculpture, and Marion E. Davis Fund (1993.61).

on its body and cover. Webb, born in England about 1666, learned his craft in London during an apprenticeship to William Denny. Denny had opened shop in London in 1679 and worked there until his death in 1709. He had just entered into business when Webb started his training in 1680, which lasted until about 1687. Denny's prominent shop filled many important commissions, and Webb was thus exposed to sophisticated English silver styles during his formative years there. It is possible that Webb stayed on in Denny's shop as a journeyman. Objects that have Denny's mark, like a monteith dated 1702 (fig. 12) and others dated about the same time, often bear the type of fluting — the tight, somewhat pinched, irregular, almost nervous fluting — that Webb must have learned in Denny's shop and brought to America. It is not known when Webb arrived in this country, although evidence places him here as early as 1704. Most other objects bearing Webb's mark, including tankards, porringers, and spoons, are simpler than the chocolate pot. Some of them have well-executed cast ornament, but none is as ambitious as the pot. However, Webb was a wealthy man when he died in 1718, and his estate inventory indicates that he owned all the tools necessary to create such a complex pot. As an English immigrant and one with specialized skills, Webb may have worked primarily as a jobber or journeyman for native-born silversmiths. Although the writer is not aware of any

Fig. 12. William Denny, monteith, London, 1702. Silver; diam. 10 in. From Georgina E. Lee, with assistance from Ronald A. Lee, *British Silver Monteith Bowls including American and European Examples* (Byfleet, Eng.: Manor House Press, 1978), 36, fig. 31. Photo, courtesy Museum of Fine Arts, Boston.

chocolate pots bearing William Denny's mark that resemble the Webb pot, some contemporaneous English work, such as an example of 1703 by William Charnelhouse of London (fig. 13), is closely related. Unfortunately, the original owner of the Webb pot is not known. The applied cartouche on the side of the pot is a later addition of uncertain, although possibly eighteenth-century, date, and the engraved initials it bears, P / TA, remain unidentified.[21]

The last two Boston colonial chocolate pots known were made by Zachariah Brigden, one in the Museum of Fine Arts (fig. 14) and the other at Historic Deerfield (fig. 15), both dated to about 1755–60 and thus made very early in Brigden's career. The MFA Brigden pot was made for Ebenezer and Mary (Edwards) Storer, who were married in 1723, and is engraved with the coat of arms used by Ebenezer.[22] The Deerfield Brigden example, which is slightly larger but otherwise very similar, was made for a member of the De(e)ring family.[23] Both have removable finials; the MFA example has an open-link chain to secure the finial when it is removed. Brigden's chocolate pots, last in the Boston series, document the survival of their kind for more than half a century, into the era when tea and coffee pots were the more common forms.

Provincial Luxury

This group of eight objects — perhaps statistically insignificant even when one considers that undoubtedly a few examples have been lost to the melting pot in

Fig. 13. William Charnelhouse (d. 1711/12), coffeepot, London, 1703/4. Silver; h. 9⁵⁄₁₆ in. Sterling and Francine Clark Art Institute, Williamstown, Massachusetts (1955.281).

Fig. 14. Zachariah Brigden (1734–1787), chocolate pot, Boston, Massachusetts, ca. 1755–60. Silver; h. 9⅞ in. Museum of Fine Arts, Boston, Gift of the Misses Rose and Elizabeth Townsend (56.676).

Fig. 15. Zachariah Brigden (1734–1787), chocolate pot, Boston, Massachusetts, ca. 1755–60. Silver; h. 10 ⅝ in. Historic Deerfield, Inc. (75.463).

the last two centuries — is of extraordinary significance when considered in light of developments in Boston in the colonial era, especially in the years 1700 to 1715 or 1720, when all but the Brigden pots were made. As the seventeenth century came to a close, changes began to be felt in the small seaport town of about ten thousand people. "The worldwide commercial interests of the town," according to the historian G. B. Warden, "did provide luxuries and diversions from Augustan England which seriously affected the town's way of life."[24] Many of these "luxuries and diversions" were brought to Boston by the succession of royal governors and other officials who administered the province's affairs after 1692. Changes in architecture, furniture, silver, and other furnishings took place, and the little cluster of chocolate pots is perhaps best seen as part of a constellation of material objects, large and small, that introduced new styles, customs, and behaviors to Boston.

The house built in 1679 by Peter Sargeant was probably the grandest house in Massachusetts in its time and for many years thereafter. In the 1710s, it was remodelled to become the fashionable city home of the colonial governors and became known as the Province House. Portraits of kings, queens, and governors hung in its council chambers, and it symbolized the existing power structure in Boston. It also was the epicenter of the increased urbanization and sophistication that characterized Boston in this period.[25]

The Foster-Hutchinson house (fig. 16), built on Garden Court Street in the

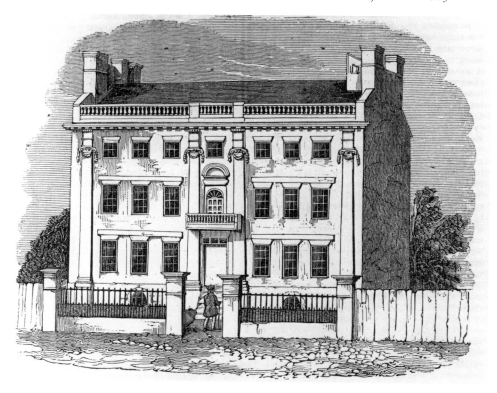

Fig. 16. Foster-Hutchinson House, Boston, Massachusetts, 1689–92. From *The American Magazine of Useful & Entertaining Knowledge* (February 1836). Courtesy of the Trustees of the Boston Public Library.

North End about 1692 (and destroyed in 1833), is representative of this new wave of change. As Abbott Lowell Cummings has observed, the Foster-Hutchinson house is the first "recorded example of the English Renaissance in Boston," with its Ionic pilasters topped by capitals of imported Portland stone.[26] The house is central to our theme because it was built by John and Abigail Foster, and descended to Mrs. Foster's nephew, the merchant-captain Thomas Hutchinson, the owner of the Winslow chocolate pot now at the Metropolitan (see fig. 8). The Foster-Hutchinson house stood next door to the Clark-Frankland house, built by the merchant William Clark about 1712. (It, too, was taken down in 1832 or 1833.) This three-story brick mansion was an even more fully developed example of the Georgian style, with its string courses, rhythmic facade, and alternating segmental and triangular pediments. Many less ambitious houses, like the Moses Pierce-Hichborn house of ca. 1711, which still stands in the North End, came from the same mold, as were collegiate buildings at Harvard and churches and civic buildings in Boston, such as the landmark building now known as the Old State House of 1712–13.[27]

Fig. 17. Chest-on-chest, Boston, Massachusetts, 1715–25. Black walnut, burl walnut veneer, eastern white pine; h. 70 ¾ in., w. 42 ¼ in., d. 21 ½ in. Museum of Fine Arts, Boston, Gift of a Friend of the Department of American Decorative Arts and Sculpture, and Otis Norcross Fund (1986.240).

Fig. 18. Desk and bookcase, Boston, Massachusetts, ca. 1715–20. Walnut, walnut veneer, eastern white pine; h. 88 ½ in., w. 29 ⅝ in., d. 20 ½ in. Museum of Fine Arts, Boston, The M. and M. Karolik Collection of Eighteenth-Century American Arts (39.176).

Fig. 19. John Coney (1655/56–1722), sugar box, Boston, Massachusetts, 1680–90. Silver; h. 4 13⁄16 in., w. 7 ¾ in., d. 6 in. Museum of Fine Arts, Boston, Gift of Mrs. Joseph Richmond Churchill (13.421).

These developments in architecture, in which the Georgian style supplanted the timber-frame first-period buildings of the post-medieval style, started to transform the landscape. They were mirrored in changes in furniture and furnishings that similarly began to affect domestic space. Such objects as the War-land family chest-on-chest (fig. 17) and the Reverend John Avery's desk and bookcase (fig. 18) are key to understanding Boston furniture of possibly as early as 1715. Both are very English in style, and advanced stylistically. Edward S. Cooke, Jr., has suggested that they are the cabinetmaking equivalent of the elaborate Boston silver made by Coney, Winslow, and others — silver that includes the sophisticated group of chocolate pots, as well as other notable examples of conspicuous consumption, such as the wrought candlesticks of 1690–1710 by Coney and gadrooned candlesticks by John Noyes of about 1695–1700, lighting devices rarely made in silver in this country. Other rare forms made in this period include John Coney's spectacular monteith (made about 1705–10 for rinsing and cooling wineglasses) and his simple yet elegant punch bowl of about 1710.[28]

The chocolate pots bear perhaps the most significant relationship to Boston silver sugar boxes, a similarly small group of ten known examples, including ones

Fig. 20. Edward Winslow (1669–1753), sugar box, Boston, Massachusetts, ca. 1700. Silver; h. 5 ¾ in., w. 8 ½ in., d. 6 ¹¹⁄₁₆ in. Museum of Fine Arts, Boston, The Philip Leffingwell Spalding Collection. Given in memory by Katharine Ames Spalding and Philip Spalding, Oakes Ames Spalding, Hobart Ames Spalding (42.251).

by John Coney of ca. 1685 (fig. 19) and Edward Winslow of about 1700 (fig. 20). Both forms are rare, costly, stylish, and linked to relatively short-lived customs. The chocolate pots lack the overt snake symbolism and other embellishments that are practically unique to Winslow's sugar boxes, as explained by Ed Nygren, who explored the complex iconography and sexual connotations of these objects, which are related to issues of marriage, fertility, and fecundity. Although sugar boxes were used primarily in the service of wine, one can imagine a wealthy family using sugar boxes and chocolate pots in the same household, for sugar was also important as a sweetener for the otherwise bitter chocolate.[29]

Both forms also were produced by only a few craftsmen. Of the combined total of eighteen sugar boxes and chocolate pots, Coney (four sugar and two chocolate) and Winslow (five sugar and two chocolate) produced thirteen, or 72 percent; another chocolate pot was made by Peter Oliver, who was probably apprenticed to Coney. It is possible that Coney and Winslow were able to employ a journeyman with experience in London — perhaps Edward Webb or Henry Hurst — to assist in the fashioning of such stylish, sophisticated forms.[30]

The "Excellent Nectar"

Drinking chocolate was both a private and a public custom. Chocolate was taken at coffee-houses, or houses of public entertainment, in a public setting, although because of its higher price due to high duties, chocolate initially took a secondary role to coffee and was soon almost completely eclipsed by the more caffeine-laden drink. A silver chocolate pot was not necessary, of course, for even though silver's purity and thermal conductivity made it suitable for hot beverages, base-metal vessels would do as well and were commonly used in these commercial establishments.

In the home, the principal context of silver articles, chocolate was often taken in the morning, at least during the first years after its introduction, but it was undoubtedly used at many times during the day.[31] For example, Madam Sarah Kemble Knight (1666–1727) arrived in the evening in a clean, comfortable house in the Narrangansett country while en route in her famous trip from Boston to New Haven in October 1704. The owner of the home asked what Madam Knight would like to eat, and she replied, "I told her I had some Chocolett, if shee would prepare it; which with the help of some Milk, and a little clean brass Kettle, she soon effected to my satisfaction."[32] But the long-standing, fashionable tradition amongst the European-monied class, in a tradition that migrated from the Catholic countries of southern Europe, Italy, and Spain, was to take chocolate in the morning, as Samuel Sewall did at least once and undoubtedly did more frequently. The chocolate was poured, in most cases, from silver pots into ceramic chocolate cups, often small, handleless beakers imported from abroad, although smaller tea cups would serve nearly as well. No doubt a variety of drinking vessels were used. Peter Fanueil (1700–1742/43), reputed to be the wealthiest man in Boston at his death in 1743, who owned some fourteen hundred ounces of silver, served the beverage in "6 lignum vitae chocolate cups lin'd with silver," and, as we saw earlier, the Rev. Thomas Prince used a porringer.[33]

Bostonians obtained their chocolate from local merchants, such as Mrs. Hannah Boydell, who offered "Tea, Coffee, Chocolate, Loaf and Muscovado Sugars of all Sorts" at her shop on King Street in the 1730s, or the grocer John Merrett, at the sign of the Three Sugar Loaves and Canister, also on King Street, who sold "Super-fine Chocolate, Coffee, raw and roasted, [and] very choice Teas," along with all manner of sugars, spices, and other delicacies. Another merchant offered "Italian chocolate ready prepared with sugar" in 1739, and in 1769, John Goldsmith advertised "Choice Chocolate made and Sold" at his corner shop leading down John Hancock's wharf.[34]

Although chocolate contains some theobromine, a mild stimulant, it has

Un Caualier, Et vne Dame beuuant du Chocolat
Ce jeune Caualier, et cette belle Dame   Mais l'on voit dans leurs yeux vne si viue flame
Se regalent de Chocolat;   Qu'on croit qu'il leur faudroit vn mets plus delicat

Fig. 21. Robert Bonnard, published by Nicolas Bonnart, *Un Cavelier et une Dame beuvant du chocolat (Cavalier and Lady Drinking Chocolate)*, ca. 1690–1710. Engraving on paper; h. 10 11/16 in., w. 7 1/2 in. Pierpont Morgan Library, New York.

more nutritional than stimulating value. In its early days, chocolate was also thought to have medicinal value and to be an aphrodisiac.[35] (An English verse of 1652 observes that chocolate "'Twill make old women Young and Fresh; / Create new notions of the flesh / And cause them long for you know what, / If they but taste of chocolate."[36]) But within a few years, chocolate, like tea, which had similarly been given many magical and mystical powers when first introduced, became primarily a fashionable, expensive drink that did not carry a great deal of attendant symbolic meaning. Thus, the French cavalier and lady seen taking chocolate in a French print published between 1690 and 1710 (fig. 21), were primarily simply enjoying themselves in a *cabaret*.[37]

This theme of enjoyment and relaxation typifies many eighteenth-century images of chocolate drinking. A French depiction of a lady's boudoir — or possibly a brothel — features a chocolate service at its center (fig. 22), for example, with the mill (or *molinet*) clearly visible. A painting (fig. 23) by the French artist Jean-Baptiste Leprince entitled *La crainte (Fear)* (1769) depicts a woman in bed

81

Fig. 22. Jean-Baptiste Mallet (1759–1835), *La Jolie Visiteuse*, ca. 1750, Gouache; h. 10⅞ in., w. 14⅛ in. Museum of Fine Arts, Boston, Forsyth Wickes Collection (65.2585).

leaning toward her departed lover (and her chocolate pot, with its mill clearly visible, and cups). The method of drinking chocolate was to adopt a "fluid, lazy, languid motion," well typified by this young lady. Dress for taking chocolate was meant to be casual (carried to an extreme in this image).[38]

Most everything about chocolate drinking suggested ample amounts of leisure time, which is perhaps the greatest symbol of power. The Englishman William Hughes, writing in 1672, cautioned his readers that "it is not convenient, as experience hath sufficiently taught us, to eat or drink any thing else quickly after the drinking of it; or presently to use any immoderate exercise; but rather to rest awhile, whether it be taken hot or cold: because it is apt to open the Pores, and thereby it causeth the greater expence of Spirits by transpiration, and so consequently nouriseth the less."[39] In other words, take it easy. As the scholar Wolfgang Schivelbusch has observed, a long breakfast involving chocolate "does not start off a workday — rather it marks the start of a day's carefully cultivated idleness," a "morning-long awakening to the rigors of studied leisure."[40]

Such a style of life — of slow, languorous mornings — was at odds with the Puritan and Yankee modes of behavior, and this divergence may account for the small number of silver chocolate pots made in Massachusetts Bay. Certainly the Rev. Prince was not an idle aristocrat — his morning draft of chocolate inaugu-

Fig. 23. Jean-Baptiste Le Prince (1734–1781), *La crainte* (*Fear*), 1769. Oil on canvas; h. 19 ¾ in., w. 25 ¼ in. Toledo Museum of Art, Gift of Edward Drummond Libbey (1970.444).

rated a long day of scholarship and meditation. Coffee was more in tune with New England Protestantism. The silver chocolate pots of Coney, Winslow, Webb, and Oliver allow us to see a few Bostonians, in the first few years of the eighteenth century, trying on a Continental style of life that, apparently, didn't fit. Although chocolate remained a part of the culinary landscape throughout the eighteenth century, it was not afforded the exalted status of silver pouring vessels, designed and reserved just for chocolate, with the exception of the two Brigden pots made at midcentury. Other forms became more popular in silver. Based on surviving examples, for example, Massachusetts silversmiths are known to have made at least ninety-five silver teapots before about 1775. Most of these, however, were made relatively late. The earliest is one by John Coney of about 1710 and only five others are known that date before 1730. By the middle of the 1730s, there was a real spike in the production of teapots, with at least twenty-five known examples, including many by Jacob Hurd, that can be dated to ca. 1735 to ca. 1745; the numbers continue to increase during the following decades. Silver coffeepots were crafted rarely by Massachusetts silversmiths in the first half of the eighteenth century. Only about six made before 1750 survive, although at least twenty-one are known dating to the period ca. 1750 to ca. 1775. Silver coffeepots or pots of other materials may have been used for chocolate after 1720, but the era when it demanded specialization had largely passed.[41]

The historian Cary Carson, in a very lengthy study of the style of life in the eighteenth century, has observed that there was something in the air in the years just before and after 1700. The world was changing, and among the many consequences of those changes, he suggests, "none was more novel or conspicuous than the pleasure that men and women took in their physical well-being and the value they placed on material things."[42] Why this was so remains a matter of debate among historians in the academy, but it is likely that the story of Boston's silver chocolate pots might add a footnote to the ultimate resolution. Certainly people drank chocolate because it tasted good, and wealthy people apparently took pleasure in using silver vessels to do so. The surviving chocolate pots indicate that the period of 1700 to 1715 was especially significant for these changes in one small area of "cultivated gentility." Thus, aside from their intrinsic qualities as works of art, these pots have something to add to the current academic concerns about the rise of gentility and genteel behavior in America, about changes in etiquette and manners, and about the ongoing concern in American life over the pernicious effects of luxury.[43] They offer information about the consumer revolution, and no doubt, like the story of sugar as told by Sidney Mintz, they say something about power relationships based on wealth and exploitation.[44]

The thoughts expressed by William Hughes in 1672, however, probably come closer to the true meaning of chocolate to people of the eighteenth century than do our latter-day theoretical speculations. In his volume entitled *The American Physitian, or. A Treatise of the Roots, Plants, Trees, Shrubs, Fruit, Herbes, &c. Growing in the English Plantations in America, . . . whereunto is added a Discourse of the Cacao-Nut-Tree, And the use of its Fruit; with all the ways of making Chocolate, the like never extant before*, Hughes wrote "But what shall I say more of this excellent Nectar? It is a very good aliment, a clear *Pabulum multi nutriment*: that it doth fatten . . . is undeniable; and that it nouriseth . . . is without dispute . . . [I]t revives the drooping spirits, and chears those that are ready to faint; expelling sorrow, trouble, care, and all perturbrations of the minde: it is an Ambrosia: And finally, in a word, it cannot be too much praised."[45]

Notes

1. As an enormously popular food, chocolate is surrounded by a vast literature of uneven quality. Particularly helpful for understanding the origins and early history of chocolate are Sophie D. Coe, *America's First Cuisines* (Austin: University of Texas Press, 1994), 50–58; Sophie D. Coe and Michael D. Coe, *The True History of Chocolate* (New York: Thames and Hudson, 1996); Maguelonne Toussaint-Samat, *A History of Food*, trans. Anthea Bell (Cambridge, Mass.: Blackwell Publishers, 1992), chap. 18; and Fernand Braudel, *Civilization and Capitalism, 15th–18th*

Century, vol. 1, *The Structures of Everyday Life: The Limits of the Possible*, trans. Siân Reynolds (New York: Harper & Row, 1981), 249–60. Quotation from Abraham Rees, *The Cyclopaedia; or, Universal Dictionary of Arts, Sciences, and Literature*, 41 vols. (Philadelphia: Samuel F. Bradford and Murray, Fairman and Co., 1810–24), s.v. "Chocolate." The form is discussed in many places: see especially Edward Wenham, "Silver Chocolate Pots," *Antiques* 42, no. 5 (November 1942): 248; G. B. Hughes, "Silver Pots for Chocolate," *Country Life* 128, no. 3320 (October 20, 1960): 856–57.

2. See such disparate sources as *Cocoa and Chocolate: A Short History of Their Production and Use* (Dorchester, Mass: Walter Baker & Co., 1886), 39; Frederic Morton and Marcia Morton, *Chocolate: An Illustrated History* (New York: Crown, 1986), 59; and the introduction to chocolate, coffee, and tea in Beth Carver Wees, *English, Irish, and Scottish Silver in the Sterling and Francine Clark Art Institute* (New York: Hudson Hills Press, 1997), 267–72.

3. *The Diary of Samuel Pepys*, ed. Robert Latham and William Matthews, 11 vols. (Berkeley and Los Angeles: University of California Press, 1970–83), 5:139. See also references for June 19, 1660 (1:178), October 17, 1662 (3:226–27), January 6, 1663 (4:5), February 26, 1664 (5:64), and November 24, 1664 (5:329).

4. *The Diaries of John Hull, Mint-Master and Treasurer of the Colony of Massachusetts Bay* (Boston: John Wilson and Son, 1857), 158; *A Report of the Record Commissioners of the City of Boston Containing the Boston Records from 1660 to 1701* (Boston: Rockwell and Churchill, 1881), 58; see also 60, 64, 68, 73, and ten subsequent references.

5. See Harrison T. Meserole, ed., *Seventeenth-Century American Poetry* (New York: W. W. Norton, 1968), 225–29.

6. M. Halsey Thomas, ed., *The Diary of Samuel Sewall, 1674–1729*, 2 vols. (New York: Farrar, Straus and Giroux, 1973), 1:380.

7. *Diary of Samuel Sewall*, 2:626.

8. Samuel Sewall, *Letter-Book*, Collections of the Massachusetts Historical Society, 6th ser., vols. 1 and 2 (Boston, 1886), 1:46.

9. *Diary of Samuel Sewall*, 1:570; Sewall, *Letter-Book*, 2:157. See also *Diary of Samuel Sewall*, 1:476, 563–64.

10. Manuscript notes printed in Hamilton Andrews Hill, *History of the Old South Church (Third Church), Boston, 1669–1684*, 2 vols. (Boston: Houghton, Mifflin, 1890), 1:398, and in F. E. Blake, *History of Princeton* (Boston, 1915), 110. The Virginian William Byrd (1674–1744) recorded that he drank chocolate for breakfast about once every three weeks from February 1709 through September 1712; see *The Secret Diary of William Byrd of Westover, 1709–1712*, ed. Louis B. Wright and Marion Tinling (Richmond, Va.: Dietz Press, 1941), 1 and 67 subsequent references.

11. John Worlidge, as quoted in John D. Davis, *English Silver at Williamsburg* (Williamsburg, Va.: Colonial Williamsburg Foundation, 1976), 85.

12. As cited in Michael Clayton, *The Collector's Dictionary of the Silver and Gold of Great Britain and North America* (New York: World Publishing Co., 1971), s.v. "chocolate pot."

13. Patricia E. Kane, ed., *Colonial Massachusetts Silversmiths and Jewelers: A Biographical Dictionary* (New Haven: Yale University Art Gallery, 1998). An object by Edward Winslow is listed in this source (p. 977) as a chocolate pot. However, in the entry on the Yale Winslow chocolate pot, Kathryn C. Buhler and Graham Hood discuss the various known chocolate pots known at that time, and note that "Winslow made a later coffee pot (privately owned) in the tapered-cylindrical, Queen Anne style, which is apparently engraved with the Saltonstall arms," citing the Yale

University Art Gallery files as their source; see Kathryn C. Buhler and Graham Hood, *American Silver: Garvan and Other Collections in the Yale University Art Gallery*, 2 vols. (New Haven: Yale University Press for the Yale University Art Gallery, 1970), 1:56 (cat. no. 49). Its present whereabouts is unknown to this writer. Inquiries to current members of the Saltonstall family have not been successful in locating the object. For the purposes of this essay, it will be regarded as a coffeepot.

14. Kathryn C. Buhler, *American Silver, 1655–1825, in the Museum of Fine Arts, Boston*, 2 vols. (Boston: Museum of Fine Arts, Boston, 1972), cat. no. 50.

15. Patricia E. Kane, "Furniture Owned by the Massachusetts Historical Society," *Antiques* 109, no. 5 (May 1976): 960, fig. 3; Harriet Ropes Cabot, *Handbook of the Bostonian Society* (Boston: Old State House, 1979), 10 (left).

16. See entry by Barbara McLean Ward in *The American Craftsman and the European Tradition, 1620 to 1820*, ed. Francis J. Puig and Michael Conforti (Minneapolis: Minneapolis Institute of Arts, 1989), 77–79 (Dighton); *Antiques* 155, no. 1 (January 1999): 104 (Garthorne pot); Clayton, *Collector's Dictionary*, fig. 124 (Williamson).

17. Jonathan L. Fairbanks, "A Decade of Collecting Decorative Arts and Sculpture at the Museum of Fine Arts, Boston, " *Antiques* 120, no. 3 (September 1981): 627, pl. 42 (right); Jonathan L. Fairbanks et al., *Collecting American Decorative Arts and Sculpture, 1971–1991* (Boston: Museum of Fine Arts, Boston, 1991), 70; Clayton, *Collector's Dictionary*, fig. 127.

18. C. Louise Avery, *American Silver of the Seventeenth and Eighteenth Centuries: A Study Based on the Clearwater Collection* (New York: Metropolitan Museum of Art, 1920), cat. no. 11, 21–24. John Marshall Phillips, *American Silver* (New York: Chanticleer Press, 1949), 57–58.

19. Buhler and Hood, *American Silver: Garvan and Other Collections*, cat. no. 49. Annette Townsend, *The Auchmuty Family of Scotland and America* (New York: Grafton Press, 1932), illustrates portraits of Auchmuty and his coat of arms.

20. Kathryn C. Buhler, *Colonial Silversmiths: Masters and Apprentices* (Boston: Museum of Fine Arts, Boston, 1956), cat. no. 111; illus. fig. 45.

21. For Webb, see the biography by Barbara McLean Ward in *Colonial Massachusetts Silversmiths and Jewelers*, 951–57. For Denny, see Arthur G. Grimwade, *London Goldsmiths, 1697–1837: Their Marks and Lives*, 2d ed. (London: Faber and Faber, 1982), 490. Monteith bowls with related fluting are illustrated in: ad of S. Wyler, Inc., in *Antiques* 154, no. 4 (October 1998): 459; Georgina E. Lee, with assistance from Ronald A. Lee, *British Silver Monteith Bowls including American and European Examples* (Byfleet, Eng.: Manor House Press, 1978), fig. 32 and appropriate entries in Appendix II; *Catalogue of Fine English Silver Plate of the 17th and 18th Centuries, The Property of Captain H.C.S. Ward* (London: Christie, Manson, and Wood, 1914), lot 44. Other forms with related decoration are illustrated in David Revere McFadden and Mark A. Clark, *Treasures for the Table: Silver from the Chrysler Museum* (New York: Hudson Hills Press in association with The American Federation of Arts, 1989), cat. no. 28; Charles James Jackson, *An Illustrated History of English Plate*, 2 vols. (1911; reprint, New York: Dover Publications, 1969), 1:272–73. A chocolate pot by Denny of 1705 bears no visual relationship to the Webb example; see Michael Clayton, *Christie's Pictorial History of English and American Silver* (Oxford: Phaidon/Christie's, 1985), p. 122, fig. 1; and Clayton, *Collector's Dictionary*, fig. 129. The Charnelhouse pot is discussed in Wees, *English, Irish, and Scottish Silver*, cat. no. 182. Other English pots related in style to the Webb pot are illustrated Robert Peake, London, 1702, illustrated in Peter Waldron, *The Price Guide to Antique Silver*, 2d ed. (Woodbridge, England: Antique Collectors' Club, 1982), p. 257, fig. 812.

22. Buhler, *American Silver*, cat. no. 326.

23. Henry N. Flynt and Martha Gandy Fales, *The Heritage Foundation Collection of Silver, with Biographical Sketches of New England Silversmiths, 1625–1825* (Old Deerfield, Mass.: Heritage Foundation, 1968), 100–101, fig. 79.

24. G. B. Warden, *Boston, 1689–1776* (Boston: Little, Brown and Co., 1970), 24.

25. See the special issue devoted to the Province house of *Old-Time New England* 62, no. 4 (Spring 1972).

26. Abbott Lowell Cummings, "The Domestic Architecture of Boston, 1660–1725," *Archives of American Art Journal* 9, no. 4 (1971): 1–16; quotation p. 7; see also Abbott Lowell Cummings, "The Foster-Hutchinson House," *Old-Time New England* 54, no. 3 (January-March 1964): 59–76.

27. Cummings, "Domestic Architecture," fig. 11 (Clark-Frankland), fig. 10 (Moses Pierce-Hichborn).

28. Entry by Edward S. Cooke, Jr., in Fairbanks, *Collecting*, p. 32. See also Benno M. Forman, *American Seating Furniture, 1630–1730: An Interpretive Catalogue* (New York: W.W. Norton, 1988).

29. Edward J. Nygren, "Edward Winslow's Sugar Boxes: Colonial Echoes of Courtly Love," *Yale University Art Gallery Bulletin* 33, no. 2 (Autumn 1971): 38–52.

30. See Barbara McLean Ward, "Boston Goldsmiths, 1690–1730," in *The Craftsman in Early America*, ed. Ian M. G. Quimby (New York: W. W. Norton for the Henry Francis du Pont Winterthur Museum, 1984), 126–57, esp. pp. 144–50.

31. Many of the sources cited in this essay contain information on the use of chocolate and the various recipes and other accoutrements used in its preparation. An invaluable guide to the period literature is Barbara Ketchum Wheaton and Patricia Kelly, *Bibliography of Culinary History: Food Resources in Eastern Massachusetts* (Boston: G. K. Hall & Co., n.d.). See also Peter B. Brown, *In Praise of Hot Liquors: The Study of Chocolate, Coffee, and Tea-Drinking, 1600–1850* (York, England: Fairfax House, 1995 and Julie Emerson, *Coffee, Tea, and Chocolate Wares in the Collection of the Seattle Art Museum* (Seattle, Wash.: Seattle Art Museum, 1991). The various types of stirring rod (sometimes called molinet, mill, muddler, or stirrer), made of silver, wood, or glass, are discussed in Edward H. Pinto, *Treen and Other Wooden Bygones: An Encyclopedia and Social History* (London: G. Bell and Sons, 1969), 291, pl. 312; and Harold Newman, *An Illustrated Dictionary of Silverware* (New York: Thames and Hudson, 1987), 214. A late example of ca. 1830–50 from New Mexico is pictured in Jonathan L. Fairbanks et al., *Frontier America: The Far West* (Boston: Museum of Fine Arts, Boston, 1975), 148.

32. *The Journal of Madam Knight* (Boston: David R. Godine, 1972), 9.

33. Quoted in Jonathan L. Fairbanks et al., *Paul Revere's Boston: 1735–1818* (Boston: Museum of Fine Arts, Boston, 1975), 29, cat. no. 26.

34. Contemporary newspaper advertisements as reprinted in George Francis Dow, comp., *The Arts and Crafts in New England, 1704–1775* (Topsfield, Mass.: Wayside Press, 1927), 209 (Boydell), 263–64 (Merrett), 292–93; 294 (Italian); and *Boston Gazette*, January 2, 1769 (Goldsmith).

35. On the substance's special properties, see the section entitled "The Psychopharmacology of Chocolate" in Diane Ackerman, *A Natural History of the Senses* (New York: Random House, 1990), 153–57, and Wolfgang Schivelbusch, *Tastes of Paradise: A Social History of Spices, Stimulants, and Intoxicants* (New York: Pantheon Books, 1992), especially chap. 3.

36. James Wadsworth, *A curious History of the Nature and Quality of Chocolate* (1652), as quoted in Brown, *In Praise of Hot Liquors*, 18.

37. Robert P. Maccubbin and Martha Hamilton-Phillips, eds., *The Age of William III and Mary II: Power, Politics, and Patronage, 1688–1702* (Williamsburg, Va.: College of William and Mary in Virginia; New York: Grolier Club; Washington, D.C.: Folger Shakespeare Library, 1989), xxxii. For tea, see Rodris Roth, *Tea Drinking in Eighteenth-Century America: Its Etiquette and Equipage*, United States Museum Bulletin 225, Contributions from the Museum of History and Technology, paper 14, 1–30 (Washington, D.C.: Smithsonian Institution, 1961).

38. Schivelbusch, *Tastes of Paradise*, 91, is especially good on the aristocratic manner of drinking chocolate. For the pictures illustrated, see Jeffrey H. Munger et al., *The Forsyth Wickes Collection in the Museum of Fine Arts, Boston* (Boston: Museum of Fine Arts, Boston, 1992), cat. no. 73; and Pierre Rosenberg, *The Age of Louis XV: French Painting, 1710–1774* (Toledo, Ohio: Toledo Museum of Art, 1975), cat. no. 66.

39. W. Hughes, *The American Physitian; or, A Treatise of the Roots, Plants, Trees, Shrubs, Fruit, Herbs, &c. Growing in the English Plantations in America* (London: Printed by J.C. for William Crook, at the Green Dragon Without Temple Bar, 1672), 141 (copy at American Antiquarian Society, Worcester, Mass.).

40. Schivelbusch, *Tastes of Paradise*, 91.

41. Specialized chocolate forms continue to appear in documents throughout the eighteenth century, often in base metals. For example, the architect Peter Harrison had a copper chocolate pot valued at 16*s.* in his estate when he died in New Haven, Connecticut, in 1775; see Carl Bridenbaugh, *Peter Harrison: First American Architect* (Chapel Hill: University of North Carolina Press, 1949), 176. Outside of New England, Lord Botetourt of Williamsburg, Virginia, owned 24 pounds of chocolate and had "3 chocolate pots with four mills" in his 1770 estate; see Graham Hood, *The Governor's Palace in Williamsburg: A Cultural Study* (Williamsburg, Va.: Colonial Williamsburg Foundation, 1991), 287–89.

42. Cary Carson, "The Consumer Revolution in Colonial America," in *Of Consuming Interests: The Style of Life in the Eighteenth Century*, ed. Cary Carson, Ronald Hoffman, and Peter J. Albert (Charlottesville: University Press of Virginia for the United States Capitol Historical Society, 1994), 483–697; quotation p. 494.

43. See Kevin M. Sweeney, "High-Style Vernacular: Lifestyles of the Colonial Elite," in Carson, Hoffman, and Albert, *Of Consuming Interests*, 1–58. The chocolate pots suggest that Boston was ahead of the changes that Sweeney finds in "many areas in the late 1710s and the 1720s" by perhaps a decade (see p. 5). The symbolic meanings of drinking are discussed in David W. Conroy, *In Public Houses: Drink and the Revolution of Authority in Colonial Massachusetts* (Chapel Hill and London: University of North Carolina Press for the Institute of Early American History and Culture, 1995), 22–23.

44. Sidney W. Mintz, *Sweetness and Power: The Place of Sugar in Modern History* (New York: Penguin Books, 1986), esp. 106–39.

45. Hughes, *American Physitian*, 148.

Ecclesiastical Silver

"We owe something more than prayers":
Elizabeth Porter Phelps's Gift of Church Silver and Her Quest for Christian Fellowship

KAREN PARSONS

. . . may we ever remember that we owe something more than prayers even
on offering to the Lord that they who preach the Gospel shall be supported.

–Elizabeth Porter Phelps to
Elizabeth Phelps Huntington,
August 21, 1811

SOMETIME IN THE YEARS from 1811 through 1813, Elizabeth Porter Phelps, a wealthy Hadley townswoman, donated two communion vessels to the congregation at the Church of Christ (fig. 1). Such gifts of silver, especially when inscribed with the donor's name, expressed something about the giver to her community. One convention of material culture criticism ascribes the gesture primarily to the desire to demonstrate status. Since Phelps belonged to a prominent, monied Massachusetts family, it would be easy to see these cups as nothing other than a display of class identity. A careful examination of the context in which Phelps made the gift, however, reveals the complexity of the role that church silver played in early-nineteenth-century New England life. In this broader view, it becomes evident that the gift brought together the social networks in which Phelps traveled as a wealthy woman with her intense dedication to her religious principles and community. The meaning of the communion vessels in particular is revealed in that context, since the Hadley congregation advocated a very open and inclusive communion ritual. Furthermore, the time at which Phelps gave the cups coincided with a membership crisis in the church in the years following the death of their beloved pastor, Rev. Samuel Hopkins.

Taken only at face value, Phelps's gift can be read as an expression of status simply by virtue of her family wealth and the high profile she maintained in her church. The family's wealth was certainly no secret to those who worshiped at the Church of Christ. Elizabeth's husband, Charles, owned six hundred acres, making him the largest landowner in town; in 1799 he paid almost twice as much land tax as the next largest property owner.[1] The Phelpses employed

Fig. 1. Thomas C. Fletcher (1787–1866) and Sidney Gardiner (1791–1869), two-handled communion cups, Boston, Massachusetts, 1808–13. Silver; h. 5 ¼ in. Courtesy, First Congregational Church, U.C.C., Hadley, Massachusetts.

Fig. 2. Forty Acres (Porter-Phelps-Huntington House Museum), Hadley, Massachusetts.

Fig. 3. Fletcher and Gardiner's mark on cups illustrated in fig. 1. Photo, courtesy First Congregational Church, U.C.C., Hadley, Massachusetts.

church members and local residents as farm workers, domestic servants, and skilled craftspeople at their estate, Forty Acres (fig. 2).[2] The couple's activities within their church also demonstrated, intentionally or not, their financial well-being. Charles, who served as a deacon and played an important role in the 1807–1808 construction of the third meetinghouse, sold pews in this new meetinghouse to church members.[3] He also owned three pews: numbers 26 and 28 each valued at $200, and number 70 — which he probably rented out — valued at $24 in 1817.[4]

Befitting their financial position, the Phelpses communicated a taste for decor that was fashionable, genteel, and urban: while the surrounding area supplied their household labor, by 1800 the Phelpses looked often to Boston, not to Hadley, to furnish their home.[5] Not insignificantly, the cups themselves were of Boston manufacture, making it all the more likely that Elizabeth's fellow churchgoers would have associated the cups with her social station. Each of the two five-inch tall cups bears a footed base, two strap handles projecting more than an inch and a half from its body, and an inscription that reads "Presented / by Elizabeth Phelps to the / Church of Christ in Hadley. / Feby. 1813." On the underside of one cup's base appears the stamp "F.&G." in a rectangular surround — the mark of the silversmithing firm Fletcher and Gardiner (fig. 3). Thomas Fletcher and Sidney Gardiner ran a shop and retail store in Boston between 1808 and 1811. They sold goods produced by other metalworkers but found their greatest profit in merchandising wares made in their own silversmithing shop.[6] Aside from the conflict in evidence — maker's mark versus inscribed date — Phelps apparently made the gift in the 1811 to 1813 time period.[7]

Considerable evidence and analysis about the social value of material culture appears in a pivotal exhibition catalogue entitled *The Great River: Art and Society of the Connecticut Valley*. In her discussion of how silver objects functioned to display the affluence of the area's elite, Barbara McLean Ward noted

Fig. 4. Unknown maker, flagon, probably England, 1824. Silver fused-plate; h. 11 ½ in. Courtesy of First Congregational Church, U.C.C., Hadley, Massachusetts.

that gifts of expensive communion silver "made [the donor's] power and position manifest to all . . . their neighbors."[8] In his contribution to the book, Robert Blair St. George asserted that the wealthy elite "preserved the image of corporate communalism to their own advantage" by making generous donations of church plate. Churches had no choice but to be subservient to these donors who, according to St. George, made "calculated acts of largesse" and thus maintained a level of control over their congregations.[9] The Hadley church certainly did obtain its silver through a particular social network that included Phelps and a number of her friends. In the 1780s Lucretia Colt Walker gave two cups in memory of her first husband, Benjamin Colt.[10] John Hopkins, another close friend of Phelps and the son of Rev. Hopkins, gave an enormous gift of silver fused-plate in 1824.[11] The set was comprised of eight cups, four plates, two flagons, and one baptismal basin (fig. 4). Church records note that "two tankards and some cups were given by Major Erastus Smith" (fig. 5) on the same day that Hopkins presented his gift: "On July 4, 1824 . . . the church voted 'thanks to Major E. Smith and Captain John Hopkins for furniture for the communion table.'"[12] Phelps also counted Smith among her convivial group of friends.

While many churchgoers certainly recognized Phelps's wealth and her social position as they drank from the cups she had given, that perception does not necessarily encompass the meaning that the objects would have carried for Phelps herself. Phelps's diary and letters reveal that her primary motivation for

Fig. 5. Unknown maker, two-handled communion cup, probably England, 1824. Silver fused-plate; h. 5⅜ in. Courtesy of First Congregational Church, U.C.C., Hadley, Massachusetts.

the gift was not to make a public statement about her wealth nor to gain power within the church community. The tenor of her spiritual life as she recorded it in these documents, as well as the many acts of Christian fellowship she performed, suggest that Phelps prioritized building and maintaining Christian fellowship above all or most other goals. Probably inspired by her friendship with Rev. Hopkins, the gift may have been intended to embody his beliefs about communion participation — a belief manifested in the very design of the cups and the way they functioned during the communion service.

Phelps's day-to-day life was very much a product of her fellowship in Hopkins's congregation. She lived her piety, integrating rigorous spiritual self-examination and dedicated discipleship into most everything she did. Her forty-nine years of highly introspective diary entries and numerous letters recount her noble deeds, moments of self-doubt, and concern for others' personal salvation. Phelps ardently pursued fellowship through daily acts of generosity — aiding the poor, the parentless, and the distressed. She actively looked to create spiritual fellowship with her husband, her household, townspeople, women in the community, and with Christians around the globe.

A testament to how closely Phelps wished to integrate religion into her daily life appears in her thoughts about her husband, who did not share her focus on spiritual matters. Charles apparently had little tolerance for religion that swayed from traditional Calvinism. In an 1807 letter to her daughter Elizabeth Phelps Huntington, Phelps reported that "we had Mr. Montague all day, a baptist preacher — your father stood it pretty well."[13] Worse yet, Charles often failed to engage in spiritual introspection, and possibly her greatest disappointment resulted from their inability to share thoughts about religion. On the thirty-seventh anniversary of their wedding, Elizabeth reflected,

> my feelings on this day have been tender & solemn — when I remember, what my expectations were before I married, respecting a life of religious conversation, & mutual enjoyment of the things of God — I am almost ready to sink in discouragement — my husband has treated me with that reserve & distance which I little expected . . . he finds not that inducement to converse upon experimental religion perhaps, which is requisite to a free Union & endearing interchanging of tho'ts & affections. — O how ought my heart to be humbled, low in the dust before God, that the privilege which I so ardently desired, & confidently expected, has been almost wholly denied me.[14]

Elizabeth's relationship with Hopkins may have satisfied her desires to "converse upon experimental religion" and acquired special significance as a result.

Phelps created other opportunities to foster Christian fellowship in her household, especially in the work spaces at Forty Acres, where she interacted with her domestic servants and their children. Approximately thirty women worked and lived at Forty Acres over two decades.[15] Like the church community, this household staff was diverse, including white, African American, and Native American women. Most were young, at least two arrived at Forty Acres unwed and with an infant in their arms, and still others became pregnant while in Phelps's service.[16] Phelps extended concern to these young mothers and in particular to their children. She and her husband sponsored two-and-a-half-year-old Submit West, the daughter of former servant Susanna Whipple, for baptism in the Hadley church in 1794.[17] Later, Phelps kept Submit, or Mitte as she was called, off the town's pauper rolls by repeatedly securing her employment; bad behavior cost the teenaged Mitte four jobs in eighteen months.[18]

Phelps also showed special concern for two elderly German paupers, George and Mary Andries. Elizabeth cared for Mary in December 1783 when Andries believed she had been poisoned.[19] In 1785, 1788, and 1793, Charles and Elizabeth Phelps visited the Andries in "their humble cottage at the edge of the woods opposite Forty Acres" to "eat Christmas supper," a German tradition not shared in the eighteenth century by most New England Congregationalists.[20] After George's death in 1809, Phelps visited the eighty-five-year-old invalid Mary and "told her she must come live with me but that she must leave all her dirt & rags" behind.[21] Speaking little English, in poor health, and unable to dress herself, Mary brought new challenges to the household. But to Phelps's delight, this poor widow sought God's help while resting at Forty Acres.

> [S]he appears to be in prayer a great part of her time, uplifted eyes, with folded hands. . . . [H]ow should I feel was I such a poor helpless creature in a strange land without any person to depend on? [N]o where else but on clear, pure providence, indeed I can't but hope her eyes are fixed & trusting on God. . . . She says, "all is good, all is good."[22]

Evidence of such religious devotion apparently fulfilled Phelps's goals for her charitable work. All of her deeds tended toward bringing Christians together in a greater awareness of God's presence in their daily lives.

These deeds rarely passed without Phelps's self-evaluation of intentions and results. Often she emerged from this introspection humbled and more committed to her goals of spiritual fellowship. Phelps looked to God and through prayer for solace in these dark moments of self doubt. The birth of Submit West's mulatto child in January 1810, just after Mitte's nineteenth birthday, drew Phelps into a month-long flurry of reflection. She wrote, "Lord it is a sore grief to me, may my sin be set before me — my neglects be forgiven." Four weeks later she recorded,

> we have been taught by experience so often that when we were endeavouring to do our best it has eventually been productive of the most unhappiness. . . . Oh Lord we desire to look to thee for direction. . . . if thou seest best that we should be more tryed, & grieved by her misconduct may we say in truth, they will be done. Lord there is one favour for [Mitte], which I may beg for . . . may the riches of sovereign Grace be exalted, in the salvation of her & her poor destitute child — we have dedicated her to the Lord in baptism & . . . where is so ever we have done wrong, may we all be forgiven & have true repentance.[23]

Outside of her home, Phelps propogated Christian fellowship no less ardently. She worked closely within her church's congregation in a number of capacities and pursued a discipleship well beyond it. Her efforts within her church ranged from finite tasks to ongoing and much more active organizing. When the congregation built its third meetinghouse, Elizabeth participated in the effort to furnish the new building with textiles. In July of 1809 she "rode into town of arrands. Carried a tablecloth to deacon Smiths for the communion table."[24] On a broader scale, she vigorously organized Hadley women for church patronage and prayer meetings. During 1808, Phelps asked women to join a subscription for dressing the pulpit in the new meetinghouse. She traveled to "the Mills" and the town's Back Street — areas that held some dissension among the residents about where the new building should be located — and she asked the female inhabitants to put aside their differences and unite with women across town.[25] In the spring of 1810, Phelps joined "the good women [who] had agreed to keep as a day of fasting & prayer for a blessing upon their families & others."[26]

While Phelps physically assembled with women for patronage and prayer, she also organized female believers to pray simultaneously, but in the isolation of their own homes. To celebrate the dedication of the new meetinghouse and, more importantly, the resolution of the divisions that had threatened the community, Elizabeth and other women "agreed to Join in a certain hour (altho' at our respective homes) & offer up our . . . thanks, to the great God who we think has answer'd our prayers."[27] Phelps later invited women from different towns in the river valley, including a neighboring "pious widow" and a family member living in Middletown, Connecticut, to join in prayer at ten o'clock on Saturday evenings. She hoped these women, separated by geography but united in faith, would offer prayers for "our near relations."[28] Phelps's enthusiasm for this dispersed prayer meeting indicates that she enjoyed fellowship on a spiritual level: she envisioned a Christian community that maintained its fellowship even when it could not gather together.[29]

As evidenced in her diary, Phelps also pursued her religious ideals with a missionary zeal, working and praying always for the winning of new souls to God. In 1805, for example, Phelps and other Hadley women took special interest in the "deranged" soul of local resident Samuel Porter: after prayer session on the Old Street, as Phelps wrote, "a number of women retir'd into a room [and] pray'd — this meeting called upon Lawyer Porters account who continues to be in distress for his soul."[30] During a prayer meeting the following year, Elizabeth was overwhelmed by "a sudden & earnest desire . . . that a dear friend . . . might be fitted for, & brought to the Lords table, & faith immediately followed it — that it would soon be so."[31] By 1807 Porter "appeared a very bright Christian" and in 1809 he joined the church.[32] Phelps remarked that this was the "fulfillment of the faith which was so strongly impressed on my mind . . . in 1806."[33]

During the winter of 1810, Phelps witnessed the "signs of an . . . outpouring of the spirit" in Hadley that excited her hopes: "some are under convictions, may they . . . endure to the end & be saved."[34] Two months later, she enthusiastically reported that two teenage girls "are very much altered, they are together several hours a day with their bibles alone. — have no conversation with anybody, tell none of their feelings unless to each other . . . the Lord is surely carrying on his own work & we will rejoice in it."[35] At the same time that she hoped for increased faith in Hadley, she held great optimism for an apparent "outpouring of the spirit" across New England and even around the globe. She longed to hear reports about religion's impact. She asked her daughter Elizabeth, who lived in Middletown, Connecticut, to "tell in your next, how the small awakening process, in those few families by the river, & how religion is with you, as a town — O may there be many sons & daughters born into the *real* family of Christ."[36] The Phelpses hosted regional Missionary Committee meetings at their home, and attended numerous ordinations and lectures by missionaries who worked around the globe.[37] In December 1811, a jubilant Elizabeth reported, "O what good tidings are constantly saluting our ears, from many parts of the world. . . . [O]ur hearts leap for Joy when we hear how many instruments God is raising up."[38] In many ways, her desires for the advancement of the gospel seemed to be fulfilled, in Hadley and beyond.

The inspiration for Phelps's hard work and ardent discipleship took shape in the Church of Christ congregation and specifically under the teachings of Rev. Hopkins, who was called to the pulpit in Hadley in 1755, just a few months after Elizabeth turned seven years old.[39] He remained her pastor well into her adult life and became an important friend as well. In her diary, Phelps recorded numerous visits to Hopkins's home and wrote enthusiastically about these visits and his preaching. The ideal he inculcated in his congregants all those years was primarily one of religious fellowship. Some years later his successor, Rev. John Woodbridge, would recall Hopkins as a "distinguished . . . cultivator of peace among his people."[40]

The religious community Hopkins fostered practiced diversity in a variety of ways — not only by including the unconverted along with the converted, but also without discrimination as to race or denominational leanings. Hopkins welcomed African Americans to full membership in this overwhelmingly white congregation. At least five African Americans, four of whom were slaves, were admitted to full church membership between 1765 and 1776.[41] Hopkins performed at least five marriages for African American couples from 1766 to 1808.[42] Evidence suggests that the black congregants were segregated from whites in the meetinghouse: from the mid-eighteenth century, they sat in the gallery's back seats or in the "high pews in the corners over the stairs, which were very conspicious."[43] No evidence survives revealing where they sat in the third meetinghouse, dedicated in 1808. Despite being physically marginalized from the rest of the congregation, and despite their small numbers, some African Americans were fully integrated into the spiritual fellowship of Hopkins's church. During a June 1768 worship service, "Ralf Way [a free African American] desired prayers for his child sick of the canker which is called the Throat Distemper . . . and has swept away a great many children."[44] Between 1799 and 1809 at least four funerals of African Americans and one of a mulatto girl took place in Hadley. Elizabeth Porter Phelps attended these or burials and prayer meetings for the deceased.[45]

Hopkins also kept his church open to Christians with denominational leanings different from Congregationalism and thus deterred splinter churches from forming. A nineteenth-century Hadley native noted that "in Hopkins's day, it was a great point of interest to keep out other sects. And no small part of the minister's duty was to watch against interlopers."[46] The most significant threat to church unity during his tenure came from Baptists. In 1805, Hopkins encouraged churchgoers to "mark them who cause divisions and offences, contrary to the doctrine which ye have learned," and, more specifically, "those who [are] commonly called Baptists among us." These persons sought to separate themselves from the congregation over differing ideas on the appropriateness of infant and adult baptism. Hopkins adamantly opposed the potential division. He argued that "Those . . . Baptists have no pretence of any sufficient ground for separation from our churches, save such of them as behold we are not churches of Christ, because baptized in infancy and that therefore they cannot partake with us at the table of the Lord." Hopkins urged his people to broaden the place of the baptismal ritual in the Hadley meetinghouse and to give the so-called Baptists no sufficient grounds for leaving the congregation. He stated that "we are ready to baptize [these people], at the age, and in the mode, they think proper; and when baptized, to receive them to our communion."[47] Hopkins made it a priority to preserve the congregation's unity by identifying and promoting the common beliefs among groups. He thus managed not only to build fellowship within his congregation but also to keep other churches from forming in the town.

The communion ritual that Hopkins unfailingly kept open to a broad range of individuals played a vital role in his quest for religious unity.[48] He consistently welcomed "all persons of a sober moral life" to the communion table, "whether they did or did not profess to have been subjected to renewed grace."[49] The diverse group invited to this ritual, one of Christianity's most sacred, included the town's social elite, paupers, African Americans, churchgoers with Baptist leanings, conservative Congregationalists, and most importantly, individuals for whom the communion service offered an opportunity to experience conversion, not affirm an already publicly professed faith. Hopkins and his two predecessors, Isaac Chauncey and Chester Williams, all viewed this sacrament as a converting ordinance, not a reward for those who had publicly disclosed their conversion experience. These ministers, who maintained the church between 1695 and 1809, welcomed the converted and unconverted to full participation in the Lord's Supper.[50]

After Phelps's donation, the church owned six two-handled vessels and used this form exclusively until 1824. Although no evidence reveals who selected Phelps's Fletcher and Gardiner cups for the Church of Christ, whoever made the choice — Phelps or the church deacons — clearly referenced the communion silver already used in the meetinghouse. The church owned four two-handled cups by 1800.[51] In her essay "'In a Feasting Posture': Communion Vessels and Community Values in Seventeenth- and Eighteenth-Century New England," Barbara McLean Ward suggested that a preference for a single form of communion vessel can indicate a congregation's desire to blur social distinctions among church patrons and members of the congregation.[52] Since this reading could easily apply to the Hadley church, given its efforts to erase spiritual distinctions among participants during the communion ritual, it helps to explain the church's apparent preference for two-handled vessels in the absence of any

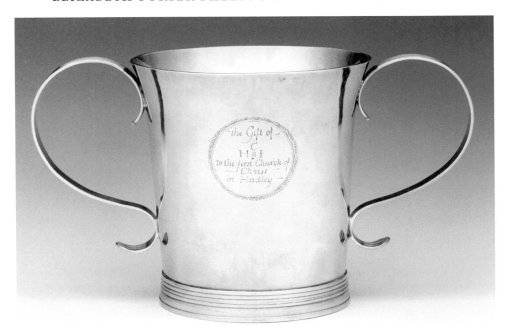

Fig. 6. John Dixwell (1680/81–1725), two-handled communion cup, Boston, Massachusetts, 1724. Silver; h. 5 ½ in. Courtesy of First Congregational Church, U.C.C., Hadley, Massachusetts, on loan to the Museum of Fine Arts, Boston. Photo, courtesy Museum of Fine Arts, Boston.

other documentation. Its earliest ritual vessels were probably pewter and part of a set acquired after the town's settlement in 1659. Unfortunately, these no longer survive in the church collection.[53] Beginning with the items extant from the eighteenth century, however, a relationship seems to appear between the church's emerging doctrine of an open communion and its preference for the two-handled communion vessels. In 1723, Peter Montague donated a two-handled silver cup made by Boston silversmith John Dixwell (fig. 6). Roughly half a century later, the church received another silver cup, made by Zachariah Brigden in Boston, bearing these oversized handles (fig. 7). Between 1781 and 1784, Lucretia Colt gave two silver fused-plate cups to the church in memory of her husband, Benjamin Colt (fig. 8). Silver and silver fused-plate vessels remained in use at the Hadley church until 1906, when small individual glass cups were introduced.[54]

Among the unusually diverse population in Hopkins's meetinghouse, the passing of the communion vessel from one congregant to the next would have constituted in itself an act of spiritual fellowship. The communion ritual began with the minister's blessing of the wine, after which he poured it from a large vessel into the smaller cups. The blessed wine then stood for the blood Christ

Fig. 7. Zachariah Brigden (1734–1787), two-handled communion cup, Boston, Massachusetts, 1723. Silver; h. 4½ in. Courtesy of the First Congregational Church, U.C.C., Hadley, Massachusetts, on loan to the Museum of Fine Arts, Boston. Photo, courtesy Museum of Fine Arts, Boston.

Fig. 8. Unknown maker, two-handled communion cup, probably England, 1781–84. Silver fused-plate; h. 6 in. Courtesy of First Congregational Church, U.C.C., Hadley, Massachusetts.

shed to forgive the sins of mankind and secure the promise of everlasting life. Thus bearing, in metaphor, the blood of Christ, the two-handled cups traveled through the congregation — "worthy deacons and communicants . . . passed them from hand to hand and from lip to lip as they took the cup and gave thanks."[55] Drinking from the vessel, each communicant embraced this promise simultaneously with an entire congregation. Each time a participant transferred the cup to the next believer, a moment occurred when two members held the cup together, each grasping one of the handles. In the same way that the promise of an eternal spiritual life held meaning for the group as well as the individual, these two-handled cups facilitated a single participant's communion experience and linked it to that of others in the meetinghouse. Clearly, the two-handled cups favored by the Hadley congregation helped to promote Hopkins's vision of congregational unity.

This inclusive invitation to church rituals had not always been in effect in Hadley. The town's first minister, John Russell, who served from 1659 to 1692, subscribed to more conservative ideas about who was eligible for the church's sacraments. The town's founding in 1659 resulted from a disagreement in the church in Hartford, Connecticut, partly over who could present their children for baptism. A minority in the Hartford congregation held fast to conservative teachings of their recently deceased pastor, Thomas Hooker, and believed that only full church members were entitled to baptize their children. These traditional Congregationalists rejected the less rigid view of their current minister, Samuel Stone. As Stone promoted the Half-way Covenant — this loosening of the rules governing baptism — the minority withdrew from the church, aligned with Rev. John Russell of Wethersfield, and removed to Massachusetts. As the first minister in the new town of Hadley, Russell enforced "strict Congregationalism" by allowing only members of the church in full communion to present their children for baptism and by administering communion only to "those who gave some evidence of faith and repentance."[56]

A less exclusive perspective about the church community came to the Hadley congregation after Russell's death in 1692 and with the calling of Isaac Chauncey three years later. Chauncey and his two successors, Chester Williams and Samuel Hopkins, subscribed to the theology advocated by Solomon Stoddard, minister in the neighboring town of Northampton from 1669 to 1712. Stoddard, who in his youth had experienced a conversion during a communion service, promoted "open communion" for all worshippers as a means by which they might feel that "'mighty change' in the heart."[57] He did not require a public affirmation of faith for membership in the Northampton church; one needed only "evidence of good behavior[,] . . . a simple profession of faith," and Stoddard's approval in order to gain access to the communion ritual. Stoddard believed that individuals could experience conversion after "extensive preparation through baptism, education, prayer, communion and much consideration of God's word."[58]

During his lifetime, Stoddard gained limited support in the Connecticut River Valley for redefining the role of the communion service and the part that ministers could play — because they administered that ritual — in conversion. Staunch support came from some nearby churches and their ministers, especially Isaac Chauncey of Hadley and William Williams of Hatfield.[59] After Stoddard's death, however, his views were challenged by his successor and grandson, Jonathan Edwards. Under Edwards's leadership, the Northampton church returned to strict Congregrationalist views requiring "those received into the church [to] make a credible profession of piety."[60] This reversal contributed to great controversy in the church and resulted in Edwards's dismissal in 1750. Chester Williams, Hadley's minister at the time, sat on a county-wide ministerial council that heard Edwards's case. Williams voted for the preacher's dismissal, honoring Hadley's longtime allegiance to an open communion.[61] In 1755, when Hopkins took his place at the Hadley pulpit, he joined with a congregation already well versed in the welcoming theology he espoused.

Despite the legacy of decades that gave foundation to Hopkins's principles, the Hadley congregation went into a crisis when they lost his leadership. In 1809 he suffered a number of strokes; about one, Phelps noted in her diary that he "had another shock, one side nearly dead."[62] Paralysis forced him to retire from active ministry, although he remained the senior pastor at the church in name.[63] Elizabeth visited him regularly over the next two years when immobility confined him to his bed. During the week before his death in March 1811, Phelps sat with him for at least two days.[64] Less than a day after his death she was "at the meetinghouse to see about putting the pulpit in black."[65] She later wrote, "Tuesday we attended the funeral of Dr. Hopkins — a dear good friend to us & to all mankind. May all follow him as he followed Christ."[66] Phelps's first opportunity to take communion after Hopkins's death prompted an especially painful moment of self-examination. She wrote in her diary,

> one more opportunity at the Lords table can it be that there is one spark of true grace — Lord awake this dead, hard, stupid, heart[.] [W]hat can, what shall I do, but endeavour, & really take my place, at the foot of the cross — Lord if I perish; I perish, surely it will be just — the Sovereign God has a sovereign right to chose who he pleases — to make one vessel to honour & another to dishonour.[67]

The loss was certainly a profound and personal one for Phelps, but she took no less personally the threat to the congregation that he had ministered so carefully. After a lifetime of trying to live and support Hopkins's ideals, Phelps would do all she could to bolster the community's commitment after his death. In this context, it became clear that the communion vessels she gave sometime between 1811 and 1813 evoked Hopkins's vision of a unified church dedicated to an inclusive communion ritual. The gift must also have inspired helpful memories for the congregation as it found itself in a membership crisis.

Phelps's concern about threats to the congregation had already become evident a few years earlier, when the construction of the new meetinghouse stirred disagreement in Hadley. At that time, a number of Back Street residents refused to buy pews in the new building, and six months into the project less than half of the seating had been purchased.[68] With great relief, Elizabeth reported that by the 1808 dedication of the meetinghouse,

> those people who have been greatly displeased, & said many hard & bitter things against . . . those who have built the house, are now so far reconciled, that almost the whole of them, are coming into the new meeting-house, & either buying or hireing pews.[69]

It was clear to Elizabeth why this change of heart occurred. "This is the Lord's doing. It is marvelous in our eyes . . . we have long been sending up [our prayers] to the throne of grace for this very change of sentiment & conduct."[70]

Just as the church appeared unified after the meetinghouse dedication, and the Lord's good works were apparent in town, Hopkins's illness and death precipitated a dramatic membership crisis. Once Hopkins became bedridden in 1809, the junior pastor, Rev. Woodbridge, took over the pulpit; he did not earn popularity in town quickly. Phelps described him as "very much an orritor . . . [who] has too many gestures" and remarked that he gave "thanks very pathetically."[71] By 1811, the year of Hopkins's death, a frustrated Woodbridge noted in his records that "the church diminishes with rapidity." He added an ominous warning: "Consider ye that slight the Lord. Presume his wrath anon."[72] That year the congregation lost twenty-three members to death.[73] Despite an extraordinary increase in new members — a four-fold increase over the previous year in new adult memberships, with thirteen new believers — the church's losses to death in 1811 were almost twice the number of new communicants.[74] The following year brought only one new member to the church, and in 1813 only three adults joined.

Phelps focused her energies on the individuals who did join. She recorded their admissions in her diary and distinguished those who joined by adult baptism, and she took particular interest in the young women, who accounted for eleven — or 85 percent — of these new members.[75] In May 1811 she wrote, "we have had a number join'd to the church . . . Polly Shipman is one [and] I suppose by what I see [and] have heard, she rejoices greatly in the Lord. O may there be many sons [and] daughters, born into the *real* family of Christ."[76] Four months later, Phelps visited Betsey Smith shortly after her baptism and reflected,

> I rode out east, the middle way to a cloathers — stopt a few moments at Sereno Smiths — [His wife] was taken into the church last Lords day — was baptized herself & three children, Lord Jesus was not my heart drawn forth in Love to thee, & thy members.[77]

The sentiment she expressed here, the dedicated effort to further the growth of the church, provides us with the context so easily overlooked in the standard analysis of church donations. Perhaps Phelps hoped her donation of communion vessels would buoy the spirits of a flagging congregation, drawing churchgoers' hearts closer to Jesus and to their fellow members, as she had felt during her visit with Smith.

The cups physically increased access to Hadley's communion ritual and built fellowship among the congregation. At the same time, they pledged support for the enlargement of a spiritual fellowship around the globe. While Phelps struggled in her life and writings to balance worldly concerns with the promise of eternal life, she clearly stated her belief in salvation through Christian fellowship with her gift of communion silver. In offering "something more than prayers" to Hadley's Church of Christ, Elizabeth Porter Phelps brought together her material and spiritual realms in these cups, and furthered her lifelong pursuit of Christian fellowship.

Notes

1. Christopher Clark, *The Roots of Rural Capitalism: Western Massachusetts, 1780–1860* (Ithaca: Cornell University Press, 1990), 41; Sylvester Judd, *Selected Papers from the Sylvester Judd Manuscripts*, comp. Gregory H. Nobles and Herbert L. Zarov (Northampton, Mass.: Forbes Library, 1976), 1:523.

2. Marla Miller, "Crossing the Threshold: Interpreting Women and Community in the Phelps Household, 1770–1816," paper given at "Through Women's Eyes: A Colloquium Presenting New Research on Women at 'Forty Acres,' 1750–1850: The Reinterpretation Initiative Phase II," Porter-Phelps-Huntington Museum, Hadley, Mass., September 24, 1994; Margaret Mary Fitzpatrick, "Forty Acres: A New England Homestead and Its Owners, 1752–1814" (M.A. thesis, University of Delaware, 1977), 62, 66, 75; Clark, *Roots of Rural Capitalism*, 111.

3. James Lincoln Huntington, *Forty Acres: The Story of the Bishop Huntington House* (New York: Hastings House, 1949), 21; Elizabeth Porter Phelps, Diary, January 18, 1807, Box 7, Folder 3, Porter-Phelps-Huntington Family Papers at Amherst College, Amherst College Archives, Amherst, Mass. (hereafter cited as PPH Family Papers).

4. Charles Phelps Estate Division. Box 4, Folder 33, PPH Family Papers.

5. Tara L. Gleason, "The Porter-Phelps-Huntington Family: The Social Position and Material

Wealth of An Elite Family in Eighteenth-Century Hadley, Massachusetts" (senior honors thesis, Amherst College, 1994, Amherst College Archives, Amherst, Mass.), 141.

6. Thomas Fletcher to his father, February 4, 1811, Fletcher Papers, Philadelphia Athenaeum, Philadelphia, Penn.; Ian M. G. Quimby, *American Silver at Winterthur* (Winterthur: Henry Francis du Pont Winterthur Museum, 1995), 357; Elizabeth Ingram Wood, "Thomas Fletcher: A Philadelphia Entrepreneur of Presentation Silver," *Winterthur Portfolio* 3 (1967): 137.

7. Physical evidence, namely the engraved presentation date of 1813 and the silversmiths' mark used by Fletcher and Gardiner only between 1808 and 1811, presents a vexing mystery about when Phelps donated these cups to the Church of Christ. Documentary evidence is no less clear. In a letter written to her daughter in August 1811, five months after Hopkins's death, Phelps offered a clue, although vague, of her intention to donate the silver cups.

> How did my heart burn within me the day before yesterday while I was at Mr. Perkins's, hearing him & Dr. Parsons, conversing upon the opening prospects of the Glory, of the redeemers Kingdom — how animated does it make even stupid me . . . may we ever remember that we owe something more than prayers even on offering to the Lord that they who preach the Gospel shall be supported.

She continued, "the publick thanks was returned last Sabbath" (Elizabeth Porter Phelps to Elizabeth Phelps Huntington, August 21, 1811, Box 5, Folder 10, PPH Family Papers). We know from church records that church members voted thanks to other donors of communion silver. Perhaps this vote of thanks was directed to Phelps. During Fletcher and Gardiner's Boston career, Phelps made five shopping trips to this city, and although no evidence confirms this, it is possible that she purchased these cups during one of her urban excursions. A local merchant or the church deacons may have secured them from Fletcher and Gardiner at this time as well. The 1813 engraved date may have been added later by one of the six Hadley and Northampton area silversmithing firms working at that time. These craftsmen include Joel Brown, Nathaniel Fowle, Jr., John Hodge, Nathan Storrs, Huntington & Packard, and Crooks & Phelps. The misspelling of the word presented — "presnted" — on one of the cups suggests that this embellishment was done by an engraver who worked hurriedly, sloppily, or by one who was prone to errors in his work.

Very few business records survive from Fletcher and Gardiner's 1808–1811 period and only three other objects are known to have survived from these early years. They are two-handled cups virtually identical to the Elizabeth Phelps cups: a pair of communion vessels given to the Second Baptist Church in Boston by I. Shedd in 1811, and a cup given to the First Church in Plymouth, Mass., about 1810. The remarkable similarity of these objects suggests that Fletcher and Gardiner recognized and met consumer demand for this form of church silver.

No Hadley or Hadley area silversmiths' account books survive from the early nineteenth century. For information on silversmiths working in the Connecticut River Valley at this time, see Henry N. Flynt and Martha Gandy Fales, *The Heritage Foundation Collection of Silver with Biographical Sketches of New England Silversmiths, 1625–1825* (Deerfield: Heritage Foundation, 1968), and Patricia E. Kane, ed., *Colonial Massachusetts Silversmiths and Jewelers: A Biographical Dictionary* (New Haven: Yale University Art Gallery, 1998).

8. Barbara McLean Ward, "Metalwares," in *The Great River: Art and Society of the Connecticut River Valley, 1635–1820*, ed. Gerald W. R. Ward and William Hosley, Jr. (Hartford: Wadsworth Atheneum, 1985), 274.

9. Robert Blair St. George, "Artifacts of Regional Consciousness in the Connecticut River Valley, 1700–1780," in *Great River*, 35.

St. George has also suggested that Connecticut River Valley church donors hoped their gifts would preserve social power for their heirs. If Elizabeth Porter Phelps expected this from her donation, she would have been sorely disappointed. Between 1821 and 1828, her daughter

Elizabeth Huntington faced severe judgment and eventual excommunication by the Hadley church and its leader, Rev. John Woodbridge, for admitting Unitarian leanings. Although Huntington embraced her mother's and Rev. Hopkins's vision of an inclusive, harmonious church, she rejected the doctrine of the Trinity, "narrow[ing] the distance between God and believer by endowing Him with benevolent human attributes." To conservative Congregationalists, such as Woodbridge, this denial of the Trinity and allowance of "the human mind to reflect rationally on religious . . . problems" threatened the spirituality of the communion sacrament. While Hopkins actively discouraged splinter groups from forming in Hadley by welcoming diverse theological ideas into his church, Woodbridge, his successor, zealously expelled church members for violating conservative Congregationalist principles or behavior. Also excommunicated were members who were believed to have committed adultery or danced at balls, and those who were thought to be habitual drunks. Because of her views, Huntington was denied attendance at the Hadley communion table and prohibited from drinking from the very cups her mother had donated. This indicates that a donation of church silver was not enough to secure a family's long-term position in the Hadley congregation. Prevailing theological ideas — not an ancestor's status evoked by communion silver — determined who was welcomed to the church's sacraments.

In 1821, four years after Phelps's death, Woodbridge appointed a committee to inquire into each church member's "feelings with regard to religion." Huntington told the committee that she did not believe in the doctrine of the Trinity and soon after, "was exposed on communion seasons to observations which were extremely trying to her feelings." She concluded that "her presence at the Lord's Table was not desired" and asked to be dismissed from the church. "Only by excommunication," Woodbridge asserted, would Huntington be free of the church. He considered the excommunication case for six years during which Huntington did not take communion at the meetinghouse, assuming that she was not welcome there. Ironically, in 1827, Deacon Jacob Smith informed Huntington that she was to be disciplined for "withdrawing from the communion" ritual.

Facing a humiliating excommunication, Huntington offered the deacons a statement echoing the message of unity so central to the life and work of her mother and Rev. Hopkins. Church records preserve this statement:

> [Mrs. Huntington] rejoices to believe that many who judge their brethren . . . will be admitted to those mansions . . . in her heavenly Father's House — she indulges a very comforting hope, that a place will also be found there for some whose names have been cast out as evil, and who have been esteemed as . . . the disgrace of the church. Anticipating the universal diffusion of light and love through the world, she is happy in the prospect that mankind will one day love together as brethren.

On August 26, 1828, the church approved Huntington's excommunication and voted its desire to "express their disassociation of such dangerous sentiments as hers."

St. George, "Artifacts of Regional Consciousness," 35; Mary Kupiec Cayton, "Who Were the Evangelicals?: Conservative and Liberal Identity in the Unitarian Controversy in Boston, 1804–1833," *Journal of Social History* 31, no. 1 (Fall 1997):2, 3. All information about Huntington's excommunication is taken from an account written between 1825 and 1827 by Deacons Jacob Smith and Timothy Hopkins. This untitled document is held in the Archives, First Church, Hadley, Mass.

10. The cup's inscription reads "Presented / by Lucretia / Widow / Lt. Benj. Colt / to the / Christ Church in / Hadley." Colt died in 1781 and Lucretia married John Walker in 1784. See Lucius Boltwood, "Family Genealogies," in Sylvester Judd, *History of Hadley Including the Early History of Hatfield, South Hadley, Amherst and Granby* (Camden, Me.: Picton Press, 1993), 23.

11. In a letter to her daughter, dated November 13, 1810, Phelps noted that John and Lydia

Hopkins "really do treat us like parents & their friendship appears in many instances." Box 5, Folder 10, PPH Family Papers; Boltwood, "Family Genealogies," 71.

12. Book of Remembrance, Archives, First Church, Hadley, Mass.

13. Phelps to Elizabeth Phelps Huntington, March 10, 1807, Box 5, Folder 9, PPH Family Papers.

14. Phelps, Diary, June 14, 1807, Box 7, Folder 3, PPH Family Papers.

15. Miller, "Crossing the Threshold," 8.

16. Thomas Eliot Andrews, ed., "The Diary of Elizabeth (Porter) Phelps," *New England Historical and Genealogical Register* 120 (July 1966): 129; 121 (April 1967): 95, 99; Phelps, Diary, August 11, 1805, December 6, 1807, July 16, 1809, Box 7 Folder 3, PPH Family Papers. See also Phelps to Elizabeth Phelps Huntington, November 12, 1807, Box 5, Folder 9, PPH Family Papers, for her interest in pregnant unwed girls of the lowest class being admitted to the Northampton church.

17. Church records note on September 28, 1794, "Submit West in the right of Charles Phelps and his wife" was baptized. Hopkins, "Baptisms since ye Burning of my House," Archives, First Church, Hadley, Mass.; Andrews, "Diary of Elizabeth (Porter) Phelps," 120 (July 1966): 213.

18. Phelps, Diary, November 29, December 7, 1806, June 20, 1808, Box 7, Folder 3, PPH Family Papers; Phelps to Elizabeth Phelps Huntington, July 14, November 26, 1808, Box 5, Folder 9, PPH Family Papers.

19. Andrews, "Diary of Elizabeth (Porter) Phelps," 119 (April 1965): 140.

20. Huntington, *Forty Acres*, 4; Arria S. Huntington, *Under a Colonial Roof-Tree: Fireside Chronicles of Early New England* (Boston: Houghton, Mifflin and Company, 1891), 55; Andrews, "Diary of Elizabeth (Porter) Phelps," 119 (October 1965): 295, 301; 120 (July 1966): 299.

21. Phelps to Elizabeth Phelps Huntington, December 15, 1809, Box 5, Folder 9, PPH Family Papers. Evidence suggests that Phelps's home county, Hampshire County, may have been an attractive place of residence for paupers and transients because well-established networks of charitable support appear to have been in place. See Douglas Lamar Jones, "The Strolling Poor: Transiency in Eighteenth-Century Massachusetts," *Journal of Social History* 8, no. 3 (Spring 1975): 28–54.

22. Phelps to Elizabeth Phelps Huntington, December 15, 1809, Box 5, Folder 9, PPH Family Papers.

23. Phelps, Diary, January 28, February 10, 1810, Box 7, Folder 3, PPH Family Papers.

24. Phelps, Diary, July 23, 1809, Box 7, Folder 3, PPH Family Papers.

25. Phelps, Diary, May 15, 1808, August 20, 1808, Box 7, Folder 3, PPH Family Papers. See also Phelps to Elizabeth Phelps Huntington, January 21, 1808, Box 5, Folder 9, PPH Family Papers.

26. Phelps, Diary, April 1, 1810, Box 7, Folder 3, PPH Papers.

27. Phelps, Diary, October 30, 1808, Box 7, Folder 3, PPH Family Papers.

28. Phelps to Elizabeth Phelps Huntington, August 21, 1808, Box 5, Folder 9, PPH Family Papers.

29. Phelps further integrated herself into the local community with the social rituals connected to death, illness, or hardship. In 1785, for example, she drank tea with Major Williams; she later described him in her diary as "not well — has had all his Furniture and most of the family Cloaths taken for Debt and sold at Vendue." (Andrews, "Diary of Elizabeth (Porter) Phelps," 119 [July 1965]: 213.) Sometimes Phelps was called into private homes to pray for a church member when

death seemed imminent, and she attended the burials and funerals of Hadley's citizens, from those of her own peers among the social elite to those of local African Americans and paupers. (Phelps, Diary, December 20, 1807, December 3, 1809, October 21, 1810, Box 7, Folder 3, PPH Family Papers; Andrews, "Diary of Elizabeth (Porter) Phelps," 121 [April 1967]: 99; Phelps, Diary, October 14, 1804, January 19, 1806, July 9, November 19, 1809, Box 7, Folder 3, PPH Family Papers; Phelps to Elizabeth Phelps Huntington, December 15, 1809, Box 5, Folder 9, PPH Family Papers.)

30. Phelps, Diary, October 20, 1805, Box 7, Folder 3, PPH Family Papers.

31. Phelps, Diary, March 30, 1806, Box 7, Folder 3, PPH Family Papers.

32. Phelps, Diary, April 12, 1807, October 1, 1809, Box 7, Folder 3, PPH Family Papers; Rev. John Woodbridge, "Church Records," Archives, First Church, Hadley, Mass.

33. Phelps, Diary, October 1, 1809, Box 7, Folder 3, PPH Family Papers.

34. Phelps, Diary, February 25, 1810, Box 7, Folder 3, PPH Family Papers.

35. Phelps to Elizabeth Phelps Huntington, April 4, 1810, Box 5, Folder 10, PPH Family Papers.

36. Phelps to Elizabeth Phelps Huntington, May 29, 1811, Box 5, Folder 10, PPH Family Papers.

37. "Extracts and Abstracts from Reverend Enoch Hale's Diary," Judd Manuscript, Vol. X, Special Collections, Forbes Library, Northampton, Mass., 52.

38. Phelps to Elizabeth Phelps Huntington, December 14, 1811, Box 5, Folder 10, PPH Family Papers.

39. Judd, *History of Hadley*, 324–27.

40. John Woodbridge, *Two Discourses Preached in the First Church in Hadley, Lord's Day, June 24, 1860* (Northampton: Bridgman & Childs, 1861), 24.

41. Hopkins, "Baptisms since ye Burning of my House," Archives, First Church, Hadley, Mass.

42. Hopkins, "Baptisms since ye Burning of my House," Archives, First Church, Hadley, Mass.

43. Judd, *History of Hadley*, 313.

44. Andrews, "Diary of Elizabeth (Porter) Phelps," 118 (January 1964): 19.

45. Andrews, "Diary of Elizabeth (Porter) Phelps," 121 (April 1967): 99; Phelps, Diary, October 14, 1804, July 9, 1806, July 9, November 19, 1809, Box 7, Folder 3, PPH Family Papers.

46. Judd, *History of Hadley*, 327.

47. Samuel Hopkins, *Christ King in Zion: A Half Century Discourse Delivered in Hadley, March 3, 1803* (Northampton: Thos. M. Pomeroy, n.d.), 29–30.

48. Sylvester Judd notes that he was remembered for his "rare sagacity in this matter." *History of Hadley*, 327.

49. Woodbridge, "Two Discourses," 24.

50. Woodbridge, "Two Discourses," 24; Judd, *History of Hadley*, 327; "The Communion Service of Hadley," *Hampshire Gazette and Northampton Courier*, June 19, 1888. They broadened the religious community further by inviting virtually all parents, even those not baptized themselves, to present their children for baptism in the Hadley church.

51. The Hadley church was not atypical in using two-handled cups for communion during the eighteenth and nineteenth centuries. See Anthony N. B. Garvan, "American Church Silver: A

Statistical Study," in *Spanish, French, and English Traditions in the Colonial Silver of North America* (Winterthur: Henry Francis du Pont Winterthur Museum, 1968), 73–104, for a detailed study of the preference for certain forms of communion silver, including two-handled cups. See also Barbara McLean Ward and Gerald W. R. Ward, eds., *Silver in American Life: Selections from the Mabel Brady Garvan and Other Collections at Yale University* (New York: American Federation of Arts, 1979), 91; E. Alfred Jones, *The Old Silver of American Churches* (Letchworth, Eng.: Arden Press for the National Society of the Colonial Dames of America, 1913).

52. Barbara McLean Ward, "'In a Feasting Posture': Communion Vessels and Community Values in Seventeenth- and Eighteenth-Century New England," *Winterthur Portfolio* 23, no. 1 (Spring 1988): 14.

53. A church history notes that these were given to "some feeble Western church" at its formation. See "The Communion Service of Hadley," 3. For information on the tradition of giving communion vessels to fledgling churches see Peter Benes and Philip D. Zimmerman, *New England Meeting House and Church, 1630–1850* (Boston: Boston University and the Currier Gallery of Art for the Dublin Seminar for New England Folklife, 1979), 87.

54. Book of Remembrances, First Church, Hadley, Mass.

55. "The Communion Service of the First Church of Hadley," 3.

56. Judd, *History of Hadley*, 4.

57. Paul R. Lucas, "Solomon Stoddard and the Origin of the Great Awakening in New England," *The Historian* (Summer 1997): 2.

58. Lucas, "Solomon Stoddard and the Origin of the Great Awakening," 1.

59. Paul R. Lucas, *Valley of Discord: Church and Society Along the Connecticut River, 1636–1725* (Hanover: University Press of New England, 1976), 193, 257.

60. Judd, *History of Hadley*, 323.

61. Judd, *History of Hadley*, 322–23.

62. Phelps, Diary, April 23, 1809, Box 7, Folder 3, PPH Family Papers.

63. William B. Sprague, *Annals of the American Pulpit: Or Commemorative Notices of Distinguished American Clergymen of Various Denominations* (New York: Robert Carter & Brothers, 1857), 1: 521.

64. Phelps noted early in the week that Hopkins was "more unwell" and later "Thursday . . . in the eve . . . we went to see Dr. Hop: . . . he appears very low pulse hardly discernable—fryday we visit at John Hibbards. . . . there we heard Dr. Hop: died about 3 that afternoon." Phelps, Diary, March 3, 1811, Box 7, Folder 3, PPH Family Papers.

65. Phelps, Diary, March 3, 1811, Box 7, Folder 3, PPH Family Papers.

66. Phelps, Diary, March 3, 1811, Box 7, Folder 3, PPH Family Papers.

67. Phelps, Diary, April 7, 1811, Box 7, Folder 3, PPH Family Papers.

68. Phelps to Elizabeth Phelps Huntington, January 21, 1808, Box 5, Folder 9, PPH Family Papers.

69. Phelps, Diary, October 30, 1808, Box 7, Folder 3, PPH Family Papers.

70. Phelps, Diary, October 30, 1808, Box 7, Folder 3, PPH Family Papers.

71. Phelps to Elizabeth Phelps Huntington, January 3, March 28, 1810, Box 3, Folder 10, PPH Family Papers.

72. "Ministers of the First Congregational Church of Hadley," Archives, First Church, Hadley, Mass.

73. Rev. John Woodbridge, "Church Records," Archives, First Church, Hadley, Mass.

74. Woodbridge, "Church Records," Archives, First Church, Hadley, Mass.; *First Church in Hadley Confession of Faith and Catalogue of Members, April 1, 1832* (Northampton: T. W. Shepard, 1832).

75. Woodbridge, "Church Records," Archives, First Church, Hadley, Mass.; *First Church in Hadley Confession of Faith and Catalogue of Members, April 1, 1832*. The increased membership appears not to have been the result of one of the religious revivals that periodically swept the Connecticut River Valley in the early nineteenth century. In 1804, thirty-three adults joined the Hadley church during what Phelps called "an outpouring of the spirit." Rev. Woodbridge, in his 1860 sermon, "Two Discourses Preached in the First Church in Hadley," noted that a young male schoolteacher who came to Hadley in 1804 greatly fueled this revival. For evidence of other revivals in the Connecticut River Valley, see Ruth Patten, *Interesting Family Letters of the Late Mrs. Ruth Patten, of Hartford, Conn.* (Printed by D. B. Moseley, 1845), 162.

76. Phelps to Elizabeth Phelps Huntington, May 29, 1811, Box 5, Folder 10, PPH Family Papers.

77. Phelps, Diary, September 29, 1811, Box 5, Folder 10, PPH Family Papers.

Continuity and Change in New England Church Silver and Communion Practices, 1790–1840

BARBARA McLEAN WARD

URING THE FIRST HALF of the nineteenth century many New England churches melted down vessels from their collections of old communion plate. They used the resulting silver to have new vessels made. We do not know precisely why this was done; all we have as evidence are vague references to the practice. This paper seeks to explore why this process took place, and to analyze the forms of communion vessels made in the first half of the nineteenth century.

In 1826, at a meeting of the First Parish Church in Cambridge, Massachusetts, a committee was appointed for the purpose of obtaining more suitable plate for the communion table. At this time, the church had six tankards and four standing cups among its collection. The committee reported that:

> they have caused two of the [church's] Tankards and two cups to be re-cast and also two cups to be altered in such manner, as make seven cups of a uniform size and shape. They have also procured a new spoon, and six Britannia ware dishes more adapted to the use for which they are designed, than those formerly used. The expenses attendant upon these alterations and improvements have been drawn from the funds belonging to the Church, an abstract of which is hereto annexed.

Dr. Expense of re-casting 5 cups and altering two	$114.41
Making seven do	5.00
Six Britannia ware dishes	21.00
	$140.41
Cr. By 78 ounces of silver at 7/ per ounce	91.00
By 48 lb. old pewter, at 18 cts.	8.64
By Cash paid from the Church funds	40.77
	$140.41

> Your committee are of the opinion, that by thus taking from the capital of the Church fund the sum of $40.77, they have added much to the value and convenience of the service of plate, for the future use of the Church.[1]

The two "altered" standing cups, on high baluster stems, were made by John Hull and Robert Sanderson of Boston about 1670, and were probably originally close in appearance to the cup made by Hull and Sanderson for the church

Fig. 1. Robert Sanderson, Sr. (1608–1693) and John Hull (1624–1683), wine cup, Boston, Massachusetts, 1674. Silver; h. 7 5/16 in. Yale University Art Gallery, Mabel Brady Garvan Collection (1936.137).

in Rehoboth, Massachusetts (fig. 1), now in the Yale University Art Gallery. The alterations to the cups were slight, and the makers' marks were still evident in the bowls of the refashioned cups. The silversmith merely shortened the stems of the cups and deepened the bowls.

What had happened to make the church members feel the need for new communion plate? Why did they believe that vessels of a different form would be more "convenient" than the old silver they already possessed? The silversmith melted the old vessels and credited the church for the value of the silver, but there was still some expense involved in making the vessels. What made the Cambridge congregation believe that these new forms were worth the trouble and expense?

The wave of refashioning communion vessels that took place in the late eighteenth and early nineteenth centuries coincides with changes in the manner and form of worship in New England's Congregational meetinghouses. By looking closely at the material culture of worship, we gain insight into the needs, desires, priorities, and unspoken concerns of a distant generation. The following analysis rests on the conviction that objects reveal the sometimes unconscious concerns and anxieties of the people who made them or who caused them to be made.[2] The choices they made when determining the arrangement of a new meetinghouse or in selecting new forms of vessels for the communion table were not random acts without significance. Each alteration of the status quo represents a new solution to a problem. The changes that took place in New England meetinghouses and their furnishings between 1780 and 1840 represent a subtle manipulation of object assemblages and formal arrangements of space that resulted in a paradigm shift in the material culture of American Protestantism.[3] It is hoped that this analysis can provide fruitful material for a greater understanding of the complex interrelationship between artifact and belief — both civil and religious — and demonstrate how objects and spaces both reflected and communicated prevailing ideas about the proper order of things. Forms that appear in churches suggest that there is a connection between religious diversity and social conformity, and help us to understand why, and for what purpose, such connections may have existed.

Changes as subtle as those that transformed the look of communion vessels in the early nineteenth century can not be understood without an exploration of the material sources and their meanings. Because the meetinghouse was the stage on which the performance of repeated rituals such as communion took place, this article will begin with an examination of meetinghouse and church architecture, with a focus on New England Congregational meetinghouses, their colonial Anglican counterparts — particularly in Virginia — and the English sources that inspired them. It will then combine these insights with an analysis of the communion plate from both regions and their English sources.

In the seventeenth and eighteenth century most New England meetinghouses were unassuming structures used for both civic and religious purposes. In contrast to the parish churches the Puritan settlers had left behind in England, these were austere buildings. Stripped of the trappings of popery, such as stained glass windows, altars, and altar screens, these meetinghouses were powerful testimonies to the Puritan — and Congregationalist — belief in the power of the preaching of God's word to effect the conversion of men and women into visible saints. The interiors of these meetinghouses, although plain, were highly structured, and their arrangement served to undergird the most important principles of the Puritan faith.

The focal point of the New England meetinghouse was the pulpit. Rising high above the pews, the pulpit put the minister in a commanding position vis-à-vis his parishioners. But lest he forget from whence his position was derived, the pews flanking the minister, and facing the main body of the congregation, were filled with the community's most prestigious members. In the earliest meetinghouses, such as the First Church in New Haven, Connecticut, the pul-

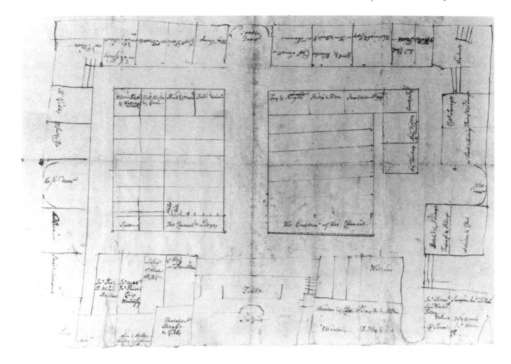

Fig. 2. Seating plan of Boston's Third ("Old South") Church, 1675. Old South Meetinghouse. Photo, Robert Blair St. George.

pit was actually thrust into the middle of the congregation, with large pews on either side to accommodate the "chief" members of the congregation. The 1675 seating plan of Boston's Third, or Old South Church (fig. 2), shows a building in which this seating arrangement was perpetuated.[4]

These square-plan meetinghouses were not consecrated or sacred structures, but served as centers of community life, and were used for town meetings and the proceedings of the Quarterly courts as well as for religious services. By their sheer size, these buildings dominated New England's towns. The Great Awakening, and the renewed emphasis on the conversion experience that it inspired, divided many congregations and resulted in the creation of new churches. Population growth also created a need for new churches. By the mid-eighteenth century, congregations were erecting new structures dedicated to purely religious purposes, and towns were building separate townhouses and court houses to house civic activities.[5] These new meetinghouses were rectangular, and had the appearance of large houses. Parishioners entered these buildings through doors on the long side of the structure, and the pulpit was placed directly across from the main entrance. Some meetinghouses had adjacent bell towers, and by the 1760s and 1770s it was becoming increasingly common for

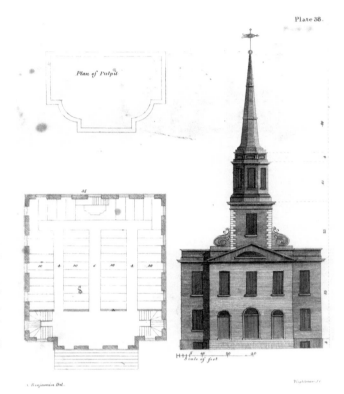

Fig. 3. "Plan and elevation for a meetinghouse." From Asher Benjamin, *The American Builder's Companion; or A New System of Architecture* (Boston: Etheridge and Bliss, 1806), plate 38. Courtesy, The Winterthur Library: Printed Book and Periodical Collection.

builders to construct new meetinghouses with bell towers attached to the main body of the structure. The innovative design of the 1772 North Church in Salem, which placed the main entrance under the attached bell tower, began a trend which would gather momentum after the Revolutionary War. Communion table and pulpit were now located together on the short end of the building. The pulpit was to one side or above the altar or communion table, and both occupied a central position and thus dominated the parishioner's view as he or she entered the meetinghouse. By the time Asher Benjamin wrote his *American Builder's Companion* (1806) (fig. 3), this type of church-plan meetinghouse was widespread in New England.

Communion vessels also underwent changes during this period. From an analysis of more than one thousand communion vessels owned by New England churches before 1780, in an earlier article I concluded that most New England congregational churches assembled groups of communion vessels that mirrored the values of their communities.[6] The deacons of a Congregational church were charged with overseeing the "temporal" matters of the church's existence, and therefore were the members who decided how to utilize gifts made to the church. In doing so, they made decisions about which objects were

117

most appropriate or "convenient" for their congregation's way of practicing the Lord's Supper. Some churches collected large numbers of communion vessels because they believed in admitting nearly all adults to the communion table. But these same churches, by collecting vessels in a variety of different forms — from prestigious standing cups to simple beakers — could continue to maintain social distinctions among the communicants even as they liberalized their communion policy. Thus, the vessels perpetuated the social differentiation that also was evident in the way people were seated in the meetinghouse. In rural areas, and some urban churches known for their egalitarianism, deacons seem to have preferred to slowly amass sets of matching vessels. This trend toward uniformity would continue, and gain favor, everywhere, as the century progressed. Churches where the deacons chose to inscribe communion vessels with the names of their donors also were able to perpetuate for several generations the memory of prominent patrons of the church.

The way the South Church in Andover, Massachusetts, handled the 1802 gift of two silver flagons is perhaps an extreme example of the role of objects in maintaining ties to the past. The church minutes record that the church received two silver flagons, weighing 109 ounces "by direction" of the late Lt. Gov. Samuel Phillips and by Samuel Abbott, both members of the church. Those attending the meeting were so overcome that they decided that the church should "gratefully accept the liberal and sacred donation" and the church voted "to perpetuate the memory of the Donors and express [its] gratitude" by entering the inscription on the flagons into the church records, and directing "that they be read at every annual meeting thereof forever."[7] Other churches avoided donative inscriptions, or placed them on the undersides of the vessels, where they would not be seen, rather than giving them a prominent place on the sides of these objects. These same churches generally preferred to assemble groups of communion vessels that were all of the same general form — such as the group of communion cups, in the form of caudle cups, owned by the first church in Farmington, Connecticut (fig. 4), or the set of beakers owned by the first church in Ipswich, Massachusetts.[8]

In both types of Congregational churches — those that owned mixed sets of vessels, and those that had matching sets of vessels — the objects for the communion table generally were not acquired at one time, and many churches used pewter and silver objects together. Typically, a congregation first purchased pewter flagons, plates, and cups, and gradually replaced these with objects of silver.[9] The first items to be acquired in silver were the various forms of vessels used to partake the communion wine. Favorite forms — most with domestic counterparts — included tankards, standing cups, two-handled cups, beakers, caudle cups, and mugs or canns. The next items to be acquired in silver were

Fig. 4. Silver caudle cups owned by the First Church in Farmington, Connecticut. Various Boston makers; h. (gadrooned cup) 4¼ in. From E. Alfred Jones, *The Old Silver of American Churches* (Letchworth, Eng.: Arden Press for the National Society of the Colonial Dames of America, 1913), plate LXI. Photo, courtesy Museum of Fine Arts, Boston.

usually the flagons used to refill the "cups" with wine. And the forms most likely to be made of pewter throughout the life of a church were the plates for the communion bread. Baptismal basins, used in the only other sacrament recognized by Congregationalists, seem to have been acquired in silver only if a donor came forward to make such a gift; church members did not vote common church funds for this purpose.

Drinking vessels known generically as "cups," from the use of the term in the Bible, had greater symbolic importance for Protestants than did plates for the communion bread. Communion cups helped Protestants to differentiate themselves from Roman Catholics. Roman Catholics believed that the wine was reserved for the clergy alone. The Protestant Church "restored the cup to the laity" and communicants were allowed to drink the communion wine as well as eat the communion bread. The proliferation of communion cups in Protestant churches thus was a result of the belief that all communicants should receive the wine.

Within Christian churches, there are significant differences in the way communion was practiced. In the Roman Catholic Church numerous items were required in serving the mass — such as monstrances to hold the consecrated host, censers to hold incense — but only one cup was necessary, as only the priest drank the wine. Because the priest had to consume all of the wine that was consecrated, Roman Catholic chalices tended to have a small capacity.[10]

Fig. 5. Set of church silver made by Francis Garthorne of London in 1709/10, presented by Queen Anne to Trinity Church, New York City. H. (flagons) 13 in. From E. Alfred Jones, *The Old Silver of American Churches* (Letchworth, Eng.: Arden Press for the National Society of the Colonial Dames of America, 1913), plate CIII. Photo, courtesy Museum of Fine Arts, Boston.

Anglicans used a standard set of church plate which included a pair of chalices and patens, a pair of flagons, and an alms basin, such as the set given to Trinity Church in New York City by Queen Anne in 1709 (fig. 5).[11] Because every adult in the congregation drank the communion wine, Anglican cups were commodious. These cups were filled from flagons on the church altar, and then presented to the communicants as they came forward, took the cup from the priest, drank, and returned the cup to the priest.[12] In the Reformed Protestant tradition – which includes Congregationalists, Presbyterians, Baptists, Church of Scotland, and Dutch Reformed – until the mid-eighteenth century communion was restricted to those individuals who had made a relation of saving faith and had been admitted to the church as members in full communion. In these churches there was a great deal of emphasis on passing the cup among the communicants, with each person who was eligible to participate in communion receiving the cup directly from another "saved" individual. Numerous cups were used, and tankards and standing cups appear to have been reserved for use by the most prestigious members of the church, while beakers and canns were passed to the others.[13]

In analyzing the nature of assemblages of communion vessels in New England Congregational churches, I originally decided to confine my study to churches whose earliest communion vessels dated before 1780. I did this because I noted some trends that seemed to indicate that the categories into which objects fell, and the meanings attached to certain types of objects, changed significantly after the Revolution. These changes coincided with an increase in the number of new meetinghouses being constructed with a long axis, or church plan. The coincidence of changes in both the church plans and in the form, variety, and source of communion vessels suggested that the changes were due to more than just fashion, although fashion certainly may have been a significant factor.

Discussions preserved in church records, and a close examination of the material evidence, reveal that communities defined social order in distinctly different ways. This article attempts to examine, through the use of material evidence, how the emerging emphasis on economic status in the middle of the eighteenth century was affected by revolutionary ideas and the dislocations of war. The new order of Protestant denominations in New England that followed the Revolution created diversity, but this diversity was frequently mediated by a sense of shared purpose such as in the development of broad-based nondenominational charitable organizations during the early decades of the nineteenth century.[14] While this sense of shared purpose among New England's Protestants may seem predictable for a fledgling republic, the material form this new order assumed reflects a complex interplay of Congregational and Anglican ideals.

The move toward a "church" plan in New England ecclesiastical architecture can be compared to the experience in Virginia, where the Anglican church was the established church. New England congregationalism developed as an attempt to purify the Church of England, and early adherents made a conscious effort to differentiate their meetinghouses from the Anglican parish churches they had known at home. By contrast, Virginians drew heavily on the church forms that they knew back in England. Dell Upton, in his study of Anglican parish churches in Virginia, shows that in the earliest years of settlement, churches like St. Luke's Church in Isle of Wight County, retained many of the elements of the Anglican parish church. In addition to an elaborate window on the chancel end of the church, St. Luke's also utilized altar screens to visually separate the altar and choir from the congregation. By the early eighteenth century the plans used for Virginia's Anglican churches varied considerably, with the auditory church — in which the pulpit occupies the most important position — being by far the most common. Nearly all Anglican churches in Virginia appear to have been built without towers.[15] The main differences between these Anglican churches, and the traditional eighteenth-century New England meetinghouse, was that in Virginia the communion table occupied a place directly opposite at least one entrance, usually the main one, while in New England meetinghouses the pulpit occupied this prominent position. In Virginia the communion table was sometimes surrounded by special pews for communicants, and often was isolated from the main body of the church in a "communion place" which, although not a true chancel, was set off from the nave by a

Fig. 6. Interior of Christ Church in Lancaster County, Virginia. From Dell Upton, *Holy Things and Profane: Anglican Parish Churches in Colonial Virginia* (Cambridge, Mass.: MIT Press, 1986), 179, fig. 212. Photo, courtesy Museum of Fine Arts, Boston.

communion railing. The pulpit, elevated and often elaborately decorated, was usually to one side or, in cruciform churches, such as Christ Church in Lancaster County, Virginia (fig. 6), thrust into the center of the church by being placed on one corner of the intersection of the arms. These churches were expanded and altered in the nineteenth century; Upton's research shows that many evolved so that the pulpit and communion table came to be located on the same short side of the building (with the pulpit to one side), and towers were added to the short ends of the buildings.[16] The resulting plan closely resembles the "church" solution arrived at by progressive New England congregations by the turn of the nineteenth century.

In both the New England meetinghouse and the Virginia Anglican Church, box pews (see fig. 6), with seats running around three sides, were the preferred form of seating for the most prominent members. In both New England and Virginia committees drawn from among the male members of the congregation determined who should sit where in the house of worship. This practice, known as "seating" the meetinghouse, was intended to ensure that the hierarchy established in the church mirrored the social, political, and economic hierarchy of the town or parish. Although the means of distinguishing what constituted the "best seats in the house" varied from one locale to the next, parishioners knew the meaning of the seating arrangements in their churches. By the middle of the eighteenth century, as established churches in both areas faced challenges from dissenting sects, there was an increasing tendency to raise money to build new churches by auctioning pews in the prospective building to the highest bidders. By the beginning of the nineteenth century, the old custom of seating people according to their worth to the community was set aside in favor of economic considerations. The wealthiest people could buy the seats they wanted—some could choose to remain inconspicuous, while others may have preferred prominent seats.[17] Established families with less disposable income than newly arrived merchants might choose to spend a greater proportion of their income on a desirable pew, rather than risk losing status to a newcomer. What effect this may have had on social relations within towns is uncertain, and more analysis of seating plans is needed before we fully understand the dynamics of this change. In Virginia, while pew assignments and seating were based on similar criteria to those used in New England, by the second half of the eighteenth century some leading planters were going to even greater lengths to separate themselves from the common folk during religious services. Vestry committees, dominated by one or two families, were responsible for designing and financing many of Virginia's parish churches. Increasingly, these wealthy planters chose to seat themselves in specially built galleries that literally lifted them above their less well-to-do neighbors, and these distinctions lasted up until the Revolution.[18]

If we imagine what it was like to attend these houses of worship — in both New England and Virginia — we can see that every week, and in New England sometimes more than once a week, the members of a church congregation spent one or more hours face-to-face with their neighbors in a large space that was laid out as a social and economic map of their entire community. Once a congregation opted to sell pews rather than assign them, the "best pews" went to the highest bidders. Because pews were real property, they could be bought, sold, or bequeathed to one's heirs. Under this system, prestige and power were no longer subject to periodic review, and could become hereditary. By the eve of the Revolution, in most New England towns, therefore, the "meetinghouse map" reflected whose family had money (or had had money). It was no longer the traditional measure of which citizens were thought to be the most useful and important to the town, or a guide to the most religious and pious members of the community. We have no comparable situations today, unless we might say that the common folk sit in the bleachers at Fenway Park and the influential and powerful members of the community own box seats. The arrangement in the church or meetinghouse, however, had additional power, because, existing as it did within God's house, this enactment of social difference and social connectedness, or social distance, was backed by a conviction that such distinctions mirrored God's plan for humankind and underscored the Bible's message that some were meant to occupy places lower on the social ladder than others. Whether conscious or not, changes in how people were seated within their meetinghouses help us to understand how eighteenth-century New Englanders ordered the world around them, and help us to determine the nature of what they believed to be a divinely ordained social order.

On the interior, the seating plans and disposition of pews in New England churches show a subtle but significant change after the Revolution. Early Congregational seating plans, such as the 1675 plan for the Third Church in Boston, known as the Old South Church (fig. 2), show many pews that are actually *behind* the pulpit, in a space regarded as sanctified in English parish churches. These pews, generally reserved for the most important church members, actually *faced* the congregation. Dell Upton found that, in Virginia's Anglican churches, the most important parishoners occupied the space between the communion table and the pulpit (which was usually located on an axis 45 degrees from the communion table). As in Congregational churches, these prominent members faced the less important members of the congregation during the service. Either the preparation of the communion table or the preaching of the Word, therefore, would actually take place behind some of the occupants of these pews.[19] In a New England meetinghouse the most prestigious seats generally were around the outside edges of the building, and the least important seats, the benches, were located at the dead center, in what would seem to us to be the "best" seats from which to view the preacher.[20] Imagine the impact of this seating arrangement, however, on a Sunday, when the people who occupied the benches found themselves confronted by the eyes of the more esteemed members of the congregation bearing down on them from all sides. By contrast, in a Virginia Anglican Church outsiders and newcomers were allowed more anonymity, being expected to occupy the seats at the rear of the nave.[21]

The gradual reorientation of the New England meetinghouse, and of the Virginia parish church, so that the pulpit was on one end, and all seats were oriented toward the pulpit, created a new relationship among the members of the congregation. In the New England meetinghouse the deacons and some privileged members of the congregation still faced the body of the congregation, and a few of these important church members occupied pews on either side of the pulpit, but most looked toward the minister, and toward the preaching of the word. The same change took place in Anglican parish churches in Virginia, but there, as Upton has pointed out, the most prominent members of the community not only stopped facing their neighbors, they also sometimes separated themselves completely from the rest of the community, preferring to sit literally "above" them, and "above" the clergyman.[22]

If we were to graph the acquisition of communion vessels by New England's Congregational churches during the seventeenth and eighteenth centuries we would notice a slow curve upward during the first decades of settlement as new towns and new churches were established across the region. There is then a sharp rise in acquisitions during the 1720s, 1730s, and 1740s, in part because of the new evangelism of the Great Awakening and the converts it attracted, and in part because of the church schisms that occurred in the aftermath of religious fervor. There is then a sharp downward plunge in the number of vessels acquired during the next three decades. Acquisitions were particularly low during the 1770s and early 1780s, but began to increase gradually in the first years of the new republic. Another sharp upward curve occurs in the first three decades of the nineteenth century.[23]

To what can we attribute this new upward curve? The increase coincides with the period known as the Second Great Awakening during which large numbers of new converts became members of America's Protestant denominations. By all accounts, however, Congregational and Unitarian churches were not the fastest growing denominations. Why then, did they add communion vessels to their possessions? Why did some churches add silver vessels while keeping older collections (sometimes quite extensive ones) virtually intact?

In having its communion vessels "recast," the church in Cambridge did what many other New England churches would do in the early nineteenth century — the church not only increased the number of cups available for communion, it also increased the number of cups of a single form available to the church. The church in Middletown, Connecticut, for instance, decided to add several new beakers to its communion set in 1784 and 1785.[24] The deacons chose a form for these six new beakers which differed from their earliest beakers in being slightly raised on a molded foot. This form also appears in Anglican churches, the most beaker-like example being this "chalice" purchased by St. James Church, New London, Connecticut, from a gift presented in 1773 (fig. 7). St. James Church gave the beaker to the Berkeley Divinity School at Yale University in the nineteenth century. This cup closely resembles the Anglican chalice form found in many Virginia churches, in that it is truncated in form and was less grand in appearance than the standing cups acquired by several New England Congregational churches in the seventeenth and early eighteenth centuries.[25] By the eighteenth century many New England churches frequently chose to add to their collections chalice-like cups on high molded feet, such as the examples purchased by the First Church in Berlin, Connecticut, about 1798, or similar examples owned by the church in Derby, Connecticut (fig. 8).[26]

When Josiah Sartell died in 1784, the First Parish Church in Groton, Massachusetts, owned at least three silver communion vessels — a beaker, donated in 1720, and two tankards donated in 1729. Sartell bequeathed three farms to the

Fig 7. "Chalice" purchased by St. James Church, New London, Connecticut, from a gift made in 1773. Made by John Gardner (active ca. 1760–75), New London, Connecticut, 1773. Silver; h. 5⅛ in. From E. Alfred Jones, *The Old Silver of American Churches* (Letchworth, Eng.: Arden Press for the National Society of the Colonial Dames of America, 1913), plate XCI. Photo, courtesy Museum of Fine Arts, Boston.

Groton Church, as well as additional property, stipulating that the church was to use the income from these properties to support the town's minister. The income apparently turned out to be more than sufficient for the purpose, and the church's membership decided that some of the monies should be used to purchase seven matching silver communion cups. When Sartell's widow died in 1790, she bequeathed a tankard and fifteen pounds for the use of the church. Even though the church already owned two tankards, the deacons decided to have Mary Sartell's tankard melted down. They used the resulting silver, and her monetary bequest, to have five cups, similar in form to those inscribed with her husband's name, added to the church's collection of communion plate.[27]

In 1808, Samuel Abbott bequeathed a tankard to the South Church in Andover. This tankard was large enough to make two silver cups, and the inscription was transferred to the two cups, part of a set of twelve silver cups on high stems made for the church about 1815.[28] Insight into why the deacons chose such a course of action is provided by the records of the Third Church in Ipswich (Hamilton), Massachusetts. In 1790, Mary Holyoke, widow of the late Symonds Epes, left a tankard to the church. In 1821, the deacons voted to exchange the tankard for vessels of another form, "on account of its being a ves-

Fig. 8. Communion cups owned by the church in Derby, Connecticut. Made by Miles Gorham (active 1790–1840), New Haven, Connecticut, ca. 1804. Silver; h. 5⅝ in. From Peter Bohan and Philip Hammerslough, *Early Connecticut Silver, 1700–1840* (Middletown, Conn.: Wesleyan University Press, 1970), 150–51. Photo, courtesy Museum of Fine Arts, Boston.

sel exceedingly inconvenient for ye sisters of the church."[29] The tankard was replaced with two small canns, or mugs. The interest in accommodating the "sisters" of the church may be telling. Women were becoming more involved in the affairs of their local churches during the early nineteenth century, and may have taken a more active interest in providing the accoutrements of the communion table. Inscriptions reveal that women had always been among the donors of church plate, but after the Revolution increasing numbers of women gave communion vessels to their churches, either as life gifts, or as bequests in their wills.[30]

All of these actions, and particularly the reasons given for them, are intriguing, and perhaps instructive. During the first three decades of the nineteenth century, dozens of Congregational and emerging Unitarian churches in New England either "recast" their early communion vessels, or retained their old vessels while acquiring substantial numbers of new ones. The forms most often added by churches between 1780 and 1840 were flagons, mugs, beakers, and cups, nearly always in sets, and often by subscription of all, or a portion of, the membership. Significantly, many churches also added silver dishes or baskets for the communion bread, and baptismal basins.

The use of the words "convenient" and "suitable" appear frequently in church records in reference to the decision to take old vessels to be melted and refashioned into new ones of a different form. Clearly both qualities were taken into consideration in making these decisions, but from our modern perspective, it is not always easy to discern what these words meant in their nineteenth-century context. The members of the First Church in Hampton, New Hampshire, for instance, voted in 1744 to purchase pewter flagons with church funds, but later decided to dispose of them because they were no longer being used. In the 1780s, the church deacons apparently again changed their minds about what was suitable when they purchased four matching pewter flagons for the communion table. Four flagons could hold a significant quantity of communion wine, and the minister used these to fill the church's small silver beakers (eight made in 1713, and four made in 1744) which were used for communion throughout the nineteenth century.[31]

There is some evidence that occasionally doctrinal differences may have affected decisions about the types of communion vessels a church acquired. In 1840, Deacons J. Patch and E. Annable had two mugs added to the communion service of the Third Church in Ipswich, noting that they had had their own names inscribed on the mugs "with a view to render them more secure to the 'orthodox' part of the Church for its use for ever." The Church voted that "thanks be presented to the deacons for their efforts in providing the above communion furniture" and also for acquiring a wine flagon, two bread baskets, and two silver cups. It is curious that these two deacons had their own names inscribed on these pieces, as the records clearly state that church funds from past gifts for "supplying the table" paid for the two mugs.[32]

Whatever the stated reasons, the cups and flagons used in these churches, though they were often made in greater numbers than the cups and flagons designated for use in Anglican churches, did come to resemble the traditional Anglican cup quite closely, and manufacturers of pewter and Britannia ware marketed standardized communion sets on the old Anglican model beginning about 1830. A set of this type was owned by the Congregational church in Springfield, Massachusetts, and a very similar set, in silver plate, was the original communion set of the John Street Methodist Church in New York City, one of the country's oldest Methodist societies. In New England, the communion cup considered appropriate in both the Anglican Church and the Congregational Church was becoming gradually truncated in form.

The most progressive churches, such as Brattle Street Church in Boston, or

Fig. 9. Joseph Loring (1743–1815), covered cup, Boston, Massachusetts, ca. 1790–1800. Silver; h. 11 ⅜ in. Museum of Fine Arts, Boston, Gift of Benevolent Fraternity of Churches (13.395).

the fashionable West Church in Boston which became a Unitarian Society, even added objects to their communion services that were neoclassical in form (fig. 9). These objects, derived from pagan forms, seem more to us like trophies than like church cups, and it is difficult to imagine that they were ever actually passed among the members of the congregation. The tendency to adopt a more urn-shaped form for communion purposes, however, was not confined only to the most fashionable urban churches, for we can detect a distinctly urn-like shape in cups owned by the First Church in Killingworth, Connecticut, which were purchased by the church about 1800. The Church in North Haven, Connecticut, also purchased cups on raised bases in 1804.[33] All in all, the move was toward uniformity. The Anglican cup form, with a deep bowl and high foot, and the Congregational form, with high baluster stem and a smaller bowl, were gradually changing to become one form — a low-footed cup with a deep bowl. Communion vessels thus became more uniform in size and shape. The numbers of communion vessels increased in an effort to demonstrate inclusiveness. Congregational churches usually combined numerous cups of this type with one to four flagons. Anglicans — who broke with the Church of England after the Revolution and became Episcopalians — and dissenting sects like the

129

Methodists usually had one or two cups, and practiced communion in such a way that congregants came to the front of the church and took communion directly from the minister, in keeping with the retention of an episcopal hierarchy in both denominations. The cups used by all Protestant denominations became increasingly alike, perhaps, as some have suggested, because sectarian distinctions came to mean less to Americans than a commonality of belief in a Protestant world view.

Parallels in the changes taking place in both New England and in Virginia suggest that increasing conformity in the material culture of Protestantism may have had more to do with the response of the established church to the threat of competing dissenting sects, than it had to do with theological considerations. Faced with the need to maintain prominence while being challenged by interlopers, the established churches — Congregationalists in New England and Anglicans (Episcopalians after the Revolution) in Virginia — may have been more interested than ever before in creating church edifices that physically dominated the village landscape. They may also have placed a new emphasis on portraying the church and the community as one — on demonstrating that theirs was an inclusive rather than an exclusive church. As the nineteenth century progressed the influx of Irish and other Catholic immigrant populations increasingly threatened the hegemony of the Protestant churches. In response, American Protestants came to take comfort more in their sameness than in their differences. As the established churches of the colonial period became disestablished — Massachusetts was the last to fall in the 1830s — their members may have needed to take comfort in the fact that more communion cups were needed to accommodate their many members. These sets of cups replaced the earlier communion objects in practical use — the older cups and tankards remained on view at the time of communion only to provide for modern communicants a sense of connectedness with the past, while the newer, cups were egalitarian forms equally "convenient" for both the "brothers" and "sisters" of the congregation.

Notes

1. E. Alfred Jones, *The Old Silver of American Churches* (Letchworth, Eng.: Arden Press for the National Society of the Colonial Dames of America, 1913), 108–9.

2. Jules David Prown, "Mind in Matter: An Introduction to Material Culture Theory and Method," in Robert Blair St. George, ed., *Material Life in America, 1600–1860* (Boston: Northeastern University Press, 1988), 17–38. Jules D. Prown, "On the 'Art' in Artifacts," from Gerald L. Pocius, ed., *Living in a Material World: Canadian and American Approaches to Material Culture* (St. Johns, Newfoundland: Institute of Social and Economic Research, Memorial University of Newfoundland, 1991), 144–55.

3. This discussion refers to the principles of the development of forms over time established most notably by Henri Focillon and George Kubler, as outlined in Kubler's, *The Shape of Time: Remarks on the History of Things* (New Haven: Yale University Press, 1962). The paradigm shift mentioned has been chronicled by several writers on the subject of New England meetinghouse and church architecture. See especially, Philip D. Zimmerman, "Ecclesiastical Architecture in the Reformed Tradition in Rockingham County, New Hampshire, 1790–1860" (Ph.D. diss., Boston University, 1985); Kevin M. Sweeney, "Meetinghouses, Town Houses, and Churches: Changing Perceptions of Sacred and Secular Space in Southern New England, 1720–1850," *Winterthur Portfolio* 28, no. 1 (Spring 1993):59–93. It is my contention that their conclusions can be said to have even broader significance if we analyze the parallel developments in architecture and the furnishings of the communion table, and see both as part of a significant shift in attitude and purpose.

4. Sweeney, "Meetinghouses, Town Houses, and Churches," 61–62; Robert J. Dinkin, "Seating the Meetinghouse in Early Massachusetts," in St. George, *Material Life in America*, 407–18; Philip D. Zimmerman, "The Lord's Supper in Early New England: The Setting and the Service," in Peter Benes, ed., *New England Meeting House and Church: 1630–1850* (Boston: Boston University, 1979), 124–29.

5. Sweeney, "Meetinghouses, Town Houses, and Churches," 71, 75.

6. Barbara McLean Ward, "'In a Feasting Posture': Communion Vessels and Community Values in Seventeenth- and Eighteenth-Century New England," *Winterthur Portfolio* 23, no. 1 (Spring 1988):1–24.

7. Jones, *Old Silver of American Churches*, 4–5.

8. Jones, *Old Silver of American Churches*, 178–79 (pl. LXI) and 222–26 (pl. LXXVIII).

9. Jones, *Old Silver of American Churches*, 178–79 (pl. LXI) and 222–26 (pl. LXXVIII).

10. Heidi Roehig Kaufmann and Elaine K. Bryson, *Eucharistic Vessels of the Middle Ages* (Cambridge, Mass.: Busch-Reisinger Museum, 1975).

11. Jones, *Old Silver of American Churches*, 332–33, pl. CIII.

12. Charles Oman, *English Church Plate, 597–1830* (London: Oxford University Press, 1957).

13. E. Brooks Holifield, *The Covenant Sealed: The Development of Puritan Sacramental Theology in Old and New England, 1570–1720* (New Haven and London: Yale University Press, 1974), 109–68.

14. Conrad Edick Wright, *The Transformation of Charity in Postrevolutionary New England* (Boston: Northeastern University Press, 1992), 77–95.

15. Dell Upton, *Holy Things and Profane: Anglican Parish Churches in Colonial Virginia* (Cambridge, Mass.: MIT Press, 1986), 56–57, 61. The only church known to have been built with an integral tower was St. Luke's Church, Isle of Wight County, Va., which Upton dates to 1685. Upton illustrates the variety of church plans common in Virginia on p. 97 (fig. 117).

16. Upton, *Holy Things*, 47–98; Christ Church, Lancaster County is discussed on pp. 84–85; fig. 90 is a floor plan of the church.

17. Dinkin, "Seating the Meetinghouse," 410–15.

18. Upton, *Holy Things*, 186–88, 222–25.

19. Upton, *Holy Things*, 186–88.

20. See seating plans illustrated in Dinkin, "Seating the Meetinghouse," 409–16, and seating plans in the Records of the First Congregational Church, Hampton, N.H., in the possession of the church.

21. Upton, *Holy Things*, 186–87.

22. Upton, *Holy Things*, 222–25.

23. This analysis is based principally on the data provided by Jones, *Old Silver of American Churches*.

24. Jones, *Old Silver of American Churches*, 281–84 (pl. XCI).

25. Jones, *Old Silver of American Churches*, 284–85 (pl. XCI); *Church Silver of Colonial Virginia* (Richmond, Va.: Virginia Museum, 1970).

26. Jones, *Old Silver of American Churches*, 139–40, 232–33; Peter Bohan and Philip Hammerslough, *Early Connecticut Silver, 1700–1840* (Middletown, Conn.: Wesleyan University Press, 1970), 126–27, 150–51.

27. Jones, *Old Silver of American Churches*, 190–92 (pl. LXIX).

28. Jones, *Old Silver of American Churches*, 3–4.

29. Jones, *Old Silver of American Churches*, 196–97 (pl. LXIX).

30. Based on figures compiled from Jones, *Old Silver of American Churches*.

31. Records of the First Congregational Church, Hampton, N.H., in the possession of the church.

32. As quoted in Jones, *Old Silver of American Churches*, 197.

33. Jones, *Old Silver of American Churches*, 357–58; Bohan and Hammerslough, *Early Connecticut Silver*, 138–39.

Social Context

Paul Revere and 1768: His Portrait and the Liberty Bowl

JONATHAN L. FAIRBANKS

T HE MUSEUM OF FINE ARTS, Boston, possesses perhaps the two greatest icons of Boston art and history: the John Singleton Copley portrait of Paul Revere and Revere's silver Sons of Liberty Bowl. These two precious objects have captivated scholars and connoisseurs as preeminent examples of their creators' skills and rare survivors from the moment of our nation's birth. Not until recent discoveries revealed that the two masters created their pieces separately but both in 1768, however, could viewers fully appreciate the meanings shared between the objects. A series of tumultuous political events made 1768 a turning point on the path toward American independence; a reexamination of the portrait and the bowl in that light brings into view previously unnoticed political symbolism — meanings otherwise lost to us but powerfully obvious to the Bostonians who lived through the events leading up to the Revolutionary War.

In 1995, in preparation for a Copley exhibition at the Museum of Fine Arts, museum staff set about cleaning the portrait of Revere (fig. 1). Jim Wright, Head of Paintings Conservation, and Jean Woodward, Associate Painting Conservator, discovered an inscription on the lower right edge of the painting (fig. 2): Copley's initials and the date, 1768, rendered in miniature. Before this discovery, generations of historians had surmised that Copley made the portrait circa 1770. Off by just a few years, the supposition had led interpreters to miss both the historical significance and emotional poignancy of the portrait.

The year 1768 constituted a turning point in Boston politics, marked particularly by the unification of Whig loyalties. Many observers understood it as the year that, under the slogan of liberty, reason became the means to persuade the colonies to band together in the resolution to free themselves from unjust demands and taxation from abroad. Whigs used every form of influence on public opinion to promote their cause: mob action, public notice, legal opinion, party caucuses, secret clubs, public celebrations and toasts, illuminations and displays, political prints, satirical songs, and newspaper editorials and all manner of written persuasion.[1] Public and private gatherings celebrated the communal values that emerged with the patriotic mindset.

Fig. 1. John Singleton Copley (1738–1815), *Paul Revere (1734–1818)*, 1768. Oil on canvas; h. 35 ⅛ in., w. 28 ½ in. Museum of Fine Arts, Boston, Gift of Joseph W., William B., and Edward H. R. Revere (30.781).

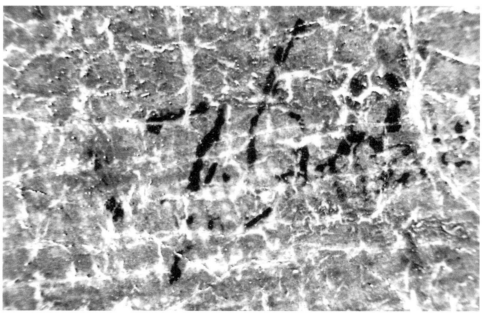

Fig. 2. Enlargement of photomicrograph of date inscribed by Copley in the lower right corner of his portrait of Revere (fig. 1).

Fig. 3. Paul Revere (1734–1818), *A Warm Place—Hell*, Boston, Massachusetts, 1768. Engraving; h. 3 ⅜ in., w. 4 ¹⁵⁄₁₆ in. Courtesy, American Antiquarian Society.

A primary rallying point for Whig sentiment arose early in the year, when the Massachusetts House of Representatives sent out a document known as the "Circular Letter" on February 11. This letter, distributed to the legislatures of all the colonies, decried the Acts of Parliament that levied taxes on the colonies.[2] By early summer, Governor Bernard demanded that House members rescind their letter; should they fail to do so, he threatened, he would dissolve the General Court. Brought to a vote on June 30, the letter won an unhesitating reaffirmation: ninety-two members voted not to rescind. For the seventeen who cooperated with the governor's demands, Revere issued a print entitled *A Warm Place — Hell* (fig. 3). It shows a devil using a pitchfork to drive seventeen men into the mouth of Hell, represented as the yawning, fiery jaws of a monster. Above flies a demon crying "push on Tim," referring to Timothy Ruggles, one of the active Loyalists.[3]

These events were accompanied in Boston by prolific debates in the press, often conducted by a few central players who guarded their identities with pseudonyms. "A True Patriot," who was Dr. Joseph Warren (see below), needled Bernard to the point that the governor hoped to have his writings declared treasonous. Sam Adams, using the name "Populous," also took part. By mid-

Fig. 4. Paul Revere (1734–1818), *The town of Boston in New-England and Brittish (*sic*) ships of war landing their troops*, Boston, Massachusetts, 1770. Engraving; h. 7⅝ in., w. 12 in. Boston Athenaeum (A/B64B6/Hil.1770x).

summer, popular protest erupted in acts violent and symbolic, including effigies hanged in the Liberty Tree. On July 11, the Liberty Song appeared in the pages of the *Boston Gazette*.

The conflict escalated even further in the fall. On September 30, ships arrived from Halifax with British Regiments and detachments of the Royal Artillery; disembarked at the Long Wharf, the soldiers occupied the city. Revere captured the outrage of Bostonians, who mostly still saw themselves as loyal British subjects invaded without just cause, in his subtle and sarcastic landing print (fig. 4). Merging mock humility and respect for authority, he dedicated the print to the earl of Hillsborough, whom he cites as the British minister responsible for the only well-planned expedition chastening the insolence of America. The print depicts an Indian princess, America, with her foot on the face of a grenadier, mocking authority. The legend describes the landing with

> the Ships of War, armed Schooners, Transports, &c. Came up the Harbour and Anchored round the TOWN; their Cannon loaded, a Spring on their Cables, as for a regular Siege. At noon on Saturday October the 1st the fourteenth & twenty-ninth Regiments, a detachment the 59th Regt. and Train of Artillery, with two pieces of Cannon, landed on the Long Wharf; there Formed and Marched with insolent Parade, Drums beating, Fifes playing, and Colours flying, up KING STREET. Each Soldier having received 16 rounds of Powder and Ball.[4]

138

The British troops would remain quartered in Boston until George Washington drove them out with cannon aimed from Dorchester Heights on March 17, 1776. Ever since, Boston has celebrated the occasion as Evacuation Day.

Seventeen sixty-eight ended unhappily in Boston, with no resolution having been reached between Whig and Tory. Through non-importation agreements, patriotic Bostonians had embarked on a campaign of boycotts, refusing to buy English-made goods, but it was only the beginning of the struggle. The increasing polarization would drive apart colonial Boston's social structure, in many cases separating otherwise friendly and compatible townspeople. The relationship between Revere and Copley was no exception, and these two representative pieces — the Liberty Bowl and the portrait of Revere — bespeak, both boldly and subtly, the commitments each man pursued as their world changed.

Copley and Revere were about thirty and thirty-three years of age respectively when they sat facing each other virtually knee to knee for this portrait. They were friends and artistic associates, but they inhabited distinctly separate professional worlds. Revere was a tradesman/craftsman; Copley aspired to raise himself above such classification to that of gentleman. That difference, however, could in no way anticipate the separation prompted by their increasingly opposed political allegiances. Revere made the decision to resist the mercantile and tax stranglehold of the mother country, choosing danger and treason over submission to tyranny — although his vindication as a victorious patriot was still years away. Copley found himself torn between loyalty to the Crown and sympathy with the colonies and his friends.[5] Within a year he would marry into a Tory family whose Loyalist connections would decide his own. In a few years the two men would be separated by the Atlantic Ocean, never to see each other again.

While one can read the events of the year very clearly in the Sons of Liberty Bowl, as demonstrated below, the presence of 1768 in the Copley painting requires a more thoughtful study. Previously widely admired as the image of an American patriot/craftsman at work or at a contemplative moment of thoughtful creativity, the portrait shows Revere in a frontal pose with tools laid out on a table before him. In his left hand, he holds a double-bellied or pear-shaped teapot, which rests on a sand-filled leather pad (fig. 5) that served as a fulcrum when a smith needed to manipulate an object for engraving.[6] The tools pictured are two wooden-handled, steel-shanked burins with sharp points for engraving, and a needle set in a wooden dowel used in preparation for engraving by scratching designs on the silver. Other details in the painting, however, suggest that Revere is not in the midst of working. In a contemplative pose, he rests his chin in his right hand. The sleeve of his luxurious white linen shirt billows below what seems to be a dark green, silk vest apparently embellished with gold buttons. These are not, as some scholars have surmised, working clothes.

Fig. 5. Detail of engraving tools in Copley's portrait of Revere (fig. 1).

At work Revere would have worn a soft leather apron, essential for rubbing clean the surfaces of his hammers. Nor is the reflective mahogany surface on which he rests his elbow a workbench.

There is, in fact, a decidedly artificial construct in the composition of Revere's pose, the polished appearance of the table, and the arrangement of some implements of his trade before him.[7] Copley seems to capture the political tensions of Boston in 1768 and the choice of loyalties both artists faced; he depicts his friend balanced between symbols of Tory and Whig — the teapot and the linen sleeve — and contemplating the highly charged situation. The boycott against goods imported from England — including tea and linen — shaped economic and social life in 1768. In response to needs for home industry, young women near Boston collaborated to produce 100 score of fine white linen to demonstrate independence from English products.[8] Is Revere's conspicuous shirt sleeve a symbol of Whig loyalty? In his other hand, however, he holds the teapot, symbolic of Tory taste.[9] No Whig in Boston would be caught serving tea. But Revere did take orders from both Whig and Tory, and possibly the manufacture of a teapot represented home industry to him. Nonetheless, he made far fewer teapots before the Revolution than after. The object seems suggestive more of Copley's affinities at this time than Revere's, and — intended or not — it provides a balance for the prominent linen sleeve. Copley's initials and date, however small, acknowledge the significance of the year and the portrait he is painting, but their diminutive size may also indicate his ambivalence: he is perhaps uneasy about seeming to be too familiar with a person whose views were radically whiggish.

During the same year that Copley painted Revere's portrait, Revere made his silver Liberty Bowl (fig. 6), commissioned by some of the Sons of Liberty, kept at Nathaniel Barber's insurance office in the North End, and used for their covert assemblages at the Bunch of Grapes Tavern and the Green Dragon

Fig. 6. Paul Revere (1734–1818), Sons of Liberty Bowl, Boston, Massachusetts, 1768. Silver; h. 5 ½ in., diam. (base) 5 ¹³⁄₁₆ in., diam. (lip) 11 in. Museum of Fine Arts, Boston, Gift by subscription and Francis Bartlett Fund (49.45).

Tavern, also in the North End. Engraved on the rim of the bowl were names of its joint owners, all radical Whigs. They were primarily merchants of the middling sort who felt their livelihoods threatened by the King's policies.[10] Most of these men later appeared in London's list of enemies. The names that appear on the rim of the bowl suggest that the movement was pluralistic — a genuine people's movement. There were modest property owners — small merchants, tradesmen, tavernkeepers, a mariner, a distiller, and a woodcarver — many of whom had their lives and work tied closely to wharves, docks, and the marketplace: Caleb Hopkins, Nathaniel Barber, John White, William Mackay, Daniel Malcolm, Benjamin Goodwin, John Welsh, Fortescue Vernon, Daniel Parker, John Marston, Ichabod Jones, John Homer, William Bowes, Peter Boyer, and Benjamin Cobb. Although influenced by more well-to-do Bostonians, the movement was not dominated by the few public figures, such as Sam Adams or Joseph Warren, who also belonged. Paul Revere himself was a small-time tradesman at the time. Only later did he become a major industrialist.

One man, Daniel Malcolm, can serve as an example of the typical Son of Liberty. Malcolm, a merchant whose wines were presumed to have been smuggled, earned the hatred of Lt. Gov. Thomas Hutchinson for his class and his political views. Much fuss occurred when customs officers attempted to seize

Malcolm's goods but found themselves barred from entering the warehouse without a search warrant. By the time they obtained the warrant, the wine had disappeared. Malcolm died on October 23, 1769; his tombstone, carved by John Homer, stands on Copp's Hill. The inscription immortalizes his support for the cause of Liberty: "A true Son of Liberty / A Friend of the Public / An enemy of Oppression / And one of the foremost in opposing the Revenue Acts on America." The marker observes further that he is buried in a stone vault ten feet deep — too deep for anyone, especially Tories, to disturb. The stone appears to be pockmarked with musket ball damage, perhaps caused by British troops using it for target practice.

Revere's work as a patriot has survived both in artifact — including but not limited to the Liberty Bowl — and of course in popular memory. He participated in many if not all of the groups dedicated to American liberty. By the 1770s he had associated with or joined the St. Andrews Lodge of Freemasons, the Loyal Nine of 1766, the North Caucus, the Long Room Club, and the Boston Committee of Correspondence. He took part in the Boston Tea Party and his name eventually appeared on the London Enemies list.[11] Only Joseph Warren belonged to as many political groups as Revere. In 1768, even the production of the Liberty Bowl constituted a daring act of defiance. Revere finished it within five weeks of the House's vote against rescinding the circular letter, which the governor considered an act of insubordination.[12] Revere's rapid production of the bowl was a remarkable feat, since it would have taken hundreds of hours of hammering on a polished anvil and stakes simply to form the bowl, let alone engrave it. Yet it does not appear in his daybooks or anywhere in the extensive Revere family papers. Because business records and papers could be seized, Revere may have needed to hide his association with the Sons of Liberty. His secrecy proves the extreme danger in which he knew himself to be living and his understanding that the Bowl itself, decorated with patriotic slogans, could be a "treasonous" object.

Revere's Sons of Liberty Bowl is monumental in scale for American silver of its period. Its design was probably inspired by the shape of a Delft punch bowl familiar to most colonials. This shape was, in turn, inspired by far eastern ceramics imported to England and the continent. The subtle s-shaped profile of its sides rises to a slightly flared lip. The foot or base is splayed and shaped with convex and concave moldings. The whole bowl stands 5 ½ inches high with a base diameter of 5 13/16 inches. The diameter at the lip is 11 inches. It weighs 43 ounces, 16 ½ pennyweight.[13] Years of polishing have exposed "fire scale," leaving a slightly cloudy coloration to the surface of the silver that makes the bowl look like it needs to be polished.

Although the bowl is the most celebrated example of American colonial sil-

Fig. 7. Detail of Paul Revere's Liberty Bowl (fig. 6).

ver even without the general public's understanding of its historical context, its most important aspects are its particular symbolic features, both those worked into its form by the smith and in its use. For the most part, that symbolism rides on two numbers: forty-five and ninety-two. The cartouche engraved on one side of the bowl (see fig. 6) contains in its center a large "N⁰, 45. / Wilkes & Liberty" over a torn page labeled "Generall / Warrants," referring to the arrest of Englishman John Wilkes, described below.[14] A liberty cap tops the cartouche and two flags flank it, one inscribed "Magna / Charta" and the other "Bill of / Rights." Revere fashioned the bowl from forty-five ounces of silver and to hold forty-five gills of rum punch.[15] The message on the other side (fig. 7) reads: "To the Memory of the glorious NINETY-TWO: Members / of the Hon[bl] House of Representatives of the Massachusetts-Bay, / who, undaunted by the insolent Menaces of Villains in Power, / from a Strict Regard to Conscience, and the LIBERTIES / of their Constituents, on the 30th of June 1768, / Voted NOT TO RESCIND."

Bostonians would well and quickly have understood the precise meanings of all these references. In volume 45 of his periodical the *North Briton*, John Wilkes, a radical Whig in England, denounced policies established by King George's servants the earls of Egremont, Halifax, and Grenville; unjust excise taxation; and "the late ignominious peace." In fact, Wilkes had established himself as a champion of liberty with the opening sentence of the first issue, where he declared that "the liberty of the Press is the birthright of a Briton and is justly esteemed the foremost bulwark of the liberties of this country." British authorities arrested Wilkes and conducted him to the Tower. Without warrant, officers of the Crown searched his house, broke into his furniture, and stole his private papers to obtain incriminating evidence. The courts put into motion Wilkes's conviction for treason. Wilkes nonetheless defended himself at trial and won his release after he proved that the royal henchman had searched his premises illegally.

Wilkes's story was well known among colonials, who read his letters to Bostonians in the *Boston Gazette*, and it made him a hero of the patriot cause. When Thomas Hutchinson wrote to Thomas Pownall, a much-liked former governor of the Massachusetts Bay Colony, in England in June 1768, he stated that

> a certain Insurance Office in the North End where one Daniel Malcolm is a principal underwriter have resolved to address Mr. John Wilkes thanking him for the glorious confusion he is putting the Government into at home and praying he would afford them his continence and encouragement in the like measures here. . . . The office keeper Nathaniel Barber some time ago christened one of his children John Wilkes and No. 45 was Figured on the breast. From this state of Anarchy Good Lord deliver first you and then us.[16]

Bostonians fully understood that the actions taken against Wilkes constituted a violation of his civil liberties as guaranteed by the Magna Carta and the Bill of Rights (fig. 8). The references to Wilkes on the bowl indicate that the Sons of Liberty felt their civil rights were threatened by the policy of taxation without representation.

On June 23, 1768, when the Sons and Daughters of Liberty met in Roxbury and traveled in an impressively large gathering of carriages to the governor's mansion in Boston, drinking their rum punch in a gesture of defiance, they further invoked John Wilkes with forty-five toasts. They addressed the first toasts, as was traditional, to "Our rightful sovereign GEORGE the Third. The QUEEN, the Prince of Wales, and the rest of the Royal Family."[17] For the fifth toast, they raised their cups for "A perpetual Union of Great-Britain and her Colonies, upon the immutable Principles of Justice and Equity," suggesting that they still saw themselves as Englishmen prepared to remain loyal subjects of the crown *if* their basic civil liberties were respected. The eleventh toast made clear their objections with the proviso that this union be based on immutable principles of justice and equity; it demanded "A speedy Repeal of unconstitutional Acts of Parliament, and a final Removal of illegal and oppressive Officers" – that is, General Gage, Governor Bernard, and other unpopular characters. Others toasts were raised to John Locke, Italian freedom fighter Pascal Paoli, John Dickinson (the Pennsylvania Farmer and author of the

Fig. 8. Detail of Paul Revere's Liberty Bowl (fig. 6).

Liberty Song), and of course to John Wilkes himself (fig. 9). The final toast cel-
ebrates the "Assemblies on this vast and rapidly populating Continent, who
have treated a late haughty and 'meerly ministerial' Mandate 'with all that
Contempt it so justly deserves'!" They concluded their festivities by singing the
Liberty Song, the first patriotic music published in America.[18] Toasts of this fes-
tive gathering were undoubtedly repeated at the Bunch of Grapes Tavern and
the Green Dragon Tavern in the presence of the Liberty Bowl.[19]

Certainly the more seditious of the two inscriptions on the bowl, the motto
celebrating "ninety-two" on the other side referred to the defiance much closer
to home — the vote in the House not to rescind the circular letter. Not Revere's
composition, the lines still resist completely reliable attribution. They do, however, betray a resemblance to writings made under the pseudonym "A True
Patriot" in the *Boston Gazette* on February 29, 1768. The overall style is consistent, and the emphatic capitalization of key words appears identical. Searching
at the Massachusetts Historical Society for the likely author of these seditious
writings, I was directed by Anne E. Bentley, the society's curator, to the papers
of Harbottle Dorr, a Son of Liberty and a Boston merchant who sold grind-

Fig. 9. Robert Sayer, *Mr. Serjeant Glyn, John Wilkes, and the Rev. Mr. John Horne*, London, 1768. Mezzotint; h. 16⅛ in., w. 19½ in. Private collection. Photo, courtesy Museum of Fine Arts, Boston.

stones on Union Street. Dorr saved newspapers and identified on each one who had written the anonymous articles. The person who called himself "A True Patriot" was none other than Revere's friend Dr. Joseph Warren, who later perished at the Battle of Bunker Hill.

Warren's articles so enraged Governor Bernard that he declared them slanderous and demanded that the House investigate and bring charges against the writer. Although Warren was careful not to name the target of his articles, everyone in Boston's small community could recognize the public officers he criticized. For example, one of his articles began "May it please your person, no age has perhaps furnished a more glaring instance of obstinate perseverance in the bath of malice than is now exhibited in your presence" — in a reference to Barnard. But the House divided on the subject, passing on the issue and noting, in words similar to those Wilkes used, that the liberty of the press is the great bulwark of liberty of the people.

While Bernard may have viewed Warren as an arch-enemy, the Whigs of colonial Boston probably embraced him as their John Wilkes. That Wilkes was

Fig. 10. John Singleton Copley
(1738–1815), *Dr. Joseph Warren
(1741–1775)*, ca. 1772–74. Oil on
canvas; h. 50 in., w. 39 ¾ in.
Museum of Fine Arts, Boston,
Gift of Buckminster Brown,
M.D., through Church M.
Matthews, Jr., Trustee (95.1366).

considered a hero is evident in his idealized image in an engraving that
appeared in 1768 for the *Boston Almanac* for 1769.[20] The image probably derived
from an elegantly framed print of Wilkes in Revere's possession, from which he
could have cut this metal relief plate. A Copley portrait of Dr. Warren (fig. 10)
may have had its prototype in William Hogarth's portrait of Wilkes (fig. 11). The
English engraver chose a less attractive representation of his subject, portraying
him with his lower extremities akimbo; Copley painted Warren in almost
exactly the same posture.[21] While Hogarth's take was distinctly unflattering to
Wilkes, Copley, by contrast, seems to praise rather than ridicule Warren.
Revere, a trained engraver and political satirist, may have thought of himself as
Boston's Hogarth.[22] In general, Bostonians considered themselves part of the
world stage on which each citizen played a role that often echoed or related to
another across the ocean.

Acquired in an era characterized by high patriotic fervor, the Liberty Bowl
came back to Boston in the same decade as Esther Forbes's Pulitzer Prize-win-
ning biography of Revere and soon after the making of sculptor C. E. Dallin's
heroic, larger-than-life, bronze midnight rider at North Square (1940). The
closely knit structure of Boston's families, the historical awareness, and the sym-

147

Fig. 11. William Hogarth (1697–1764), *John Wilkes (1727–1797)*, London, 1763. Engraving; h. 20¼ in., w. 15 in. Private collection. Photo, courtesy Museum of Fine Arts, Boston.

bolic significance of the Liberty Bowl perhaps insured that it would be preserved and eventually find its way to the Museum of Fine Arts, Boston. Along the way, it passed down among the descendants of the original associates whose names were inscribed on its rim.[23] In 1832 it became the property of William Mackay of New York City. It subsequently passed to his brother, Robert C. Mackay of Boston, who passed it in 1902 to Marian Lincoln Perry of Providence, Rhode Island, a descendant of one of the fifteen original associates. In 1949 Mrs. J. Marsden Perry offered the bowl to the Museum of Fine Arts. Not having funds sufficient to meet the asking price of $56,000, the Museum authorized a fundraising committee, headed by Mark Bortman, to solicit subscriptions. Donors, including schoolchildren, produced the necessary funds, and on February 15, 1949, Governor Paul A. Dever transmitted the bowl from Mark Bortman to Edward Jackson Holmes, president of the Museum of Fine Arts.[24] At that time the Museum put it on view in the upper rotunda with portraits of colonial notables, including Revere and Samuel Adams. It has remained on view ever since, migrating from place to place in the Museum according to changing exhibition needs and as opportunities developed.

The Copley portrait of Revere, which the Museum received from the silver-smith's descendents in 1930, has also moved around the Museum. Throughout the 1970s and 1980s it was displayed with the Sons of Liberty Bowl in a silver gallery that contained many examples of the patriot's work. Later it was moved into a gallery filled with Copley's paintings. Today the Museum exhibits the portrait and Liberty Bowl in this same gallery, where other Copley portraits of notables such as Dr. Warren, John Hancock, and Sam Adams gain context by the presence of the Liberty Bowl. Together, they bear witness to the era of the Enlightenment in which they were produced and resonate now with deep meaning.[25]

Notes

1. See Dirk Hoerder, *Crowd Action in Revolutionary Massachusetts, 1765–1780* (New York: Academic Press, 1977), 368–89.

2. An original copy of this "Circular Letter" signed by the Speaker of the House of Massachusetts Bay, Thomas Cushing, is in the "Massachusetts Papers" of the Massachusetts Historical Society.

3. Clarence S. Brigham, *Paul Revere's Engravings*, rev. ed. (New York: Atheneum, 1969), 43–49.

4. Brigham, *Paul Revere's Engravings*, 79–85.

5. That Copley had sympathy for the economic plight occasioned by the Stamp Act is suggested in a unique etching of 1765 which Pierre du Simitière (ca. 1736–84) ascribed to the painter. The etching, entitled *The Deplorable State of America*, is based on an English political cartoon of the same title. See Jonathan L. Fairbanks, Wendy Cooper, et al., *Paul Revere's Boston, 1735–1818* (Boston: Museum of Fine Arts, Boston, 1975), 114.

6. The pad is not a "hammering pillow" as recently described in David Hackett Fischer's excellent book *Paul Revere's Ride* (New York: Oxford University Press, 1994), 3. Revere's iron flat anvil used for hammering is owned by Colonial Williamsburg.

7. In her engaging essay "Carpenter, Tailor, Shoemaker, Artist: Copley and Portrait Painting around 1770," *Art Bulletin* 79, no. 2 (June 1997): 269–90, Susan Rather argues that Copley portrayed Revere as an artisan in order to distance himself as artist from this lower profession. And yet, she observes that, in a sense, the portrait is also reflective of Copley himself. While it is true that every painting is in some sense a self-portrait and that Copley was certainly conflicted about the role of the artist in colonial America, the documentary evidence from the Whig *Boston Gazette* for the year 1768 strongly supports another interpretation of the composition. The linen and the teapot seem expressive vehicles of political meaning.

8. The *Boston Gazette* announced on October 10, 1768, that "We hear from Roxbury that, one Day the Week before last, near 60 young Woman of the Place, met together at the Minister's House, early in the Morning, and gave Mrs. Adams the Materials for, and the Spinning of above 100 Score of Linnen yarn, such an unusual and beautiful Appearance drew a great number of Spectators from Town and Country, who all expressed the highest Satisfaction at such an example of industry."

9. In order to understand the painting and not miss one iota of its composition, staff of the MFA

photographically replicated it in detail. We used a genuine model for the teapot and asked staff member Steve Stenstrom to play Revere. Revere made only five teapots before the Revolution. Only two of those could qualify as the one used for the Copley portrait given the date and shape. One is now owned by Pennsylvania collector Richard Dietrich. The other possible candidate is in the collection of the Museum of Fine Arts, Boston. See Kathryn C. Buhler, *American Silver, 1655–1825, in the Museum of Fine Arts, Boston*, 2 vols. (Boston: Museum of Fine Arts, Boston, 1972), 2: no. 359. This teapot belonged to Rev. Jonathan Parsons of Connecticut. Mr. Dietrich's teapot may be for a member of the Bigelow or Call family.

10. Most of the names engraved around the rim of the Liberty Bowl have been identified as Sons of Liberty, many of whom were members of the North End Caucus. Economically they were from the lower ranks of merchants and craftsmen. For a full account of the economic situation of the Sons of Liberty, see Hoerder, *Crowd Action in Revolutionary Massachusetts*.

11. Fischer, *Paul Revere's Ride*, 20.

12. On August 8, the *Boston Gazette* noted that "We hear that the week before last was finished, by Order and for use of the Gentlemen belonging to the Insurance Office kept by Mr. Nathaniel Barber, at the North-End, an elegant silver bowl, weighing forty-five Ounces and holding forty-five Jills." The full description of the bowl noted its use as a part of genteel entertainment of the forty-five toasts concluding with the Liberty Song.

13. For a more complete description of the bowl, see Buhler, *American Silver*, 2: 408–9.

14. A silver salt cellar in the collection of the Yale University Art Gallery is also engraved with the symbolic number 45. It is possible that this piece was part of a complete service used at secret dinner meetings of the Sons of Liberty. Because many of the Sons of Liberty were also Freemasons, they might have styled the practices of this political group on the arcane rituals of the Masons. There were more such objects marked with a forty-five, some in ceramics, also probably used as parts of sets when the Sons of Liberty conducted their secret meetings.

15. The actual weight of the bowl today is just under forty-five ounces. A small amount of the original weight of silver (probably in coin) delivered to Paul Revere for fashioning the bowl was inadvertently lost in the process of workmanship. Subsequent years of polishing and wear account for some minute loss of weight.

16. Thomas Hutchinson to Thomas Pownall, June 1768, Hutchinson Papers, Massachusetts Historical Society.

17. *Boston Gazette*, August 22, 1768.

18. Vera Brodsky Lawrence, *Music for Patriots, Politicians, and Presidents: Harmonies and Discords of the First Hundred Years* (New York: Macmillan Publishing Co., 1975), 15. Dickinson based the music for the Liberty Song on the popular British tune "Hearts of Oak."

19. See Fairbanks, *Paul Revere's Boston*, fig. 167, illustrating John Johnston's watercolor of the Green Dragon Tavern in the collections of the American Antiquarian Society, Worcester.

20. A copy of *Edes & Gill's North American Almanack* for 1769 is owned by the Massachusetts Historical Society. This print has not previously been attributed to Revere.

21. In 1781 Boston engraver John Norman depicted John Hancock in an almost identical seated pose in an engraving in *An Impartial History of the War*, vol. 1 (Boston, 1781). See Wendy Wick Reaves, ed., *American Portrait Prints: Proceedings of the Tenth Annual American Prints Conference* (Charlottesville: University Press of Virginia for the National Portrait Gallery, 1984); and Georgia Brady Barnhill, ed., *Prints of New England* (Worcester: American Antiquarian Society, 1991).

22. In the fall of 1768, Revere had etched a curious allegorical frontispiece for Edes & Gill's *North American Almanack* for the following year entitled "The LORD GOD Omnipotent reigneth. let all the Earth rejoice!" The plate was struck in the fall of 1768 when newspapers reported that storms at sea were buffeting the British naval force en route to Boston. A detailed description of the plate appears on the title page:

> Two Female Figures. The principal, richly decorated, is seated on a Throne with an Imperial Diadem on her Head, and a Spear in her left Hand. The other Figure exhibits a Virgin with a Civic Crown, in the utmost Agonies of Distress and Horror. The Cap of Liberty falling from the Spear of one, and tottering to fall from the other. The Label of one, is Collidimur; of the other, Frangimur. Two Ships are represented to View in a Tempest in the Instant of dashing to Pieces against one another, and sinking between the Rocks of Sylla and Caribdis. In the Interim are seen two Arch Angels, flying as "on the Wings of the Wind." The Label of the one is, "Shall not the Lord of all the Earth do Right." The other is, "The Fool" only "hath said in his Heart there is no God." Above all, in a Glory, is inscribed these Words, "The Lord GOD Omnipotent reigneth, let the Earth rejoice!"

Seemingly an original composition by Revere, the piece shows his ability to clothe current events in a complex allegory of Biblical symbolic classicism. Brigham, *Paul Revere's Engravings*, 49–51.

23. Pedigree of the descent of the Liberty Bowl is engraved above and under its foot.

24. It bears the accession number 1949.45, the forty-fifth acquisition of the year.

25. Dennis A. Dooley, introduction to *The Glorious Ninety-Two* (Boston: n.p., 1949).

"The Pride Which Pervades thro every Class": The Customers of Paul Revere

JEANNINE FALINO

"YOU WOULD BE SURPRIZD to see the Equipage, the Furniture and expensive Living of too many, the Pride and Vanity of Dress which pervades thro every Class, confounding every Distinction between the Poor and the Rich," wrote Samuel Adams in 1785 to his cousin John.[1] The displays of material wealth that Adams lamented were caused in part by rapid changes in population, occupations, and fortunes during the revolutionary period. However inappropriate this "expensive living" may have seemed to Adams, a trend toward broad ownership of genteel goods had been underway long before the colonial struggle for independence.

The Edinburgh-trained physician Alexander Hamilton, for instance, wrote of his encounter one evening in 1744 with a man named Morrison, whom he described in appearance as "a very rough spun, forward, clownish blade, much addicted to swearing, and yet at the same time desirous to pass for a gentleman." Hamilton sensed Morrison's keen awareness of their social differences as they sat together in a Delaware tavern, and his indignation when served a coarse meal of veal scraps in the physician's presence. According to Hamilton's recollection, Morrison declared that "tho he seemed to be but a plain, homely fellow, yet he would have us know that he was able to afford better than many that went finer: he had good linnen in his bags, a pair of silver buckles, silver clasps, and gold sleeve buttons, two Holland shirts, and some neat night caps; and that his little woman att home drank tea twice a day; and he himself lived very well and expected to live better."[2]

Samuel Adams's observations and Mr. Morrison's gold buttons reflect an improved standard of living in eighteenth-century America as well as the desires of those who aspired to this better life. Scholars of consumption patterns in pre-industrial England and America have shown how a nascent, wage-based economy offered appealing alternatives to the subsistence and barter systems that had been in use since the Middle Ages. In the new, cash-based paradigm, people from all walks of life used their income to purchase goods. Even in the colonies, where currency problems were rife until the formation of the new republic, the power of the purse had an enormous impact upon the market-place, where manufactured products at all price levels soon began to enter everyday life.[3]

In eighteenth-century Boston, where vessels from abroad arrived with daily cargoes of valuable ceramics, hardware, and textiles, among countless other manufactured goods, the material life of the young province began to approach that of England. In this new Anglo-American outpost, it was not long before these items ceased to be luxury products. Instead, they became everyday objects of "comfort, convenience, and indicators of gentility," present at nearly every economic level of society.[4] Taken together, these products define the consumer revolution in its infancy.

Although silver ranked near the apex of luxury items, probate records indicate that about 20 percent of New England households owned some silver by the second quarter of the eighteenth century.[5] A close examination of who bought what from the silversmiths in the second half of the century can provide a particularly vivid picture of class and consumption in the Revolutionary era. The daybooks of Paul Revere II (1734–1818), the primary resource of this essay, will create that picture. Taken together with the data of Revere's extant silver and other published research, they demonstrate that Revere stood at an intersection of Boston's social and economic life and they reconfirm his status as Boston's most prolific and entrepreneurial craftsman.[6] At the same time, the daybooks provide a remarkable portrait of Revere himself, both as a businessman and as a local citizen (fig. 1).

The daybooks, also called wastebooks or ledgers, are two volumes that Revere maintained between 1763 and 1797 to track current orders for silver.[7] Revere recorded 588 customers in the two books, noting the charges for services that ranged from fashioning complete tea sets to making shoe buckles, from engraving Masonic certificates and bookplates to cleaning teeth, making harnesses, and performing minor repairs. As extensive as the information in the daybooks is, the volumes do not constitute a complete source for tracing all of Revere's silver; numerous pieces that he made during this period, including the Sons of Liberty Bowl, went unrecorded. To provide balance to the ledger records, the names of additional owners, gleaned from surviving objects, have been added for a total of 757 known patrons whose purchases ranged in date from 1754 to 1806.[8]

The consumption patterns of the era, described above, coincided with Revere's talents and skills as an entrepreneur. Although the entire body of Revere's silver production and the full complement of his patrons may never be fully known, the list of items and buyers noted in the daybooks can help determine how Revere's life intersected with market forces. Contrary to what one

153

Fig. 1. Paul Revere's daybook, vol. 1, January 8, 1763. Revere Papers, Massachusetts Historical Society.

might expect, Revere's business did not entirely depend on high-end purchases from wealthy clientele, although he was one of the most successful colonial silversmiths and enjoyed their patronage. Rather, smaller purchases made up the large quantity of Revere's business. As will be demonstrated, he outstripped his peers by matching silver production to meet the needs of colonial Bostonians hailing from various economic strata. At the same time, as an energetic member of many social and political groups, Revere netted roughly 20 percent of each group as clients.

A brief review of Revere's career in contrast with those of his peers demonstrates that despite a slow start after his father's death in 1754, the young patriot rapidly joined the ranks of Boston's most productive silversmiths. Zachariah Brigden (1734–1787), Benjamin Burt (1729–1805), John Coburn (1724–1803), Daniel Henchman (1730–1775), and Samuel Minott (1732–1803) were Revere's approximate equals in age and activity according to this definition. During the pre-war period, Revere made at least 175 objects, a respectable second place to the 185 made by Benjamin Burt (1729–1805), who was five years his senior and another

TABLE I. Paul Revere's Silver Production, 1761–75 vs. 1779–97.

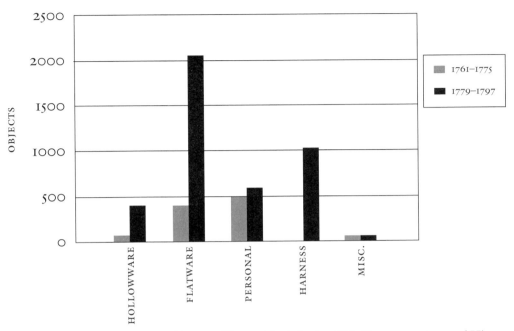

Source: Deborah Federhen, "Paul Revere, Silversmith: A Study of His Shop Operations and His Objects" (M.A. thesis, University of Delaware, 1988), table E.

silversmith's son. Revere and Burt were far ahead of Brigden, Coburn, and Henchman, whose numbers were 56, 90, and 47, respectively. Only Samuel Minott came close to approaching the volume of Burt and Revere with 105 objects.[9]

His peers, fine silversmiths all, lost their momentum primarily to age, politics, and tradition. Samuel Minott sided with the English during the war and never regained his former level of activity; Daniel Henchman and Zachariah Brigden died early. Benjamin Burt held the most promise besides Revere for a long and busy career, but a comparison between Burt and Revere offers some clues to the latter's success.[10] During the pre-Revolutionary period, Burt's clear superiority in numbers is easily appreciated by examining the most traditional forms favored at the time. He made forty canns to Revere's ten, thirty-two porringers to Revere's twenty-seven, twenty-six tankards to Revere's sixteen, and thirteen teapots to Revere's four. As years passed and the call for out-moded works declined, the situation reversed in Revere's favor. After the war, Revere proved himself capable of turning out quantities of sugar bowls, creamers, and teapots to meet the new fashion for tea equipage. Burt, by comparison, made few of these items and eventually fell far behind, never again to surpass Revere.

Revere's level of productivity was impressive; at least as remarkable was his ability to increase his business despite the disruptions of war and his own diverse activities. His ability to do so depended, again, on his entrepreneurial instinct, which led him both to maintain and exploit his many connections from many different social contexts and apparently to discern and respond to shifts in style and economy. Deborah Federhen, whose findings regarding Revere's sales activities are more complete than those gleaned from the day-books, demonstrates that Revere turned out a greater quantity of low-end goods than he did high-end. According to her research, Revere generated far more flatware, personal articles such as shoe or knee buckles, and a greater quantity of harness fittings than previously thought.

Altogether, Federhen established that between 1763 and 1797, Revere's shop sold 565 hollowware items, a fraction of his total output of 4,792 objects. Of these, 2,479 pieces were flatware, 1,074 were personal items such as shoe and knee buckles, 1,044 were harness fittings, and 195 were miscellaneous items.[11] While requests for hollowware rose somewhat after the war, flatware and harness trappings emerged as the major elements of Revere's postwar production. The number of personal accessories, such as buttons, buckles, and rings, also grew in the daybooks from a pre-war figure of 449 to 623 items purchased between 1783 and 1797; they stand for the countless individuals like the "rough spun" Mr. Morrison, who believed that these modest items heralded a better standard of living for himself and his family (table 1).[12]

As these figures demonstrate, Revere's true success lay in selling a high volume of low-end goods over a period of thirty years. If the daybooks are any indication, New England's wealthy tended to buy ambitious forms like candle-sticks and snuffer trays from abroad, and used domestic smiths such as Revere for mending and providing more common vessels and spoons. Middling patrons typically purchased small personal items, spoons, and some vessels directly from their local silversmiths. The cultivation of this clientele, which first centered on Revere's family, neighbors, and congregation and gradually widened to include a social and political network, yielded an income that may have enabled him to attempt riskier ventures later in his career.

Among Revere's buyers, as among colonial silver buyers in general, the purchase of common items such as spoons far outstripped hollowware purchases; in Revere's orders, the ratio figured at nearly five to one and constituted the bulk of silver generated by his workshop. A relatively basic household necessity, spoons of any material appeared in colonial homes across the class spectrum. While eighteenth-century Americans first used wooden, horn, and pewter spoons for everyday use, they acquired silver as time and funds permitted. Small amounts of flatware and personal accoutrements made of precious met-als first appeared in ordinary households about 1700. By the close of the century, a silver cup, a pair of spoons, or a watch could be found in all but the poorest households. In the postwar era, many modest Boston households owned at least one or two silver spoons, while those with greater incomes often owned a dozen or more. Most silversmiths at work in rural outposts produced modest quantities of spoons and little else.[13]

In contrast to the prevalence of spoons in Revere's business, hollowware constituted only 11 percent of his total output during the pre-war years and less than 9 percent in the years thereafter. Revere maintained this modest percentage by shifting hollowware production in the postwar years to sugar bowls, creamers, sugar tongs, and spoons — all newly fashionable forms of tea equipage. A review of the clientele for these more expensive items will turn up few government appointees or members of the mercantile elite, as these were the leading citizens who preferred imported goods. Revere's customers for these luxury items were, instead, prosperous merchants and tradesmen of the region. Their purchases, often made to commemorate marriage and birth, took place regardless of external events, as borne out by the seventy-five pieces of hollowware they acquired from Revere during the Revolutionary War.[14] These customers probably would have bought even more silver from Revere if political and military activities had not kept him from his bench.

With the increased business that came into his shop after the war, Revere achieved near dominance of silver teapot production.[15] He produced thirty-eight teapots during the same period that Burt and Brigden, for example, managed only five.[16] Although colonial resistance to English taxes had restricted the drinking of tea beginning in the 1770s, with the new republic this beverage quickly returned to its former popularity. Given the variety of materials then available, the popularity of silver teapots in the postwar era is all the more remarkable. Customers could choose from an ever-growing variety of materials that ranged from inexpensive ceramics, pewter, and fused or "Sheffield" plate to silver vessels made by local Boston silversmiths.

Revere probably owed his success to a variety of factors. As a mature silversmith by 1780, Revere certainly benefited by return business from old customers and new ones acquainted with him from social or political encounters. He may also have enjoyed greater visibility among the silver-purchasing public due to his revolutionary activities, though no evidence now available can prove or disprove that thesis. His high production of fluted teapots, fashioned with rolled sheet silver, demonstrates his command of a stylish and economical method that may have proved attractive to his customers.[17] Finally, Paul Revere III (1760–1813) may have revitalized his father's shop at a time when the patriot was attending to other business endeavors.

Other shifts in consumer trends also show markedly in Revere's later career.

157

Fig. 2. Paul Revere (1734–1818), ladle and tea and coffee service, Boston, Massachusetts, 1793. Silver; h. (coffee urn) 13⅝ in. Museum of Fine Arts, Boston, Arthur Mason Knapp Fund (20.1634); Gift of Henry Davis Sleeper in memory of his mother, Maria Westcote Sleeper, by exchange (60.1419–20); Pauline Revere Thayer Collection, by exchange (60.1421–22).

He took advantage of a growing desire to purchase silver in larger groups: whereas pre-war buyers usually purchased silver as single pieces, larger tea services purchased *en suite* came into vogue after the war. The broker John Templeman and his wife, Mehitable (1792), Burrell and Anne (Zeagers) Carnes (1793) (fig. 2), and merchant William Shattuck (1795) each ordered beverage services of varying sizes from Revere.[18] Other customers purchased spoons in sets of six and twelve, adding significantly to the spoon volume mentioned above. Revere also demonstrated his responsiveness to consumer trends in his mastery of the water pitcher, another form that he produced in significant numbers near the end of his silversmithing career.[19] At the end of the eighteenth century, so-called Liverpool ceramic pitchers were shipped from England in quantities to meet consumer demand in the new republic. Revere adapted the barrel-shaped form to silver beginning about 1800, thus creating a domestic source of competition for the import (fig. 3). Ebenezer Moulton of New-buryport, who hailed from the next generation of silversmiths, also took advan-

Fig. 3. Paul Revere (1734–1818), pitcher, Boston, Massachusetts, ca.1800. Silver; h. 6 ⅞ in. Museum of Fine Arts, Boston, gift of William Westfall (1991.1093).

tage of this opportunity; however, John Coburn, Benjamin Burt, and Samuel Minott, all of whom lived into the first years of the nineteenth century, failed to make this new and desirable item available to their customers.[20]

Income, Status, and Occupation

Slightly more than half of Revere's known patrons, or 361 individuals, have been identified according to their occupation and grouped according to their professional or artisanal status. To best reflect the social organization of Revere's time, this essay considers each of these groups according to the processional order used in honor of President Washington's arrival in Boston on October 19, 1789.[21] The Washington Procession gave priority to a largely educated group composed of town officials, clergymen, physicians, lawyers, merchants, traders, and masters of vessels; they were followed by the city's artisans, ordered alphabetically by craft. Of the latter group, nearly fifty different trades were represented, ranging from bakers, blacksmiths, and blockmakers to saddlers, shipbuilders, and shoemakers. In deference to his skill and accomplishments, the wealthiest artisan in each craft led that trade in the procession.

Although status and wealth do not necessarily go hand in hand, and some craftsmen ran lucrative shops, the hierarchy established for the procession does

159

give some idea of social ranking according to occupation. It matches up relatively well with Allan Kulikoff's analysis of wealth in colonial Boston, which reveals a wide disparity of income within the population. At the high end of Kulikoff's scale were merchants, with mean assessments of £1,707; lawyers, with £846; and apothecaries, with £657. Artisans had a mean assessment of wealth in 1790 that ranged from a high of £347 for a chandler to £45 for a caulker. Within that range, one finds goldsmiths assessed at £166, printers at £247, hatters at £233, and cabinetmakers at £131.[22]

The 361 individuals who transacted silver-related business in Revere's shop can be divided into a slightly unequal balance of artisan (53 per cent) and educated merchant and professional patrons (46 per cent). The tradesmen appear in proportion to their general numbers — about half of Boston's population in 1790. They were the primary consumers of the innumerable spoons and buckles that Revere sold. They also purchased many ritual goods for Masonic lodges, the odd piece of hollowware, and requested the occasional repair. Merchants and professionals figured in Revere's customer profile at almost double their percentage of the town's population. While they were an important source of orders for hollowware for Revere, they used the silversmith almost as frequently for repairs.[23]

Two men, Andrew Oliver (1731–1799) and Thomas Dennie (1756–1842), exemplify the upper echelon of Revere's patrons. A native of Salem, Massachusetts, and the son of the lieutenant governor, Andrew Oliver graduated from Harvard College in 1749. He later served as a judge to the court of common pleas and was one of the founders of the American Philosophical Society. He was also the only Loyalist in his family to remain in Massachusetts for the duration of the Revolutionary War. In 1764, his purchase from Revere of an exotic "sugar dish out of an Ostrich egg" was unheard of in the colonies. But he never repeated such a memorable request. In later years, Oliver brought porringers, teapots, and tankards to Revere for repair, perhaps choosing, like other members of this class, to purchase his silver from abroad.[24] On a different economic scale from Oliver but distinctly well-to-do was Boston wine merchant Thomas Dennie, who sat for a Gilbert Stuart portrait in 1818.[25] In 1783, Dennie ordered a pair of wine canns from Revere; nine years later he requested twelve engraved teaspoons and eight engraved tablespoons. His purchases are fairly typical for his class in that they were made on an infrequent basis and came in sets.

Shipping merchant Joseph Barrell (1740–1804), whose portrait was painted by John Singleton Copley in 1768, also shows up in Revere's daybooks. According to the inventory of his estate, Barrell owned an impressive collection of mostly imported silver including candlesticks, sconces, caster stands, and wait-

Fig. 4. Design attributed to Joseph Barrell (1740–1804), dies attributed to Joseph Callendar (1751–1821), *Columbia-Washington medal*, Boston, Massachusetts, 1787. Copper; diam. 1⅝ in. Massachusetts Historical Society, Gift of Joseph Barrell, on behalf of the merchants involved in the venture [Samuel Brown, Charles Bulfinch, John Derby, Crowell Hatch, and John Marsden Pintard], 1791.

ers that were of fused plate and wrought silver. Nonetheless, aside from numerous repairs, the daybooks do not record any silver made for Barrell by Revere except for a silver letter "B" fashioned in 1796 for the back of his "chaise." Nor does the evidence suggest that any other colonial silversmith made silver for the merchant.[26]

One unusual, albeit minor, request did come to Revere from Barrell. As one of the investors in the ship *Columbia Rediviva* and the sloop *Lady Washington*, the vessels that initiated the profitable Boston-Northwest Coast-Canton trade in 1787, Barrell employed Joseph Callendar, Revere's former apprentice, to cut the dies for a coin to commemorate "the first American Adventure on the Pacific Ocean." When difficulties arose, Barrell advised one of the recipients to "let a Silver smith file and polish the edges of your copper Medal and have it properly cleaned" (fig. 4).[27] Barrell apparently followed his own advice, for Revere's daybook records that the merchant paid five shillings for repairing the edges of ten copper medals and fifteen shillings for making six silver blanks.

In contrast to a merchant of Barrell's stature, shopkeepers of modest means constitute at least one quarter of the 120 merchants who patronized Revere, although the jobs they brought him were invariably of a more modest nature. Joshua Blanchard, who ran a wine and grocery store, bought a pair of double chapes; John Simkins, who sold upholstery and general goods, brought a pair of shoe buckles for mending. Revere charged shopkeeper Samuel Hewes in 1771 for a copper plate and two hundred prints advertising "sper'ceti Cans" (spermaceti candles) for sale. A year later, Revere "set a stone pockett," probably shorthand in the daybook for pocket buttons, set with glass, agate, or quartz, also known as "paste." No other purchases show up for these men, indicating that their income allowed for only basic repairs and business-related purchases. Nonetheless, the numbers of such small shopkeepers grew as the century progressed, making even their minor orders a significant portion of Revere's business.[28]

Fellow tradesmen, again ranging in means from relatively well-to-do to middling, constituted a similarly vital part of Revere's business. Some of these patrons knew Revere largely through professional associations, especially the Massachusetts Charitable Mechanics Association (discussed below), but some must have known the silversmith from his general reputation. Among his patrons in this sector Revere included many who were men of some wealth and well regarded by the general public. For instance, the hatter Nathaniel Balch ran a popular establishment that was frequented by many, including Governor John Hancock. Balch, whose property was assessed at £925 in 1790, led the hatters in the Washington Procession. Despite his prosperity, Balch ordered only six silver hooks and eyes and four pairs of stone sleeve buttons, as described above, from Revere.[29] Abraham Adams, a prosperous Newbury Street leather dresser and breeches maker, ordered hat bills — probably printed labels to be set into the brim — and a silver teakettle stand, a rare form in colonial silver and one which presumes ownership of a teakettle.[30] The Boston wigmaker and barber Daniel Crosby purchased a pair of stone sleeve buttons and a neck buckle.[31] Revere also did many jobs for tradesmen of lesser wealth, such as pewterer Thomas Badger of Prince Street (six silver teaspoons)[32] and sailmaker Joseph Barrett, for whom he made shoe buckles and mending sundry items, including two gold buttons.[33]

The elite group of artisans who were the core members of the Massachusetts Charitable Mechanics Association (MCMA) constituted a leading segment of the middling class, although they did not command incomes equal to those of lawyers and merchants. When these successful tradesmen and entrepreneurs formed the Association in 1795 for the support of tradesmen's activities, they elected Revere, perhaps the most notable and respected artisan in town, as the Association's first president. Membership was restricted from its earliest days to master craftsmen or shop proprietors, many of whom were also Freemasons; journeymen and apprentices were excluded. High for its day, the one-time sign-up fee of one dollar and quarterly dues of twenty-five cents selected out many with slender incomes. As a result, only about 11 percent, or 146 of the 1,259 master craftsmen known from the 1790 tax list, became MCMA members. More than 80 percent of this group were found to possess over $500 in taxable property, more than twice as much as non-members. Revere, with his holdings by this date diversified among a silversmith's shop, a hardware store, and a foundry, exemplified the MCMA artisan.[34]

As president of the association, Revere naturally counted fellow MCMA officers among his customers. Among them was the bricklayer Jonathan Hunnewell, who became the association's second president in 1800. One year after the MCMA's formation, Hunnewell ordered a silver service consisting of twelve teaspoons, one pair of sugar tongs, a teapot and stand, sugar basket, and four salt "shovels," the hollowware executed in the newly fashionable fluted neoclassical style.[35] The baker and hardware merchant Edward Tuckerman, who served as vice president of the MCMA under Revere, developed a profitable business in the North End and amassed considerable wealth. The family's rise in class status was assured in 1797 when his daughter Elizabeth married into the prosperous Worcester merchant family of Stephen Salisbury I. Revere made a tankard, a teapot, and a coffeepot for Tuckerman in the decade before the MCMA was founded. Years later, Tuckerman ordered a fluted sugar basket that was not recorded in Revere's daybook, probably for his son Edward's marriage in 1798 to Hannah Parkman.[36]

In addition to the silver that Revere made for MCMA officials Hunnewell and Tuckerman, he produced items for members in the rank and file. These smaller tradesmen used the silversmith for their business needs, sometimes adding a small personal or household purchase. For instance, hatter Samuel Barry purchased four spoons with engraved cyphers along with 310 "hatt bills," while ivory turner and musical instrument maker William Callender bought an engraved advertisement and a silver stock buckle. The painter Christopher Gore used Revere for a variety of needs, from "mending sundry" to making a nineteen-ounce silver "crane," "plating three Iron Electrical points," and fashioning a silver nutmeg grater.[37] Others simply ordered goods for themselves. Cooper Thomas Emmons ordered a pair of "stone buttons" and arranged for Revere to mend other buttons and a pair of silver knee buckles. Blacksmith Samuel Dow ordered numerous shoe buckles, small and large, silver and plated, along with a child's shoe clasp and spoon.[38]

The volume of general business from MCMA and other tradesmen was crit-ical to the success of Revere's workshop, even more so than the hollowware purchases of the wealthier tradesmen. Collectively speaking, the smaller items were an incremental and essential source of income on which Revere depended for his livelihood.

The Ties That Bind: Revere's Family, Friends, Neighbors, and Church

When young Paul Revere first set out to establish himself in his trade he did not yet have the reputation or professional ties to bring in a broad base of cus-tomers; his primary market came then from among the close circles of his fam-ily and friends. After the death in 1754 of his father, Revere garnered some orders from those who had previously patronized the elder Revere. The young man then looked to those constituencies closest to home: family and friends liv-ing nearby in the North End, the congregation of his church, and later mem-bers of the Masonic brotherhood to which he belonged and acquaintances from political alliances. Like pebbles tossed into a lake, these groups formed circles that rippled, fanned outward, and overlapped in ever-widening patterns.

A small group of customers of Paul Revere, Sr., provided the young Revere with some income beginning in the decade after his father's early death in 1754. For Thomas James Grouchy and Mary Dumaresq, for whom Revere , Sr., had made a chafing dish about the time of their 1741 wedding, Revere, Jr., made a sugar dish in 1756. Tristram Dalton purchased a pair of porringers from the elder silversmith around 1750 and a decade later returned to the son for an addi-tional pair, plus gravy spoons and butter ladles. The Salem apothecary Phillip Godfrey Kast bought a porringer from Revere, Sr., around 1750, and shortly thereafter became a devoted patron of Revere, Jr., with numerous purchases of shoe buckles, porringers, creampots, gold rings, spoons, and spatulae, in a cus-tomer relationship that lasted from 1755 until the 1780s.[39]

Shortly before his death, Paul Revere, Sr., made a creampot for his sister-in-law Mary Hichborn, the youngest sibling in the family of his wife, Deborah. Like his father, the young Revere also made silver for his extended family and received a fair amount of business from the Hichborns. Revere was close to his uncle, the boatbuilder Thomas Hichborn, Sr., whose sons Thomas, Jr., and Nathaniel followed in the same trade. Thomas, Sr., in particular purchased many small items, such as a pair of salts and six teaspoons, and brought in many items for mending, including brass snuffers and a pair of earrings. Other Hichborn relatives included William, a hatter, who purchased hundreds of hat bills from Revere, and Robert, a sailmaker, who bought knee buckles. All used Revere for modest purchases in the early 1760s, when the young silversmith was still starting out. In later years, as the family prospered, some ordered more

TABLE 2. Paul Revere's Customers: Church, Masonic, and Political Membership Patterns.

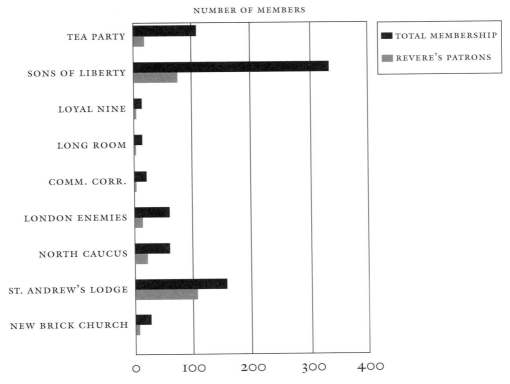

NUMBER OF MEMBERS

Sources: Ledger, New Brick Church, Massachusetts Historical Society (church); Edith J. Steblecki, *Paul Revere and Freemasonry* (Boston: Paul Revere Memorial Association, 1985), appendices 1 and 5; Henry J. Parker Index, Massachusetts Masonic Lodge (Masonic); David Hackett Fischer, *Paul Revere's Ride* (New York: Oxford University Press, 1994), appendix D; Palfrey manuscripts, Massachusetts Historical Society (political).

expensive items. Thomas Revere, Jr., purchased a cylindrical teapot in 1782. Benjamin, the youngest and only son to pursue higher education, became a lawyer and patronized his cousin beginning in the 1780s with orders for teaspoons, hardware, and a quantity of mending, thus following the usual pattern of wealthier men who purchased their silver primarily from abroad.[40]

For much of his life, Revere attended New Brick Church on Middle Street (now Hanover Street) in the North End, just a few steps away from his childhood home at the corner of Love Lane (now Tileston Street) and Middle Street. From 1787 to 1803, he belonged to the senior church committee, a measure of his prominence by that date among the congregation. Although Revere did not make silver for the church, he did find patrons among the forty-eight members who served on the New Brick Church's committee from 1755 to 1803. Fourteen of them, or 29 percent, employed Revere's services.[41] Although the

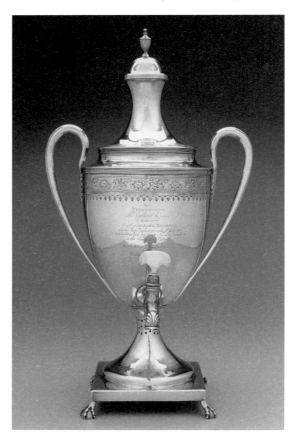

Fig. 5. Paul Revere (1734–1818), urn, Boston, Massachusetts, 1800. Silver with ivory spigot handle; h. 19 in. Massachusetts Historical Society, Gift of Helen Ford Bradford and Sarah Bradford Ross, 1933, on loan to the Museum of Fine Arts, Boston. Photo, courtesy Museum of Fine Arts, Boston.

majority of this patronage occurred during the 1790s, after his appointment to the committee, some transactions took place earlier, while Revere was an ordinary communicant of no particular rank (table 2).

Of all the orders filled by Revere for New Brick Church patrons, the most notable came from "merchant prince" Samuel Parkman, who served on the senior committee with Revere. In 1800 Parkman commissioned a presentation urn for Gamaliel Bradford, captain of the vessel *Industry* and victor in a battle with French privateers near the Straits of Gibraltar (fig. 5). Aside from the urn, Parkman purchased very little from Revere beyond ladles, two dozen spoons, a larding pin, and a pair of spectacles. He used the silversmith extensively, however, for mending his mostly imported goods, which included plated candlesticks, a tea urn (twice), a cruet (twice), and a fan, among other sundry items.[42]

Among the tradesmen at New Brick Church, the hatter William Williams ordered more than 8,500 hat bills from Revere between 1792 and 1797. Revere fashioned a teapot and knee and shoe buckles for blockmaker Thomas Lewis. For the blacksmith Enoch James, who was an active member of the church committee from 1792 to 1802, he made silver buttons, several pairs of plated knee and shoe buckles, and six teaspoons between 1789 and 1793, and did repair work including "boil[ing] and burnish[ing]" a cann in James' possession. Dr. Isaac Rand, a British sympathiser during the war and a member of the committee in 1802 and 1803, ordered a number of small items for daily use from Revere after the Revolution.[43]

Neighbors in the North End who had business dealings with Revere included such childhood friends as Josiah Flagg, Jr., who had rung bells with him at Christ Church. Flagg, a jeweller and musician, published music with engravings by Revere.[44] The hatmaker Ezra Collins (also Collings), who was a Clark's Wharf neighbor, ordered about four hundred hat bills and an engraved dog collar. This kind of patronage went both ways. Revere employed the services of the local instrument maker, ivory turner, and dentist Isaac Greenwood, who also lived on Clark's Wharf. Revere went to Greenwood for turtle shell buttons and for handles and knobs for teapots; Greenwood also turned some of Revere's vessels on the lathe, presumably to true them to proper form. In return for the favor of his business, Greenwood engaged Revere to engrave cane heads and a trade card.[45]

Some of these North End men, such as the ironware merchant Joseph Webb, who ordered trade cards from Revere, were also active Freemasons and patriots. Webb was Master of St. Andrew's Masonic Lodge and a leader, along with Revere and Joseph Warren, in the colonial resistance. Friends Josiah Flagg, shipwright Gibbens Sharp, and innholder Joshua Brackett took part in Revolutionary activities.[46] These kinds of overlapping social and political affiliations, ultimately much broader than the narrow world of the North End, gave Revere the opportunity to participate in some of the most exciting events of his time, even as he enlarged his clientele.

Political Affiliation: Freemasons, Patriots, and Loyalists

Revere's long affiliation with the fraternal organization known as Freemasons, generally known as Masons, lasted for almost fifty years, beginning in 1760 with his acceptance at age twenty-five into St. Andrew's Lodge in the North End.[47] The organization that Revere joined — a popular, respectable club that sponsored benevolent activities and general cameraderie — had developed from a secret, mystical, and ritualistic organization begun by fourteenth-century stonemasons. By Revere's day, Masonic lodges attracted men from all walks of life and in the colonies included such celebrated members as George Washington and Benjamin Franklin.

His particular lodge would have put Revere right at the center of the many communities that converged at St. Andrew's. Its North End address intensified the connections he already had with family and neighbors there. Many of the lodge's artisanal and seafaring members hailed from the North End, as did his cousins Nathaniel and Robert Hichborn. Meetings took place on Union Street at the Green Dragon Tavern, which the lodge purchased in 1764.[48] As Revere became more involved as a Masonic leader over the years – in 1795 he was appointed Grand Master of the Grand Lodge of Massachusetts – his visibility increased on Union Street and farther abroad.[49]

As a society intended for social enlightenment, Masonic lodges during the eighteenth century included men from a wide spectrum of society, from tradesmen to college-educated professionals. Although the total numbers of fraternal membership are imperfectly known, 118 of 186 men, or 64 percent of the masons in St. Andrew's Lodge alone, were his customers. Revere counted Masons among a third of his entire clientele, who were spread among at least ten different lodges. Many of these men did purchase Masonic ritual items from Revere on behalf of their lodges. Jewels such as the crossed keys and crossed pens (worn to identify officers in the society), Masonic certificates, and silver punch ladles, the latter for refreshments, were typical orders. The greater percentage of Revere's Masonic clientele, however, contracted for personal goods that ranged from tea sets and spoons to simple mending. Most Masons who patronized Revere did so for their domestic needs, ordering hollowware and flatware, shoe buckles, buttons, and practical goods such as carriage harnesses. Their numeric strength illustrates the powerful network of patronage that existed within this philanthropic brotherhood.[50]

Many of the members of St. Andrew's Lodge who sought out Revere for their silver needs were fellow tradesmen, as well as fellow Masons and regulars at the Green Dragon Tavern. The purchases of these tradesmen were fairly standard for their class: in 1766 bookbinder and stationer William McAlpine, who was later banished to Halifax, called upon Revere for a silver snuffbox; chocolate- and mustard-grinder Edward Rumney paid for a silver creampot in 1787, the same year that plumber and glazier Norton Brailsford purchased six large spoons; and cabinetmaker Simon Hall from Battery March Street engaged Revere to mend shoe buckles, a pendulum, and one gold button.[51]

Two professional men, Nathaniel Tracy, Esq., and Dr. John Warren, typified those fellow Masons who procured silver for their lodges along with first-rate goods for themselves. In 1782, Revere produced a full set of silver Masonic jewels for Tracy's Newburyport lodge and, as part of the same order, fashioned six gilded goblets for Tracy's home. The monogram "NMT" engraved on the goblets signifies Tracy and his wife, Mary Lee, daughter of the Whig merchant and shipowner Jeremiah Lee.[52] Warren, who was the Surgeon General of the Continental Army, made excellent use of Revere's skills by ordering a wide

These may certify, that
_____ has diligently
attended an entire course of my
Anatomical Lectures & Demonstrations; to-
-gether with Physiological & Surgical obser-
-vations, at the dissecting Theatre in the
American Hospital, Boston: whereby
he has had an opportunity of acquiring
an accurate knowledge in the structure
of the human body. John Warren

BOSTON

Fig. 6. Paul Revere (1734–1818), certificate of attendance at anatomical lecture, American Hospital, Boston, Massachusetts, ca. 1780. Massachusetts Historical Society, Warren Papers.

range of specialized goods for his personal, professional, and social needs. John Warren's brother Joseph, also a doctor and a Revolutionary leader, worked closely with Revere before he died in the Battle of Bunker Hill. John Warren's business relationship with Revere appears to have begun in 1783 with his purchase of a "collar for a Mason's jewel" and the mending of a tankard and a pair of canns. For his work, Warren ordered certificates for graduates of his anatomy course (fig. 6). For his home, Warren purchased a "sugar dish," a teapot, and a coffeepot.[53]

Moses Michael Hays, one of Boston's few Jewish citizens, was a prominent Mason and one of Revere's more unlikely customers. For Hays's business, Revere had to compete with colonial Jewish silversmith Myer Myers, whose relationship with Hays was familial, Masonic, and religious. Before moving to Massachusetts Hays had lived in New York City, where he had served as Master at King David's Masonic Lodge, also the lodge of silversmith and senior warden Myers. In 1766 Hays married the craftsman's sister Rachel, and the newlyweds moved first to Newport, where there was a small Jewish community, and later to Boston, where Hays operated a brokerage and insurance office. Hays

Fig. 7. Paul Revere (1734–1818), pair of sauceboats, Boston, Massachusetts, ca. 1770–85. Silver; h. (each) 5 7⁄16 in., w. 8 1⁄16 in., d. 4 3⁄8 in. Wunsch Americana Foundation, on loan to the Museum of Fine Arts, Boston. Photo, courtesy Museum of Fine Arts, Boston.

became Grand Master of the Massachusetts Grand Lodge in 1788, and again in 1791, with Revere as his Deputy Grand Master.[54]

Although Myers's shop had not recovered from the Revolution and he lived at a distance from the Hayses, it is still remarkable that the couple patronized Revere instead of a close family member. It may have been their joint involvement in Boston Freemasonry that tipped the scales in Revere's favor, bringing him Hays's quite significant business. Between 1783 and 1792 Hays ordered a "medal," probably Masonic, along with several teapots with stands, creampots, a variety of spoons and ladles, a sugar basket, gold knee buckles, a sword hilt, four goblets, and a pair of sauceboats (fig. 7).[55] David Barquist has observed that the small body of Judaica made in the colonies is based upon East European and Near Eastern style sources, while the secular forms that were purchased by colonial Jews are indistinguishable from the vast number of objects owned by gentiles of the same period.[56] In choosing to buy silver from Revere, Hays acquired Boston-made objects that would have complemented his other furnishings. At the same time, these purchases cemented a valuable social and business contact in Hays's adopted city.

While other members of St. Andrew's clearly dominate Revere's patrons within this particular circle, the web of relationships created by the Masonic order brought customers throughout New England to Revere, and prompted commissions from lodges as far away as Surinam.[57] As mentioned above, one-

170

third of Revere's total clientele belonged to one or another Masonic lodge, a percentage higher than any other in the circles of his clientele.

Although the Freemasons were not specifically political, Revere's connections from that organization inevitably overlapped with the connections he developed as his political activities increased. Unlike most silversmiths of his day, Revere fully participated in the partisan activities that swirled around Boston before and during the Revolution.[58] While serving his primary goal of aiding the patriot cause, political contacts undoubtedly brought additional revenue to his workshop. The patronage he received from political compatriots did not exceed the standard 20 percent he carved out of other social connections, but it was nonetheless an additional sector added to his clientele. Membership in New Brick Church and St. Andrew's Lodge made him familiar to a portion of the general population. Growing involvement with rebel groups both large and small may have added to his prominence and provided a competitive edge over his competitors.

Revere's customers came to him from nearly all of the revolutionary organizations in Boston, even those to which he did not belong, such as the Boston Committees of Correspondence, an elite body formed in 1772 by Samuel Adams, and the Loyal Nine, the Boston artisans and shopkeepers who formed the Sons of Liberty. The Committees directed local resistance in concert with about eighty similar groups located throughout Massachusetts and as far away as Virginia. A significant overlap in membership did nonetheless affiliate Revere closely with the members of those organizations. The Boston Committees of Correspondence, for example, shared its ranks with the Long Room Club, organized in 1773, to which Revere did belong. Both groups were comprised largely of Harvard-educated lawyers, doctors, ministers, and merchants drawn from the professional ranks. Joint members such as John Adams, Samuel Adams, John Hancock, Joseph Warren, James Otis, and Thomas Dawes formed the strategic core of the rebellion.[59]

Altogether, some 474 men have been identified as members of revolutionary groups as charted in this essay, of which 122, or 22 percent, eventually became his customers.[60] Proof of Revere's standing in these organizations can be discerned in the London Enemies List of fifty-nine men who were considered a danger to the Crown. Of these most rebellious and powerful antagonists to England, 14 men, or 24 percent of them, were patrons of Revere.

The extent of Revere's political activities and connections was ultimately very widespread. He naturally belonged to the North End Caucus (also called North Caucus), among the best organized revolutionary groups in Boston; its membership, composed of artisans, congregated at the Salutation Tavern. The large revolutionary membership of St. Andrew's Masonic Lodge convened at the Green Dragon Tavern. Cromwell's Head Tavern, run by Revere's friend Joshua Brackett, and the Bunch of Grapes Tavern were two additional watering holes frequented by Revere and receptive to colonial plans for resistance. The Long Room Club assembled in rooms over the *Boston Gazette* press operated by fellow sympathizers Benjamin Edes and John Gill.

The most prominent group in which Revere participated was probably the Sons of Liberty, formed in 1765 by the Loyal Nine, a small enclave of Boston artisans and shopkeepers opposed to the hated Stamp Act. He was among the 300 men, called the Sons of Liberty, who congregated at Dorchester's famous Liberty Tree in 1769, and in 1773, he joined with the 112 rebels, dressed in Indian garb, who have been identified as having participated in the Tea Party.[61]

As with his other networks, Revere's political involvements brought him a range of work and patrons. Revere's satirical engravings from this period are well known, but his political hollowware offers his most serious statement on the estranged relationship between the colonies and the Crown. The Sons of Liberty bowl, made in 1768, was fashioned as an act of defiance on behalf of the "glorious" ninety-two Massachusetts representatives who refused to retract ["rescind"] their denunciation of the Townshend Acts, as written in the Massachusetts Circular Letter sent that year to George III. Made at the request of fifteen patrons, whose names encircle the vessel, Revere placed his maker's mark squarely at the center of the bowl for all to see, a seditious act that would have cost him dearly had it been found.[62]

Well-to-do clients drawn from these political groups included the lawyer Perez Morton, a member of the North Caucus group and attorney-general of Massachusetts from 1811–1832. Morton married the poet Sarah Wentworth Apthorp, whose social status and fortune came from two major mercantile families of Boston. Morton must have entertained lavishly, for his name appeared in Revere's ledger numerous times from the time of his 1781 marriage until 1797.

During these years, Morton purchased a nearly complete tea equipage from Revere that included two pairs of sugar tongs, one creampot, twelve teaspoons, and a slop bowl. Morton perhaps did not order a teapot or coffeepot because he owned imported ones or possibly because Sarah, the daughter of merchant Charles Apthorp, would have brought these goods into the marriage as part of her dowry. Revere made a frame for casters, table and salt spoons, pairs of mugs and porringers, including one "large out of size" porringer, and a bookplate, for which he produced a hundred impressions. He also enhanced or repaired a number of English or foreign-made goods. Among these are the thirty-six crests that Revere engraved on spoons, the silver caps and ferrils that he added to twenty-five knives and forks, and the silver candlestick that he mended on at least two occasions.[63]

The variety of objects and amount of mending that Morton requested of Revere typifies the silversmith's transactions with other high-ranking members of these political groups. During the 1760s, Revere made a pair of canns and a tankard for John Avery of the Loyal Nine; a teapot for shipwright Gibbens Sharp of the North Caucus; and wine cups for Moses Gill of the London Enemies, plus a wide assortment of buckles, spoons, tongs, and "sundry" mending for all.[64]

Revere's involvement with the North End Caucus group probably introduced him to Scottish-born Colonel James Swan, who in 1775 fought at the Battle of Bunker Hill. A Boston merchant, Swan moved to Paris in 1787, where he flourished as an importer during the French Revolution and as an exporter of furniture that had been stripped from the fallen nobility. In the early 1780s, before his move to Paris, Swan purchased a ladle, a large group of engraved spoons, a pair of buckles, and a "cream jug" from Revere. He also paid the craftsman for many small tasks, such as cleaning and burnishing his many salts and mending rings, a punch strainer, and sugar tongs. The absence of any significant hollowware suggests that Swan probably acquired his silver from abroad.[65]

Wealthy men like Morton and Swan were two of more than one hundred other political activists who patronized Revere, hailing from all walks of life. Merchants, auctioneers, attorneys, distillers, housewrights, sailmakers, coopers, doctors, and printers were among these men. Jabez Hatch, wharfinger, purchased a pair of shoe buckles; pilot Thomas Knox bought six teaspoons along with silver and plated shoe buckles for his son Robert; scrivener Elias Parkman bought a cann; and the hatter William Boardman ordered over 2,500 hat bills.[66]

Yet Revere's visibility as a political activist and silversmith, as made manifest in the Sons of Liberty Bowl, did not necessarily create a landslide of patronage. For instance, 9 of the 15 men whose names appear around the bowl bought no other silver from him, although it is likely that they contributed toward the cost of this important symbol of resistance. And 76 men, or 22 percent of the 339 Sons of Liberty, used Revere for major and minor silversmithing needs. This 20-odd percentage is rather constant among Revere's various constituencies. It suggests that, while few populations embraced Revere overwhelmingly as their silversmith of choice, affiliations with many groups added up to a lot of business.[67]

Of course, one could easily assume that among British sympathizers, Revere would have lost rather than gained or maintained clientele. Disaffection with English policies began with the Stamp Act of 1765, but nearly all colonists considered themselves British subjects who were loyal to the Crown until 1776, when the Declaration of Independence was signed. Yet as differences grew among colonists, cordial business relations prevailed. The painter and English sympathizer John Singleton Copley, for example, accepted sitters on both sides of the political fence and treated all with respect. British commander Thomas Gage sat for Copley in 1768, the same year that Revere sat for his portrait; the year was a politically charged one, during which Boston was occupied by British troops.[68]

Like Copley, Revere could not allow politics to get in the way of his livelihood. It is doubtful that he would have had few, if any, reservations accepting commissions from royal appointees or British sympathizers. In September 1773, two months before the Boston Tea Party, Revere executed the largest commission of his career for Dr. William Paine of Worcester, who served as apothecary and physician with the British forces in America during the Revolutionary War and in 1778 was banished to Halifax. Revere produced a forty-five-piece service on the occasion of Paine's marriage to his distant relation Lois Orne, of Salem. The set included a coffeepot, teapot, tankard, two canns, two porringers, and one creamer, along with a box, presumably made to hold the silver (fig. 8).[69] Revere received £34 for his labor above the cost of materials, a considerable sum even for a service of this size.

As political tensions grew, Revere continued to make silver for acquaintances whose allegiance shifted to England. For instance, Dr. Samuel Danforth, Revere's family physician, enjoyed a reciprocal business relationship with the silversmith. Despite his Tory leanings, Danforth purchased a variety of goods from Revere before and after the Revolutionary War, while Revere engaged the doctor for his family's needs during this same period. Danforth, who graduated from Harvard in 1758, purchased domestic forms from Revere such as a silver "vissel," shoe buckles, salt spoons, a coffee urn, and a teapot. He also purchased numerous harness goods such as "pads and Winkers," and used him for mending stone buttons and his "Lancett case."[70]

ɵ

Born in modest circumstances, Revere had an ordinary start in life. As a well-trained craftsman with close ties to his family and larger community, he probably was no different from most of his fellow silversmiths or other tradesmen. However, the combination of his remarkable skills as a talented silversmith, enterprising businessman, and political operative made him uniquely prepared for the extraordinary times in which he lived. Revere lived a full life. Through his innumerable, documented contacts with customers, and his energetic embrace of social groups and revolutionary causes, he stood at the crossroads of pre- and post-Revolutionary Boston life and provided historians with a rich body of material with which to examine the colonial world.

Revere made countless pedestrian items such as spoons and shoe buckles that gave a small measure of dignity to the middling class, and surpassed his peers

Fig. 8. Paul Revere (1734–1818), Paine service, Boston, Massachusetts, 1773. Silver; h. (coffeepot) 13½ in., h. (teapot) 6⅝ in.; h. (tankard) 9⁵⁄₁₆ in. Worcester Museum of Art, Gift of Dr. and Mrs. George C. Lincoln in memory of Fanny Chandler Lincoln and Gift of Richard K. Thorndike (1937.55–58; 1959.105, 1963.338a-f, 1965.336, 1967.57).

in fabricating many examples of fine hollowware for well-to-do customers who were educated professionals or successful tradesmen like himself. Economic considerations aside, Revere's patrons can be identified according to the social relations they shared with the silversmith. Thus, the silversmith's membership in the Masonic brotherhood, his patriotic alliances, family, friends, and church relations, all had some bearing on the relative size of his customer base. Further research may define these overlapping groups with ever-greater precision and meaning, and lead us toward a better grasp of consumption in eighteenth-century American life.

Notes

Thanks to Regina Lee Blaszczyk, Jonathan Fairbanks, Patrick Leehey, Gloria Main, Michael J. Prokopow, Edith Steblecki, and Gerry Ward for reading portions of this manuscript in its early stages. Grateful thanks go to Jayne Triber for sharing her notes, to Anne E. Rogers for graciously sharing her unpublished research on the Boston Taking Books, and to Seth Vose III for providing Thwing Project data. Tara McNeil, Abby Dorman, and Myriam Gorsky assisted with Masonic and Thwing research. Nancy Wilson provided genealogical assistance.

1. Samuel Adams, cited in Alan Kulikoff, "The Progress of Inequality in Revolutionary Boston," *William and Mary Quarterly*, 3d ser., 28, no. 3 (July 1971): 375.

2. Carl F. Bridenbaugh, ed., *Gentleman's Progress: The Itinerarium of Dr. Alexander Hamilton, 1744* (Chapel Hill: University of North Carolina Press, 1948), 13.

3. There is a wealth of recent literature that addresses consumer behavior patterns in the eighteenth century. Carole Shammas, "Consumer Behavior in Colonial America," *Social Science History* 6, no. 1 (Winter 1982): 67–87; Carole Shammas, *The Pre-industrial Consumer in England and America* (Oxford: Clarendon Press, 1990); Ann Smart Martin, "Makers, Buyers, and Users, Consumerism as a Material Culture Framework," *Winterthur Portfolio* 28, no. 2/3 (Summer/Autumn 1993): 141–57; Joyce Appleby, "Consumption in Early Modern Social Thought," in *Consumption and the World of Goods*, ed. John Brewer and Roy Porter (London: Routledge, 1993), 162–73; Carole Shammas, "Changes in English and Anglo-American Consumption from 1550 to 1800," in *Consumption and the World of Goods*, 177–205; Lorna Weatherill, "The Meaning of Consumer Behaviour in Late Seventeenth- and Early Eighteenth-Century England," in *Consumption and the World of Goods*, 206–27; Cary Carson, Ronald Hoffman, and Peter J. Albert, eds., *Of Consuming Interests: The Style of Life in the Eighteenth Century* (Charlottesville: University Press of Virginia, 1994).

4. Although Daniel Horowitz addresses nineteenth- and twentieth-century consumption, I have quoted from his introduction which places this discussion in a general context. Daniel Horowitz, *The Morality of Spending: Attitudes toward the Consumer Society in America, 1875–1940* (Baltimore: Johns Hopkins University Press, 1985), xxiv.

5. Gloria L. Main, "The Distribution of Consumer Goods in Colonial New England: A Sub-regional Approach," in *Early American Probate Inventories*, ed. Peter Benes (Boston: Boston University, 1987), 153–68; Gloria L. Main, "The Standards of Living in Southern New England, 1640–1773," *William and Mary Quarterly*, 3d ser., 45, no. 1 (January 1988): 128. According to Main, "Of major significance is the fact that people of the middling rank everywhere in the sample began acquiring some, but not all, available new goods in a deliberate, selective fashion." See Table VII for a review of many luxury goods, including looking glasses, clocks, wigs, books, and silver in southern New England probate records from 1640 to 1764.

6. For modern scholarship on Revere's silversmithing career, see *Paul Revere — Artisan, Businessman, and Patriot, the Man Behind the Myth* (Boston: Paul Revere Memorial Association, 1988); Deborah Federhen, "Paul Revere, Silversmith: A Study of His Shop Operations and His Objects" (M.A. thesis, University of Delaware, 1988); Deborah Federhen, "Paul Revere, Jr. (1734–1818)," in *Colonial Massachusetts Silversmiths and Jewelers: A Biographical Dictionary*, ed. Patricia E. Kane (New Haven: Yale University Art Gallery, 1998), 795–848; Jayne E. Triber, *A True Republican: The Life of Paul Revere* (Amherst: University of Massachusetts Press, 1998). For an analogous look at the production of another enterprising New England silversmith, see Gerald W. R. Ward, "Jabez Baldwin, Silversmith-Entrepreneur of Salem, Massachusetts, 1802–1819," *Winterthur Portfolio* 23, no. 1 (Spring 1988): 54. For silver consumption in a particular region, see

Gerald W. R. Ward, "The Democratization of Precious Metal: A Note on the Ownership of Silver in Salem, 1630–1820," *Essex Institute Historical Collections* 126, no. 3 (July 1990): 171–200.

7. Paul Revere, daybooks, vols. 1–2, Revere Family Papers, Massachusetts Historical Society (cited hereafter as Daybooks). The 588 patrons and their purchases recorded in the daybooks, henceforth called the Buhler Index, are drawn from the notes of Kathryn C. Buhler, whose career at the Museum of Fine Arts, Boston, spanned five decades. Departmental Files, Art of the Americas, Museum of Fine Arts, Boston. The daybook of Zachariah Brigden offers a more limited view of one shop, its practices, and clientele. Brigden Papers, Beinecke Rare Book Library, Yale University. For an interpretation of the Brigden papers, see Hilary Anderson, "Earning a Living in Eighteenth-Century Boston: Silversmith Zachariah Brigden" (M.A. thesis, University of Delaware, 1996).

8. Additional information on patrons not recorded in the daybook is largely taken from Kane, *Colonial Massachusetts Silversmiths*, 806–45. Omitted from this list are the names of individuals who conducted non-silver transactions with Revere, and organizations such as churches and lodges, who usually ordered silver through their membership. Many duplicate names have been deleted as well.

9. Since it would be unfair to use the daybook records in a comparison of Revere's business with that of his contemporaries, the field has been leveled by relying exclusively on Kane, *Colonial Massachusetts Silversmiths*, 210–17; 228–44; 298–305; 539–43; 689–98; 806–45. This volume provides a comprehensive list of silver that has been published in American scholarly publications, auction catalogues, and advertisements. As such, it is the best resource available on silver that was made by Massachusetts silversmiths working before the Revolution.

10. The rather depressed figures for items made by these craftsmen may change in the future as additional silver comes to light. Despite Revere's admittedly large production numbers, figures may be slightly skewed in his favor due to the excessive popularity of the patriot's work among collectors in this century.

11. This analysis of Revere's production comes from Federhen, "Paul Revere, Silversmith," 80–92, tables A–E. These figures exclude engraving, printing, repairing, making tools, or the practice of dentistry.

12. Revere opened a hardware store "opposite where the Liberty Tree stood" as early as 1783, where he sold a variety of items, including shoe buckles. For the purposes of this essay, all small-work recorded in the daybooks is treated as a product of the Revere shop, regardless of their place of manufacture, in order to ascertain the breadth of his customer base.

13. Portable luxuries such as silver were frequently passed on by their owners to children or others during their own lifetime. However, probate records suggest that many retained silver until death. For a sampling, see Abbott Lowell Cummings, ed., *Rural Household Inventories: Establishing the Names, Uses and Furnishings of Rooms in the Colonial New England Home, 1675–1775* (Boston: Society for the Preservation of New England Antiquities, 1964), passim; Alice Hanson Jones, *American Colonial Wealth, Documents and Methods*, vol. 2 (New York: Arno Press, 1977). As minor as they are, small luxury goods such as spoons are important indicators of a rising level of domesticity in eighteenth-century America that has parallels in England and Scotland. For an analysis of the parallel developments of English colonies, see John Clive and Bernard Bailyn, "England's Cultural Provinces: Scotland and America," *William and Mary Quarterly*, 3d ser., 2, no. 2 (April 1954): 200–213; and Shammas, "Changes in English and Anglo-American Consumption."

14. Information about hollowware made between 1777 and 1783 has been drawn from Revere's daybooks and from Kane, *Colonial Massachusetts Silversmiths*, 806–45.

15. By this date, Henchman had already died. Minott, who had sympathized with the British during the Revolution, made no teapots and never did regain his pre-war level of productivity.

16. Revere's customers for this item ranged from fellow Mason Moses Michael Hays (1783), relatives Stephen and Isannah Bruce (1782), and New Brick Church congregant Caleb Champney (1782–85), to Robert and Mary (Ingalls) Hooper (1790), whose family was allied with the British (Daybooks 1:16, 23, 49, 50–51). Virginia Hewett Watterson, *Descendants of the Elder Richard Champney of Cambridge, Massachusetts* (Carlsbad, Calif.: privately printed, 1989), 45.

17. For an in-depth discussion of fluted teapots by Revere, and others made in smaller numbers by Benjamin Burt, and possibly by Joseph Loring, see Janine Skerry, "The Revolutionary Revere, A Critical Assessment of the Silver of Paul Revere," in *Paul Revere — Artisan, Businessman, and Patriot*, 53–55.

18. Daybooks 2:119–21 (Templeman), 134 (Carnes), 142–43 (Shattuck).

19. Fourteen pitchers by Revere have been published by Kane, *Colonial Massachusetts Silversmiths*, 819–20.

20. Kathryn C. Buhler, *American Silver, 1655–1825, in the Museum of Fine Arts, Boston* (Boston: Museum of Fine Arts, Boston, 1972), 2:470, cat. 420; 2: 517–19, cat. 461–62.

21. *Procession. Boston, Oct. 19, 1789.* Broadside, Boston, 1789. Published in *Witness to America's Past: Two Centuries of Collecting by the Massachusetts Historical Society* (Boston: Massachusetts Historical Society and the Museum of Fine Arts, Boston, 1991), cat. 90, pp. 117–18, ill. 89. Alan Kulikoff used this method to analyze Boston population (Kulikoff, "The Progress of Inequality in Revolutionary Boston," 385–88).

22. Kulikoff used the Boston Tax Taking and Rate Books for 1790 in his essay. Kulikoff, "The Progress of Inequality in Revolutionary Boston," 385, table 3.

23. This list excludes a small group of fellow silversmiths, the Revere family, and individuals who rented space from Revere but did not purchase silver. As for the balance of 283 individuals whose occupations remain unknown, future research will certainly modify the conclusions reached in this essay. Population distribution figures from Kulikoff, "The Progress of Inequality in Revolutionary Boston," 377, table 1.

24. Daybooks 1:23–24; 2:74, 89, 93, 104, 130, 136. Clifford K. Shipton, *Biographical Sketches of Those Who Attended Harvard College in the Classes 1746–1750* (Boston: Massachusetts Historical Society, 1962), 190.

25. Lawrence Park, comp., *Gilbert Stuart: An Illustrated, Descriptive List of His Works* (New York: William Edwin Rudge, 1926), 2:277, no. 234; 3: plate 234; Ann Smith Lainhart, *First Boston City Directory (1789), Including Extensive Annotations by John Haven Dexter (1791–1876)* (Boston: New England Historic and Genealogical Society, 1989)14; Kane, *Colonial Massachusetts Silversmiths*, 809. The Taking Books of 1790, the Assessor's record of wealth among Boston residents, lists Dennie as a merchant who lived in Ward 7, and in 1793 as "at sea." Taking Book data throughout this essay has been kindly provided by Anne Rogers.

26. Middlesex County Probate Records, docket 1142, in Barrell Papers [microfilm], Massachusetts Historical Society; Daybooks 2:75, 127, 130, 156; Lainhart, *First Boston City Directory*, 37. The Taking Books of 1790 record Barrell as a merchant who lived in Ward 11, whose house was valued at £1400 and pasture land at £200. Kane, *Colonial Massachusetts Silversmiths*, does not identify any other colonial silver owned by Barrell.

27. *Witness to America's Past*, 129–30, cat. 99, fig. 99.

28. Daybooks 2:86 (Blanchard), 113 (Simpkins); 1:37, 40, 42 (Hewes). The meaning of "double

chapes" is unclear, but it appears to be a metal cover of some sort or the part of a buckle used to fasten it to a strap or belt. *Compact Oxford English Dictionary* (Oxford: Oxford University Press, 1987), 379.

29. By comparison to Balch, the mean assessment for hatters in 1790 was £240. The Taking Books of 1790 record Balch as a hatter of Ward 9 and a property owner in that location from 1779 to 1784. Thwing Project, no. 4062; Daybooks 1:44–45, 67; Kulikoff, "The Progress of Inequality in Revolutionary Boston," 388. Kane, *Colonial Massachusetts Silversmiths*, does not identify any other Massachusetts silver made for Balch.

30. The Taking Books for 1780 and 1790 list Abraham Adams as a leatherdresser in Ward 12. In 1784, Adams engaged Revere to engrave two plates for hat bills and to print 200 of same, which suggests that Adams also made hats. His purchase was paid for with old silver, which is to say, damaged or unfashionable goods that were remelted and used for the new item. Daybooks 2:19; Lainhart, *First Boston City Directory*, 8; Kane, *Colonial Massachusetts Silversmiths*, 298. Kane, *Colonial Massachusetts Silversmiths*, does not identify any Massachusetts silver owned by Adams.

31. Crosby was listed in the 1780 and 1790 Taking Books as a barber living in ward 11. Daybooks 1:12, 15; Lainhart, *First Boston City Directory*, 33. Kane, *Colonial Massachusetts Silversmiths*, does not identify any Massachusetts silver owned by Crosby.

32. Taking Books, 1780, 1788, 1789, 1791, 1793, and 1799. Badger was called a "small" or "very small pewterer," with one half house and shop in Ward 1. "T. Badger" purchased six silver teaspoons from Revere in 1784. Daybooks 2:20; Lainhart, *First Boston City Directory*, 13. Kane, *Colonial Massachusetts Silversmiths*, does not identify any Massachusetts silver owned by Badger.

33. Joseph Barrett, sailmaker, was listed in the 1790 Taking Books as owning a house and loft in Ward 4, each valued at £75. Daybooks 1:66, 71; 2: 56, 127, 130. The 1789 Boston city directory lists a Joseph W. Barrett, sail-maker, of Batterymarch St. Lainhart, *First Boston City Directory*, 14. Kane, *Colonial Massachusetts Silversmiths*, does not identify any Massachusetts silver owned by Barrett.

34. Gary John Kornblith, "From Artisans to Businessmen: Master Mechanics in New England, 1789–1850" (Ph.D. thesis, Princeton University, 1983), 96–103.

35. Hunnewell was listed as a mason in Ward 12 according to the 1790 Taking Books. He received a pitcher by Revere as a gift of the association in 1806. Martha Gandy Fales, "Samuel Gilbert's Revere Pitcher," *Antiques* 75, no. 5 (May 1959): 476–77. Daybooks 2:153–54; *Annals of the Massachusetts Charitable Mechanic Association, 1795–1892* (Boston: Press of Rockwell and Churchill, 1892), 26–27. The teapot stand and sugar basket are in the Metropolitan Museum of Art. C. Louise Avery, *American Silver of the Seventeenth and Eighteenth Centuries: A Study Based on the Clearwater Collection* (New York: Metropolitan Museum of Art, 1920), nos. 302–3.

36. Tuckerman appears as a Ward 12 baker in the Taking Books of 1780 and 1790. Park, *Gilbert Stuart*, 2:661–62, no. 728, 730; Buhler, *American Silver, 1655–1825*, 2:463, cat. 413.

37. The *Compact Oxford English Dictionary*, 594, offers several definitions of the word "crane" that were in use before Revere's day. The most likely is the siphon, "a bent tube used to draw liquor out of a vessel."

38. Daybooks 2:135, 141 (Samuel Barry), 73 (William Callender; Callendar was listed as a turner in Wards 4 and 10 from 1784 until 1798), 125, 128, 131, 140 (Christopher Gore); 1:41, 44, 45 (Thomas Emmons; Emmons appeared in the Taking Books in 1790 as a cooper and journeyman of Ward 12), 77; 2:68–69, 73, 77 (Samuel Dow; Dow was listed in the 1780 Taking Books as a "continental smith" in Ward 12); Lainhart, *First Boston City Directory*, 26, 39, 49. Some of these purchases were made prior to the formation of the MCMA.

39. Daybooks 1:9–10, 15, 21–22, 26–28, 32, 34–38, 44–45, 47–48, 53–54, 59, 77; Kane, *Colonial Massachusetts Silversmiths*, 820, 826, 849–52.

40. For Hichborn (also spelled Hitchborn and Hichbourn) family purchases, see Daybooks 1: 14, 17–19, 21, 23, 28, 32, 71–72, 76; 2:6, 19, 38, 52, 54, 58, 60, 61, 69, 70, 73–74, 79, 83, 115. For Mary Hitchborn's creampot, see Kathryn C. Buhler, *American Silver from the Colonial Period through the Early Republic in the Worcester Art Museum* (Worcester: Worcester Art Museum, 1979), 24, cat. 18. For Benjamin Hichborn, see Triber, *A True Republican*, 9.

41. Ledger, New Brick Church, Collection of the Massachusetts Historical Society.

42. As one of the investors in Joseph Barrell's ship *Columbia*'s second voyage to the Northwest coast, it is likely that Parkman owned the vessel *Industry*. Daybooks 2:80, 85, 117, 122, 128, 132, 141, 144, 147, 163, 165–66; Park, *Gilbert Stuart*, 2:570, no. 608; *Witness to America's Past*, 134–35, cat. 104. The urn is not recorded in Revere's daybook; Lainhart, *First Boston City Directory*, 77.

43. William Williams's purchases from Revere in Daybooks 2:118, 122, 123, 128, 130, 132, 136, 140, 141, 148, 151, 154, 158, 161; Thomas Lewis, in Daybooks 1:11; 2:121, 132; Enoch James in Daybooks 2:75, 79, 80, 84, 91, 97, 106, 107, 129. Lainhart, *First Boston City Directory*, 60, 65, 107. The Taking Books for 1790 lists William Williams, hatter, in Ward 5, and owner of half a shop and half a house. Thomas Lewis is probably the blockmaker of Ward 3 listed in the Taking Books of 1780, and wharfinger, Ward 3, of 1790. Dr. Rand was listed in the Taking Books of 1780 and 1790 as a doctor living in Ward 4; Lainhart, *First Boston City Directory*, 83; Daybooks 2:52, 57, 85–86, 88.

44. Music published by Revere and Flagg is treated by Clarence S. Brigham, *Paul Revere's Engravings* (Worcester, Mass.: American Antiquarian Society, 1954), 16–18, 36–38, 80–82.

45. Daybooks 1:11, 16, 25, 49; James Henry Stark, *The Loyalists of Massachusetts and the Other Side of the American Revolution* (Boston: W. B. Clarke, 1910), 503; Triber, *A True Republican*, 26; Kane, *Colonial Massachusetts Silversmiths*, 800.

46. Daybooks 1:32 (Sharp), 5, 9, 15, 65, 76 (Brackett), 44, 48, 51, 54 (Collins); Col. William Palfrey, "An alphabetical list of the sons of Liberty who din'd at Liberty Tree Dorchester, Aug. 14, 1769," Miscellaneous bound manuscript, Massachusetts Historical Society. Gibbens Sharp was recorded by the Taking Books of 1800 as a shipwright in Ward 4; in 1790, he was listed as a gentleman. Brigham, *Paul Revere's Engravings*, 66, 120; Edith J. Steblecki, *Paul Revere and Freemasonry* (Boston: Paul Revere Memorial Association, 1985), 100–101; Triber, *A True Republican*, 29.

47. Steblecki, *Paul Revere and Freemasonry*, 10.

48. Walter Muir Whitehill, *Boston: A Topographical History* (Cambridge: The Belknap Press of Harvard University Press, 1959), 112–13; Nathaniel Bradstreet Shurtleff, *A Topographical and Historical Description of Boston,* 3rd ed. (Boston: Rockwell and Churchill, City Printers, 1891), 605–14.

49. For a comprehensive look at Revere and his fraternal activities, see Steblecki, *Paul Revere and Freemasonry*, esp. 100–101, app. 1, 5; Edith J. Steblecki, "Fraternity, Philanthropy, and Revolution, Paul Revere and Freemasonry," in *Paul Revere — Artisan, Businessman, and Patriot*, 117–47, n. 27.

50. Additional membership information was drawn from the Henry J. Parker Index, Massachusetts Masonic Lodge. Out of 309 patrons that Steblecki identified, 146, or nearly half, were Masons. This author has identified a total of 753 patrons of Revere, of whom 241, or one-third, were Masons.

51. Daybooks 1:29; 2:54, 88, 106, 110, 113, 132, 136. The Taking Books from 1784 to 1791 record Brailsford as a glazier from Ward 5. Rumney was listed as a trader in Ward 4 between 1784 and 1791 with a house and shops that grew in number. This apparently preceded his business selling chocolate and mustard, as recorded in the 1789 Boston city directory. Hall was recorded in the

taking books as a cabinetmaker of Ward 4 during the 1790s. According to the Parker Index, McAlpine was a member of St. Andrew's in 1761. He fled to Scotland, his country of birth, where he died in 1788. Lainhart, *First Boston City Directory*, 22, 53, 86.

52. For Tracy, see Daybooks 1:67–69, 71. Buhler, *American Silver, 1655–1825*, 2:421, cat. 369.

53. Daybooks 1:74, 78; 2:32–33, 38, 102, 153; Allen Johnson, ed., *Dictionary of American Biography* (New York: Charles Scribner's Sons, 1928), 19:479–80, 482–83; Brigham, *Paul Revere's Engravings*, 102–5, plate 48. John Warren was among the founders of the Boston Medical Society, and the first professor of anatomy and surgery at Harvard College. From 1783 to 1784 and in 1787 he served as Grand Master of the Massachusetts Grand Lodge of Free and Accepted Masons.

54. Steblecki, *Paul Revere and Freemasonry*, 52.

55. Jane Bortman, "Moses Hays and His Revere Silver," *Antiques* 66, no. 4 (October 1954): 304–5. Jeannette W. Rosenbaum, *Myer Myers, Goldsmith, 1723–1795* (Philadelphia: Jewish Publication Society of America, 1954), 40, 60. For a few of the Hays commissions, see Kathryn C. Buhler, *Masterpieces of American Silver* (Richmond: Virginia Museum of Fine Arts, 1960), 64–65, cat. 119; Jonathan Fairbanks, Wendy A. Cooper et al., *Paul Revere's Boston: 1735–1818* (Boston: Museum of Fine Arts, Boston, 1975), 186–87, figs. 288–89.

56. David Barquist, *Myer Myers*, forthcoming. I am grateful to David Barquist for his observations on Myer Myers.

57. For the Surinam commission, see Daybooks 1:31.

58. There were about seventy-five silversmiths and jewelers in Boston during the late colonial period, of whom Josiah Flagg, Paul Revere, Samuel Minott, and Daniel Parker (later a distiller) were politically active. Patricia E. Kane, "Artistry in Boston Silver of the Colonial Period," in Kane, *Colonial Massachusetts Silversmiths*, 86.

59. David Hackett Fischer, *Paul Revere's Ride* (New York: Oxford University Press, 1994), 20.

60. The revolutionary groups included in this sample are the Loyal Nine, North Caucus, Tea Party, Long Room, Committees of Correspondence, Sons of Liberty, and London Enemies. Fischer, *Paul Revere's Ride*, 301–7, app. D; Palfrey, "Alphabetical list of the sons of Liberty."

61. Palfrey, "Alphabetical list of the sons of Liberty." The names of all the Sons of Liberty may never be known, but the Palfrey list is one of the few surviving texts written by a known participant. Brigham, *Paul Revere's Engravings*, 21–25, plate 6; Buhler, *American Silver, 1655–1825*, 2: 408–9, cat. 356; Fischer, *Paul Revere's Ride*, 301–7, app. D.

62. For a full discussion of the origins and significance of the bowl, see the essay in this volume by Jonathan L. Fairbanks. For a small salt with related engraving, see Kathryn C. Buhler and Graham Hood, *American Silver: Garvan and Other Collections in the Yale University Art Gallery*, 2 vols. (New Haven: Yale University Press for the Yale Art Gallery, 1970), 1:187, cat. 241.

63. Park, *Gilbert Stuart*, 1:534–35, no. 561; 3:plate 561; Lainhart, *First Boston City Directory*, 8, 12. No holloware is listed among Revere's list of repairs for the Mortons, and a review of Kane, *Colonial Massachusetts Silversmiths*, reveals no holloware or flatware made for the couple by any other Massachusetts silversmith of the period. Daybooks 1:59–63, 65; 2: 12, 15, 18, 20, 42–43, 56, 68, 75, 116, 144, 147–48, 152, 153, 154, 157, 159, 161, 164. Brigham, *Paul Revere's Engravings*, 113, plate 53.

64. According to the annotated 1789 Boston city directory, John Avery was Secretary of the State, with an office in the Province House. The Taking Books of 1790 lists him as John Avery, Jr., Esq., of Ward 12, who owned "1 chaise, no horse, secretary." Fischer, *Paul Revere's Ride*, 306, lists "Gibbens Sharp" as a member of the North Caucus; the Taking Books for 1780 records a Gibbins

Sharp, shipwright, of Ward 4, and in 1790 lists Gibbons Sharp, also of Ward 4, as a gentleman. Sharp is recorded as a shipwright in the 1789 Boston city directory. Moses Gill was a brazier who later became acting governor of Massachusetts. According to the 1790 Taking Books, Gill lived in Ward 10 and served as a councillor and merchant whose property was assessed at £1,000; his double store on Spears Wharf was assessed at £200. The Museum of Fine Arts, Boston, recently acquired a stylish Boston rococo side chair owned originally by Gill.

65. Park, *Gilbert Stuart*, 2:729–32, ill. 4:504–5. Much of Swan's French furniture is in the Museum of Fine Arts, Boston. See Jeffrey H. Munger, "Royal French Furniture in Eighteenth-Century Boston," *Versailles: French Court Style and Its Influence* (Toronto: University of Toronto, 1992), 113–25. Daybooks 1:71; 2: 8, 10, 13, 18, 20, 24, 31, 40, 42, 55. If Swan patronized other Massachusetts silversmiths, they have not yet been identified.

66. Daybooks 1:59–60 (Jabez Hatch). The Taking Books of 1780 and 1790 list Hatch as a wharfinger living in Ward 12. In 1790 his wood wharf was assessed at £250, and his house at £350. Daybooks 2:109–10, 114, 116, 121 (Thomas Knox); 1:76 (Elias Parkman). The 1780 Taking Books list Elias Parkman as a captain in Ward 2. By 1790, he was listed in the same ward, but "poor." Daybooks 1:43–44, 46, 49, 78; 2:44, 57, 73, 83, 98, 106, 112, 114, 117, 122, 126, 130, 134, 141, 147, 148, 155, 157, 162, 165 (William Boardman). The 1790 Taking Books record a Deacon William Boardman, hatter, as living in Ward 5.

67. The fifteen men whose names are engraved on the bowl are Nathaniel Barber, William Bowes, Peter Boyer, Benjamin Cobb, Benjamin Goodwin, John Homer, Caleb Hopkins, Ichabod Jones, William Mackay, Daniel Malcolm, John Marston, Daniel Parker, Fortescue Vernon, John Welsh, and John White. Of these, only Homer, Hopkins, Mackay, Vernon, and Welsh patronized Revere for additional silver purchases.

68. For a breakdown of Copley's sitters according to their political alliances see Jules David Prown, *John Singleton Copley*, 2 vols. (Washington: National Gallery of Art, 1965), 1:102–37. Prown notes that 55 percent of Tories and 45 percent of Whigs sat for Copley, a closely divided constituency that had recourse to few other portrait painters at the time. Revere probably had fewer Tories since it would have been far easier for them to import their silver than travel abroad to sit for their portrait.

69. Daybooks 1:46–47; Buhler, *American Silver from the Colonial Period through the Early Republic*, 42–47, cat. 50–57; *American Portraits, 1620–1825, Found in Massachusetts*, 2 vols. (Boston: Historical Records Survey, Works Progress Administration, 1939), 2:297, no. 1584.

70. Daybooks 1:42, 44–46, 49, 50, 54, 76–77; 2:3, 6, 75, 79, 83, 87, 116, 129. Clifford S. Shipton, *Sibley's Harvard Graduates*, 14:251–54; Triber, *A True Republican*, 84, 89. Danforth was president of the Massachusetts Medical Society from 1795 to 1798. No evidence exists that the two men bartered their services with one another.

"Ancient and Valuable Gifts": Silver at Colonial Harvard

JANINE E. SKERRY

I
N 1991, a *Harvard Magazine* editorial entitled "A Sterling Occasion" commented on the inauguration of the university's new president:

> The installation of Neil L. Rudenstine as Harvard's 26th president on October 18 was one of the four or five most considerable public occasions at Harvard so far this century. What could be more normal at such a time than to bring out one's favorite silverware — not to be used, but to be regarded? Proof that one has been around for a while. Evidence of wealth beyond the temporal . . . "These treasured pieces of silver symbolize Harvard's continuity with its past," University marshal Richard M. Hunt told the Installation-Day audience. "They are brought out only on special occasions such as this, when institutional memory sets the stage for . . . the future."[1]

Throughout America's history, the ownership of large quantities of silver has been regarded as a sign of high social status, wealth, and heritage. Possession of silver usually denotes class and continuity with regard to individuals or families, but the association of these traits with institutions is also possible. Such is the case with Harvard College, which used an exhibition of antique plate at the installation of its president to reinforce its elite position as the nation's oldest institution of higher learning. The display of Harvard's colonial silver at ceremonial occasions tangibly demonstrates the College's awareness of these artifacts as embodiments of its past. Although the symbolic nature of these vessels is widely and unquestioningly recognized by the College administration, little is known about their original context and function within the Harvard community.[2]

Much of the College's antique silver has been published and exhibited throughout the twentieth century but the objects have been treated principally as relics or art works. For example, in the 1888 publication *Old Plate, Ecclesiastical, Decorative, and Domestic: Its Makers and Marks*, John H. Buck described Harvard's Stoughton cup as a good example of early-eighteenth-century silver. He also noted that the cup bore the "the well-known London maker's mark, IC" — a mark now recognized for more than ninety years as that of John Coney of Boston. Despite this early error of attribution, Buck deserves recognition as the first authority to acknowledge in print the importance of American silver; he included a chapter on the topic and rightly gave credit for Harvard's Browne cup to the Boston silversmith John Burt. In the hundred years since this early book, pieces of Harvard-associated silver have been published innumerable times, but the rationale behind the use of silver within an American collegiate context has never been extensively explored. This essay will focus on the specific practices pertaining to the ownership of silver within Harvard during the colonial period. Observations have been gleaned from a close study of Harvard's archives, published college laws and histories, diaries, and surviving objects. Brief but important work done on this topic by William C. Lane in 1921 and by Kathryn C. Buhler in 1955 has also been utilized.[3]

During the colonial period, the practice of presenting a piece of plate to Harvard or its faculty occurred within one of three categories. Corporate silver, given to the College proper, was usually donated or bequeathed by an alumnus or benefactor in appreciation and acknowledgment. Fellow commoner silver was also given directly to the College. This category of items fulfilled contractual obligations from students who had been granted specific perquisites in return for the payment of fees and tribute. Finally, students bestowed tutorial plate upon Harvard instructors as partial compensation when classes concluded their studies. Today, this latter category of silver survives in the greatest quantities, but the corporate gifts and fellow commoner silver play the most important symbolic role within Harvard.[4]

Of the three primary categories of colonial silver associated with Harvard, corporate gifts were among the most ephemeral in nature. The bestowal of a gift upon the College was entirely dependent upon the good will of an individual toward the institution. Records of seventeenth- and eighteenth-century donations indicate the College was indeed blessed with the generosity of numerous benefactors, but the majority of the gifts were in the form of books for the library, lands or commodities that could produce revenue, or sums of money in pounds sterling.[5] Nevertheless, some of the donations to the College were considered singular enough even in the early nineteenth century to have merited note in Harvard's first published history:

> In looking over the list of early benefactions to the College, we are amused, when we read of a number of sheep bequeathed by one man, a quantity of cotton cloth worth nine shillings presented by another, a pewter flagon worth ten shillings by a third, a fruit dish, a sugar-spoon, a silver-tipt jug, one great salt, one small trencher-salt, by others; and of presents or legacies amounting severally to five shillings, nine shillings, one pound, two pounds, & c., all faithfully recorded with the names of their respective donors.[6]

From such references it appears gifts of silver tableware to the College cor-

Fig. 1. Unknown maker, The Great Salt, London, 1629–38. Gift to Harvard College from Richard Harris, 1644. Silver; h. 4 13/16 in. Courtesy, Fogg Art Museum, Harvard University Art Museums, Loan from Harvard University (881.1927). © President and Fellows of Harvard College, Harvard University.

poration were not commonplace and may have been regarded by donor and recipient alike as having significant commemorative value. Three pieces of colonial corporate plate are still extant today. The earliest silver object that survives with Harvard associations is the "great salt" of circa 1629–38 made in London and given by Richard Harris (fig. 1). The precise circumstances of its presentation to Harvard are unknown, and it is uncertain whether the gift was made prior to Harris's death in 1644 or as a subsequent bequest. Although the great salt has been identified on several occasions as a piece of fellow commoner silver, this does not appear to be the case. No evidence has yet been put forth that Richard Harris was a matriculating student at Harvard, nor is he described in any college records as a fellow commoner. Therefore, this object is most appropriately placed in the category of corporate plate. The great salt is revered today at Harvard primarily for two reasons: it is the oldest surviving silver artifact given to the College and it is associated, albeit indirectly, with Harvard's first president, the Reverend Henry Dunster.[7]

Second in pride of place among silver donors to Harvard is the Honorable

185

Fig. 2 a (*front*) and b (*back*). John Coney (1655/56–1722), The Stoughton Cup, Boston, Massachusetts, 1701. Gift to Harvard College from the Honorable William Stoughton, 1701. Silver; h. 10 in. Courtesy, Fogg Art Museum, Harvard University Art Museums, Loan from Harvard University (877.1927). © President and Fellows of Harvard College, Harvard University.

William Stoughton, lieutenant governor and chief justice of Massachusetts. Stoughton was one of Harvard's greatest early benefactors, having personally provided £1,000 sterling in 1699 to construct a brick building containing chambers for sixteen students. Although Stoughton Hall was torn down in 1780,[8] the monumental piece of corporate silver donated by this alumnus still survives today as testimony of his generosity toward Harvard. The large two-handled cup with cover was made by John Coney about 1700/01 and is engraved with the arms of its donor (fig. 2). As with Harris's gift of the great salt, records of the actual presentation of Stoughton's cup do not survive among Harvard's papers. Fortunately, however, the date and occasion of the presentation of Stoughton's gift are preserved in the diary of Samuel Sewall:

> Monday, June 30 [1701]. Lt Govr said would go to the [Harvard] Commence-ment once more in his life-time; so would adjourn the Court to Friday, and did so. But was very much pain'd going home. Mr. Nelson, Secretary, and I visit him on Tuesday to disswade him from going, lest some ill consequence should hap-pen. He consented, and order'd us to present his Bowl. After Dinner and singing, I took it, had it fill'd up, and drunk to the president, saying that by reason of the absence of him who was the Firmament and Ornament of the Province, and that Society I presented that Grace-cup *pro more Academiarum in Anglia*.[9]

Latest in date among the extant colonial corporate silver is the two-handled covered cup made in the early 1730s as the result of the bequest of Colonel Samuel Browne (fig. 3). Like Stoughton, Browne was a generous benefactor to Harvard. His final gift, which also included two hundred acres of improved land, was entered into Harvard's College Book IV on September 2, 1731:

Fig. 3 a (*front*) and b (*back*). John Burt (1692/93–1745/46), The Browne Cup (two-handled cup with cover), Boston, Massachusetts, ca. 1731. Silver; 11½ in. Courtesy, Fogg Art Museum, Harvard University Art Museums, Loan from Harvard University (882.1927). © President and Fellows of Harvard College, Harvard University.

An Extract taken from ye last Will & Testament of the Honble Samuel Brown Esqr, late of Salem in the County of Essex, deceased, viz.

Item, I give to Harvard College in Cambridge Sixty Pounds to be Improved for purchasing an hansom piece of Plate for the College, with my Coat of Arms upon it . . . [10]

It is dangerous to read too much into the symbolic function of just three pieces of silver, but it is worth noting that both forms represented in the corporate plate — the great salt and the two covered cups — are generally considered to have been symbols of status. A standing salt was the focal point of a dining or banqueting table from the medieval period until the decline of the form in the second half of the seventeenth century. Far more important than its function of holding salt for seasoning food, its location on the table identified to the assembled diners who was the master of the household and who were the most honored guests. Ownership of such an object represented both wealth and social station. Similarly, two-handled covered cups were also statements of power and prestige. The earliest rituals of courtly dining that evolved in Britain during the medieval period strictly dictated who had the prerogative of using covered dishes and cups. Long after such formulaic rituals had dissipated, covered cups continued to be regarded as symbols of honor and recognition suitable for presentation upon important occasions. The covered cup was both commemorative and communal, and in America, it is among the largest and most ostentatious of the silver forms that survive from the early colonial period.[11]

The second category of colonial silver at Harvard, that of the fellow commoners, provides insights into a socially elite category of students virtually unknown today. Patterning itself upon Oxford and Cambridge, Harvard admitted young men who were entitled to certain perquisites and absolved from certain chores. Although fellow commoners were linked in the first Harvard College laws of 1642–46 with those who were "a Knights Eldest Sonne or of Superior Nobility," a chief concern for attaining this status seems to have been financial.[12] The revised Harvard College Laws of 1734 describe the obligations and privileges of such students as follows:

> None shall be admitted fellow commoner, unless he first pay one hundred pounds to the College Treasurer, for the time being; being for the use of the College; and every fellow commoner shall pay double tuition-money.
> Fellow commoners shall have the privilege of dining and supping with the fellows [that is, the faculty] at their table in the hall, and shall be excused from going on errands, shall have the title of Masters, and shall have the privilege of wearing their hats as masters do, but shall attend all duties and exercises with the rest of the Class, and be alike subject to the Laws and Government of the College; and shall sit with their own Class, and in their place in the Class at the worship of God in the hall and meeting-house.[13]

Following traditions established at Oxford and Cambridge, Harvard made a further demand upon such students in its Laws of 1655, requiring that:

> Every Fellow Comoner shall bring a peice of Silver plate to the Colledge to the value (at the least) of three poundes with his Name ingraven thereupon, which hee may have the use of whilest hee shall abide in the Colledge and shall leave it to the propriety of the Colledge when hee departs from it.[14]

Although dining with the faculty and being exempted from running errands for the upperclassmen may not seem like matters of consequence today, it meant fellow commoners probably ate better than most students (dining at the head table meant more food and hotter food) and that fellow commoners probably didn't have to perform tasks such as delivering messages very often.

Estimates of the number of fellow commoners at Harvard during the seventeenth and eighteenth centuries vary from nine to thirteen. Surviving documents and artifacts suggest that not all fellow commoners fulfilled the obligation of presenting a piece of silver to the College.[15] Compliance seems to have been highest during the 1650s, when the practice of accepting such privileged students was most common. References to fellow commoners appear in the Harvard Laws as late as 1767 but the last student granted this status was George Ball of the class of 1734; there is no indication he ever presented a piece of plate to the College.[16] Early fellow commoner silver mentioned in College inventories from 1654 onward includes such items as a "beer bowle," a "fruite dish," a "sugar spoon," and a "stone pott tipt with silver," the latter no doubt a piece of heavy German stoneware with silver mounts.[17] Alas, we know the College's

Fig. 4. Edward Winslow (1669–1753), The Hedge Tankard, Boston, Massachusetts, ca. 1689–1710. Silver; h. 5 13/16 in. Courtesy of the Fogg Art Museum, Harvard University Art Museums, Loan from Harvard University (879.1927). © President and Fellows of Harvard College, Harvard University.

stone pot must have been broken, or at least stripped of its mounts, by 1683. The inventory of that year includes "2 silver wine bowls" followed by the notation "1 Earthen jugge tipped with silver – of this ye 2 wine bowls abo[ve] mentioned were made."[18] These new wine bowls were probably the small, light-weight dram cups or wine tasters that were popular during the late seventeenth century.

Only three pieces of Harvard fellow commoner silver still survive. The oldest piece has the most anonymous association with this exalted category of student; it is a tankard of circa 1690–1710, made by Edward Winslow of Boston and simply engraved "Harvard College" on its base (fig. 4). The early history of this object is unknown and its identification as fellow commoner silver rests upon indirect evidence. It is probably the "Lesser Tankard, not mark'd" which was recorded as weighing twenty-two and a half troy ounces in the 1736 inventory of Harvard's plate.[19] Although the Winslow tankard does not bear the name of its donor, a fellow commoner seems most likely. It does not correspond to any corporate gifts recorded in the Harvard Donation Books, nor does its inscription conform to the norms for tutorial silver.[20] A letter written in 1828 by Professor Levi Hedge to the college treasurer regarding Harvard property helps to confirm its attribution, however. Hedge stated:

> I have . . . in my possession a silver tankard, the history of which is the following. In the early times of the College, the sons of such gentlemen as claimed privileges of nobility, were distinguished from the other students by the privilege of dieting at the Tutor's table in the Commons Hall. When these young gentlemen left the College, it was common for them to make some present to the gentlemen, as a body, in whose society they had been thus distinguished; and in this way several tankards and other articles of plate had been collected as ornaments for the Tutors' table. On the discontinuance of this distinction, the articles collected were distributed among the officers, to be used as common property by them and their successors. When I was elected Tutor, in January 1795, I found the tankard . . . in the chamber of my predecessor. The tankard was damaged by long use — it was bruised in sundry places, and the lid was off. I have had it repaired by a silver smith, so that it is in a better state now than when it came into my hands. I have regarded . . . the tankard . . . as departmental property, to be transmitted to my successor in office.[21]

In contrast, the tankards given by the brothers John and William Vassall (class of 1732 and 1733 respectively) are very straightforward fellow commoner gifts (fig. 5). The tankards bear inscriptions on their bases which read "Donum Joannis Vaſsale Commensalis A: D: 1729" and "Donum Guilielmi Vaſsale Commensalis A: D: 1729."[22] "Commensalis" is the Latin term commonly used to designate a fellow commoner at both Cambridge and Oxford; the term was frequently used at colonial Harvard as well. The 1729 date in the inscription records the year in which the brothers were accorded the status of fellow commoners.[23] In addition to the inscriptions, the canting (or punning) arms of the Vassall family are also engraved on both tankards.

The final category of silver associated with Harvard during the colonial period was tutorial plate. Unlike corporate gifts and the tribute demanded from fellow commoners, tutorial silver was given by the students not to Harvard, but to their instructors or tutors. Tutorial silver would have been the category of plate that most involved the students at colonial Harvard, and it is the type of collegiate silver that survives in the greatest quantities. Yet ironically, it is the category least imbued with symbolic meaning at Harvard today. This lack of extraordinary associational value no doubt results from the fact that tutorial silver was never meant to be the property of Harvard *per se*, but only of its faculty.

As with fellow commoner silver, the practice of presenting tutorial plate originated at Oxford and Cambridge and was carried over to Harvard with one very important distinction. Tutorial silver at Oxford and Cambridge became the property of the colleges, not the tutors. Each class of students entering Harvard

Fig. 5. Joseph Kneeland (1698/99–1740), The John Vassall Tankard, Boston, Massachusetts, ca. 1729. Silver; h. 6 13/16 in. Joseph Kneeland, The William Vassall Tankard, Boston, Massachusetts, ca. 1729. Silver; h. 6 13/16 in. Gifts to Harvard College from John Vassall (Class of 1732) and William Vassall (Class of 1733) in 1729. Courtesy, Fogg Art Museum, Harvard University Art Museums, Loans from Harvard University (873.1927, 874.1927). © President and Fellows of Harvard College, Harvard University.

was assigned to the care of one tutor, who, barring occasional exceptions, instructed that class in its studies throughout its four undergraduate years. A tutor's income consisted of a salary from the College and a fixed amount from each student determined on a uniform basis by the school. Gifts of silver, often of a significant value, further supplemented a tutor's remuneration. Since tutors were responsible for important decisions such as the placing (or ranking) of students within their class and the advancement of individuals in their studies, the presentation of private gifts and tutorial plate no doubt included some self-serving aspects on the part of Harvard students and their families.

Requirements for being appointed as a tutor included having at least a bac-calaureate degree, an intention to take the pulpit (that is, to become a minister), and being unmarried. Throughout the seventeenth and eighteenth centuries, two to four tutors were in residence at Harvard at any one time, with the College president occasionally serving in such a capacity in addition to his administrative duties. Although qualifications for the post remained intact, the Harvard College Laws of 1767 reformed the tutorial system and required individuals to specialize in specific areas of instruction. At this point the practice of presenting "public gifts" — that is, tutorial silver — was also discarded, and the levying of "one shilling and nine pence lawful money quarterly, in addition to the tuition-money" from each scholar made up the loss of income to the tutors.[24] Thus, it is clear that at least by 1767, Harvard College recognized that gifts of tutorial plate had been a very real and expected part of an instructor's salary. Not surprisingly, given the reform of Harvard's system of instruction, the practice of presenting tutorial silver seems to have died out in the early 1770s.

The earliest known piece of tutorial silver still extant is a basin made by Jeremiah Dummer and presented to William Brattle in 1695 (fig. 6). In his will dated June 21, 1716, Brattle stipulated that "I bequeath and present to the Church of Christ in Cambridge for a baptismal basin, my great silver basin, an inscription upon which I leave to the prudence of the Revd President [of Harvard College, John Leverett] and the R^d Mr. Simon Bradstreet." The basin is inscribed "Ex dono Pupillorum 1695 A Baptismall Bassin consecrated, bequeath^d & presented to the Church of Christ in Cambridge, his Dearly beloved Flock, by the Rev^d. Mr Wm Brattle Pas^t of the S^d Church: Who was translated from his Charge to his Crown, Febr 15:1716/17."[25] Despite its later use within the church, this basin was not initially meant to be an ecclesiastical object. As a piece of tutorial silver, it was intended for the personal, domestic use of the tutor.

Among the best-known pieces of tutorial silver are those given to Nicholas Sever. Many of Sever's silver objects remained in the possession of his descendants into the twentieth century and were the subject of a brief monograph written by Richard Hale in 1931. Nicholas Sever's tenure as a Harvard tutor extended from 1716 until 1728; over the course of those twelve years he amassed approximately thirty-five pieces of silver. For example, a pair of candlesticks (fig. 7), a pair of chafing dishes, and a small tazza were presented to Sever in 1724; they are all engraved with that date and "Donum Pupillorum."[26] This Latin phrase, or the variant "ex donum pupillorum," is the most frequently found inscription on tutorial silver. It translates as "the gift of the students." The majority of the pieces of Sever silver that survived into the twentieth century were the work of John Burt. Although this may be a coincidence, it seems more likely that Nicholas Sever had some influence on the choice of silversmith.

Harvard's longest-standing tutor, Henry Flynt, held office for fifty-five years and his personal diaries offer valuable insight into the practices associated with tutorial silver. Each year, seniors apparently selected one of their number to collect money for the tutor's gift. Although Harvard's regulations of 1732 stated "that the summ given by each pupil may not Exceed 20*s* and that each pupil

Fig. 6. Jeremiah Dummer (1645–1718), basin, Boston, Massachusetts, 1695. Silver; diam. 14 ⅝ in. First Parish Church, Cambridge, Massachusetts, on loan to the Museum of Fine Arts, Boston. Photo, courtesy Museum of Fine Arts, Boston.

may be at his Liberty to give any thing or not, *any custom not withstanding*," entries in Flynt's diaries suggest he often knew in advance of the actual presentation who had contributed to the gift (and how much), its total monetary value, and the form it was to take.[27] This perhaps explains the apparent patronage of a small number of silversmiths by longtime tutors such as Sever and Flynt.[28]

Given the largess bestowed upon Nicholas Sever during twelve years at Harvard, it is not surprising that Henry Flynt attained an even greater cupboard of plate during his extensive association with the college. In 1716 Tutor Flynt received a pair of candlesticks made by John Coney; they are now in the collection of Historic Deerfield (fig. 8). Two years later, the students presented Flynt with an impressive two-handled covered cup, also by John Coney and weighing in excess of thirty-seven troy ounces (fig. 9). Father Flynt, as he was called by his young charges, eventually also accumulated a tankard, porringer, teapot, and coffeepot, among other items. According to an 1851 publication by

193

Fig. 7. John Burt (1692/93–1745/46), pair of candlesticks, Boston, Massachusetts, 1724. Silver; h. (each) 7 3/16 in. Courtesy, Winterthur Museum, bequest of H. F. du Pont (1967.1443.1-.2).

John Bartlett, Harvard students — perhaps in desperation — even presented Flynt with a silver chamber pot in a morocco leather case after parading it through the streets of Cambridge on commencement day. Sadly, despite the determined efforts of several scholars, the Flynt thunder mug has never been located.[29]

By the 1760s, gifts of tutorial silver became more standardized and the presentation of a tankard and a pair of canns became the norm. Stephen Scales received a tankard, now in the collection of the Museum of Fine Arts, Boston, from his students in 1768 (fig. 10). It is in extraordinary condition, with placement lines for the engraving still visible on the front of the body. The R. W. Norton Art Gallery in Shreveport, Louisiana, owns the matching pair of canns (fig. 11). As noted before, the Latin inscriptions that recorded its presentation distinguish tutorial silver. Gifts from early in the colonial period tended to be engraved simply with "ex dono pupillorum," a date, and perhaps the tutor's arms if space permitted. Pieces from the 1760s and 1770s, however, show a marked tendency toward lengthier and more florid inscriptions. The tankard and pair of canns made by Samuel Minott for presentation to Joseph Willard in 1770 are among the latest pieces of tutorial silver known to have survived. The tankard and one cann are now in the Museum of Fine Arts, Boston; the Yale University Art Gallery owns the second cann. The Latin inscription on the tankard's body opposite the handle is five lines long and more engraving covers the tankard's base (fig. 12).

Fig. 8. John Coney (1655/56–1722), pair of candlesticks, Boston, Massachusetts, 1716. Silver; h. (each) 7 in. On permanent loan to Historic Deerfield, Inc., from Henry N. Flynt, Jr. (62.43a,b)

Fig. 9. John Coney (1655/56–1722), two-handled covered cup, Boston, Massachusetts, 1718. Silver; h. 10 in. Courtesy of the R. W. Norton Art Gallery, Shreveport, Louisiana (F1104).

195

Fig. 10a. Paul Revere (1734–1818), tankard, Boston, Massachusetts, 1768. Silver; h. 9 ⅛ in. Museum of Fine Arts, Boston, Gift of Edward N. Lamson, Barbara T. Lamson, Edward F. Lamson, Howard J. Lamson and Susan L. Strickler (1986.678).

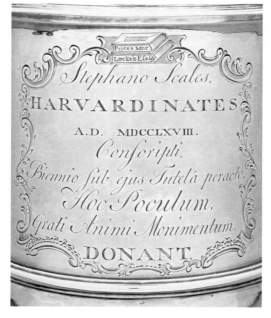

Fig. 10b. Detail of engraving on Revere tankard illustrated in fig. 10a.

Fig. 11. Paul Revere (1734–1818), pair of canns, Boston, Massachusetts, 1768. Silver; h. (each) 5 in. Courtesy of the R.W. Norton Art Gallery, Shreveport, Louisiana (F1210–11).

Fig. 12. Samuel Minott (1732–1803), tankard, Boston, Massachusetts, 1770. Silver; h. 8 ⅞ in. Museum of Fine Arts, Boston, The Philip Leffingwell Spalding Collection. Given in his memory by Katharine Ames Spalding and Philip Spalding, Oakes Ames Spalding, Hobart Ames Spalding (1942.246).

A wealth of documentation for Harvard's colonial silver abounds in the College's official records, in diaries, and in letters. A privately owned artifact is considered to have an exceptionally detailed provenance if its descent from one individual to another can be traced, but the more specific facts of how that teapot or tankard was used, where it was stored, and whether it was valued are almost never discernible. Yet it is precisely such information that can be teased from the written records of Harvard's silver.

Six inventories of Harvard's plate survive from the colonial period; four were compiled in the seventeenth century (1654, 1656, 1674, and 1683) and two in the eighteenth century (1736 and 1781). While the content and format of each inventory varies, collectively they contain descriptions of each object, names or initials of donors, values, weights, and physical locations. Although it is not known precisely why these lists were drawn up, it seems noteworthy that, with the exception of the 1656 account, each inventory was conducted within one year of a transition in Harvard's presidency. This suggests that the president was invested with the fiduciary responsibility for the school's tangible assets, including its silver. However, such a supposition raises questions about the absence of inventories for the other years in which administrative transitions occurred. Disregarding the motivations behind the creation of these inventories, the richness and variety of their details offers insights into the use and function of silver at Harvard College and raises questions as well. The terminology employed by the various inventory-takers suggests that certain forms had, at least initially, specific uses. For example, the "beer bowle" cited in 1654 retained this identity (with spelling variations) until 1683, when it became simply a "bowle." Fifty-three years later in the next accounting it had disappeared without a trace.

The inventories also indicate the plate at Harvard was usually kept in the College Buttery during the seventeenth century.[30] This conformed with "Certain Orders by the Schollars & officers of the Colledge to bee observed. written 28 March 1650," which stipulated the butler and cook were to deliver a written inventory of all "vessels & utensils great & smal" to the president every quarter, and that scholars would be fined for taking vessels without the butler's permission. If a student did not return an item in time for the next meal, he would be charged for its full cost; if a piece was damaged or lost, double its value would be levied. Should a vessel in the care of the butler be stolen, the guilty student would be penalized for four times the object's value.[31]

Although only two inventories of Harvard's silver survive from the eighteenth century, much information concerning the functional role of the College plate can be gleaned from these documents. Together with references from other records such as the College Books and personal diaries, a portrait of change from the usage of the previous century emerges. President Benjamin

Wadsworth, who was in office from 1725 to 1737, compiled an index to College Book II which included the entry "College Plate . . . to be lodg'd wth ye President," indicating perhaps that the butler was no longer responsible for the direct oversight of the silver.[32] This notation also suggests that by Wadsworth's time the College plate was not being used regularly at the head table in Commons, as had been the case during the earlier period.

Tutor Henry Flynt's diary offers clues to the dispensatory power which the College's president wielded by the eighteenth century. On June 25, 1729, Flynt recorded that "President [Benjamin Wadsworth] of his own Motion Sent mee by a Freshman Browns beaker."[33] The beaker in question was undoubtedly the piece of fellow commoner silver noted two years earlier in Wadsworth's diary:

> Sr Brown Senr, July 5. 1727 Having taken his Degree ye preceeding week, and now going to abide at home, brought a Silver Cup or long Beaker, as a gift of his Father's ye Honble Coll. Samuel Brown to ye College, in consideration yt ye said Sr Brown in his first year at College, was excus'd from serving as Freshmen usually do.[34]

Although Flynt's diary entry does not stipulate if Wadsworth gave him the beaker outright or simply consigned it to his use temporarily, the beaker is not listed among the College plate in the 1736 inventory, nor does it appear in subsequent compilations. The disappearance of this object from Harvard records, which postdate Flynt's diary notation, suggests that the transaction was considered permanent.

Harvard Librarian Andrew Eliot in "An Account of Grants, Donations, and Bequests to Harvard College" drew up an eighteenth-century compilation of earlier inventories, with dates for the acquisition and/or first record of each object. Midway through the summary compilation of Harvard's silver, this source contains the marginal notation "Several of these pieces of Plate are not now to be found." Check marks next to entries in the list conform, with one exception, to objects that are still extant today.[35] If indeed President Wadsworth's presentation of Brown[e]'s beaker to Tutor Flynt was indicative of an acceptable disposition of the College's plate, the practice may account for the missing objects.

Extensive supporting materials for the 1781 inventory provide insights into the dispersal of Harvard's silver during the late eighteenth century. On April 4, 1780, the Harvard Corporation empowered a committee to receive from the executrix of the late Professor Winthrop "any Mathematical Instruments, Books, Plate, or any other articles in her possession belonging to the College." One week later the Corporation met again and, after hearing the committee's report,

> Voted. That the Tankard received by them remain with the President till farther

orders; & that the same Comtee. be continued & desir'd to receive any articles that may yet remain in the hands of the Executrix. & to make enquiry respecting the Plate belonging to the College, for what uses, & by whom it was given, & in whose hands it is now deposited, & make Report at the next Meeting in order that a fair acco. of the whole may be recorded in the Corporation books.[36]

Apparently the committee was not able to accomplish their mission by the next meeting of the Corporation for no report was entered on their behalf. This may have been due to the resignation of President Samuel Langdon, for on September 15, 1780, the Corporation voted "That the late President Langdon be desired to deliver to Mr. Professor Wigglesworth the Cabinet, with all the books & papers belonging to the College, the Plate in his possession to remain till further order."[37] On July 4, 1781, a charge was given once again "That Mr. Wigglesworth & Mr. Williams be a Committee to take an inventory of the College plate to be recorded in the College books, and to take receipts of each of the Governors of the College, for any part they may have in their hands." At the same meeting, it was also agreed "That Mr. Professor Williams have the use of a small silver tankard, which was formerly in the possession of the Honble. Dr. Winthrop (deceased), he giving a receipt in the College books."[38]

Finally, on August 28, 1781, the Corporation accepted the report inventorying the plate, more than sixteen months after the initial charge had been issued.[39] During the interim a new College President had been appointed, and one piece of silver (the tankard inscribed "Harvard College") had been retrieved from the estate of one faculty member and had been signed out to the use of another. The five individuals who were recorded as in possession of the College silver were all members of the Corporation. By 1781 when the inventory was completed, Edward Wigglesworth was both acting president of Harvard and the Hollis Professor of Divinity. Not surprisingly, most of the plate was in Wigglesworth's care, including the out-of-fashion great salt and the two covered cups given by Governor Stoughton and Colonel Browne. More functional forms for personal use were assigned to the other Corporation members. Samuel Williams, Hollis Professor of Mathematics and Natural History from 1780 to 1788, was in possession of the tankard marked "Harvard College" on its base. Each of the three tutors was also given the use of a drinking vessel. John Mellen and William Bentley, who both served as tutors from 1780 to 1783, had the Vassall tankards. Charles Stearns, whose tutorial tenure at Harvard was limited to 1780–81, held "A large Tankard with a variety of Arms."[40]

Although no formal inventories are extant from the nineteenth century, a variety of records suggest a continuation of the pattern of settling Harvard's accounts during the transition to a new presidential administration. Within these documents are details that reveal how the College plate was being used and who had custodial responsibility for it. A volume of original letters to Corporation officers from a transition year is entitled "College Property within the Walls – 1828." In response to the request for personal accounts of all Harvard possessions scattered between the faculty and officers of the school, it is filled with lists of books, furniture, scientific apparatus, and even skeletal specimens!

Four entries contain information relevant to Harvard's silver. The first pertinent missive is an inventory dated 1828 and signed by the outgoing president, John Thornton Kirkland. In a postscript to the list, Kirkland added "Two silver Tankards, and one silver salt-cellar."[41] The postscript addendum of the three pieces of College plate suggests they may have been forgotten items amidst the jumble of furnishings. A later and more expanded list of College possessions compiled by President Kirkland on April 15, 1828, offers a similar sense of oversight. It commences with the salutation "To the Committee of the Corporation of Harvard College, appointed to receive the Papers, Books, & other articles of College Property, in the hands of the President," and contains an extensive, detailed, room-by-room list of furnishings. The west parlor, east parlor, east back room, lower front entry, front chamber west end, dressing room of the east front chamber, and back study are all duly inventoried. Once again, at the end of the list, a final notation is added: "The Communion service, a Christening Bowl & two Urns used at Commencement, in the closet of [the] back chamber, East end."[42] These entries reveal that Harvard's president had personal custody of some of the school's silver, including the great salt, two tankards (probably those given by the Vassalls), and the two covered cups given by Stoughton and Browne. The latter, now called "urns," were apparently ceremonially used or displayed at Commencement by 1828. By that point Harvard had also established a College chapel, and the silver for that office was also stored in the president's custody.

But what of the remainder of Harvard's plate? Henry Ware, Hollis Professor of Divinity, served as acting President during the transition year of 1828–29. It appears that he assumed custody of all of Harvard's plate during that period, for one last entry in the receipts of 1828 links him with the College's silver. It lists seven pieces of "Plate belonging to the Chapel" and six pieces of "Old Plate belonging to the College." The latter list specified two urns with covers, three tankards with covers, and one salt; all of these items were "Delivered to the Rev. Dr. Ware April 15. 1828. by the Committee of the Corporation."[43] One year later the silver was recalled and delivered to the new president.[44]

The 1830s and 1840s were a time of introspection for Harvard College. In 1833 the first history of the school was posthumously published; the work of Harvard Librarian Benjamin Peirce, it was entitled *A History of Harvard*

University from Its Foundation, in the Year 1636, to the Period of the American Revolution. In recognition of the two hundredth anniversary of the College, in 1836 the Corporation requested President Josiah Quincy to write an official history. His two-volume *History of Harvard University* appeared in 1840. The self-reflection generated by these works may have been responsible, at least in part, for the earnest interest in Harvard's colonial plate that is evident in the archival records pertaining to 1847. Additional factors also engendered an awareness of symbolic links with Harvard's past. The year of 1845–46 had been a period of presidential transition once again, and the installation of Edward Everett as the new president was accompanied by much public fanfare.[45] Everett's inauguration ceremony was patterned after the earliest known description of such an occasion at Harvard. When John Leverett was installed as the school's president in 1708, the College record books, charter, seal, and keys were prominently featured as symbols of office.[46] The latter items were undoubtedly the keys to the College buttery where the silver was then stored; long since lost, the originals were replaced at Everett's installation with a set of oversize silver keys, inscribed in Latin, which were commissioned from Obadiah Rich (working ca. 1830–50) of Boston by Harvard's Steward, William Gordon Stearns, in 1846.

A letter of March 5, 1847, from Stearns to President Everett suggests that the records of the College silver were in disarray, and that efforts were being made to correct the situation:

> Mr. Whitney informs me that he gave to Mr. Francis, former Treasurer of the College, in or about the year 1830, a receipt for the plate used in the Commons viz. the spoons; but that he has never given any receipt for any other articles of plate. If this receipt so given to Mr. Francis cannot be found, Mr. Whitney is willing to give a new one.
>
> The nine large spoons marked "H.C." are used only at Commencement dinners, and may, if you desire it, be placed with the other articles not used in the halls.
>
> As there is no room in the Bank vault for the plate chest, I would respectfully suggest that an order be penned "that the plate be kept in Gore Hall."
>
> I send herewith a Copy of the schedule made by Dr. Harris.[47]

Harvard Librarian Thaddeus William Harris drew up the attached compilation; it includes a mixture of chapel silver, colonial plate, and newer items (such as the spoons) that were in current use in the dining hall. Harris's list is noteworthy for being the first to include silversmiths' marks as identifying features. His choice of terminology (e.g., goblet for tankard) is both curious and confusing:

2 Bread Plates
1 Large Urn, marked, on the bottom, "John Burt."
1   do.   "   on the side I.C. [these initials are enclosed in an oval]

1 Goblet, marked on the bottom "Donum Gululmi Vassall, Commensalis, 1729."
1 do.   marked the same, except "Johannis" for "Gululmi."
1 old Goblet, on the bottom "Harvard College." (Repaired)
1 Salt, marked I^GE [these initials are enclosed in a square]
 4 Drinking vessels, for Communion.
12 [this appears to be a total of the number of items listed above]
72 large silver spoons, College Arms.
 9   "   "   "   "H.C."
189 (originally 192) silver tea spoons, College Stamp.[48]

Harris's personal interest in Harvard's plate is reflected in a letter that he wrote to President Everett on March 5, 1847, the same date as Stearns's epistle:

> The College plate, which has been in the hands of a silver-smith, was brought to the Library this morning, and was unpacked in my presence, & compared with the list, & found to correspond with it. . . .
>
> I venture to suggest . . . that the Donor's names should be graven on all the articles, which are not so marked already. The donor of the large covered bowl or vase, I determined immediately on examination, to have been Govr. Stoughton. Probably the Corporation books, and the coats of arms & cyphers on the plate, will enable you to ascertain the names of other donors.[49]

Harris's letter provides the source for the decision to embellish Harvard's colonial plate with mid-nineteenth-century inscriptions recording donors' names. The resulting upside-down legend engraved on the great salt is indicative of the form's unfamiliarity by 1847 (fig. 13). Although Harris correctly identified it in his listing of plate, the great salt was old-fashioned enough to cause confusion about its orientation. However, the letter's initial reference to the plate being with a silversmith is unclear. Was it stored there? Or had it been sent to a craftsman for repair and cleaning?

Surely the latter was the case later in the year, when Harris's suggestion was acted upon. In a letter of August 27, 1847, to President Everett, Harris describes the inscriptions which were added to the great salt and to the gifts of Stoughton and Browne; he identifies the cups as "the two large vessels of silver, set upon your table in the College Hall, on Commencement day, [that] may be called vases." The missive continues:

> The inscriptions are beautifully engraved, and the glass dish, made to fit the "old salt," is very neat and appropriate. These three vessels, with the two tankards, given by the Vassals, and another tankard, of very ancient pattern, the gift of an unknown donor, were much admired yesterday (Thursday), when they were displayed for examination on a table in the Library. I am sorry that the College Keys [given in 1846 by Stearns] were not at hand to be shown at the same time. . . .
>
> It was my intention to have sent my history of the salt seller, with some account of the vases to the Cambridge Chronicle; and I am glad that you propose to include the former, entire, in your report of the remarks made at the dinner.

Fig. 13. The Great Salt (see fig. 1) as engraved and photographed upside down.

> Until last winter, when these ancient & valuable gifts were brought from their hiding-places, there were not two persons belonging to College who knew anything about them, and their history was entirely forgotten.[50]

Harris's need to identify the correct name for the vessels displayed at the President's table on Commencement day and his remarks associating the new silver keys with the older objects indicates the transformed function of the colonial plate as signifiers of history and status. It mattered little if the original use of the great salt was misunderstood; its role as a symbol of continuity with the past was sufficient. Certainly this was its effect on the noted chronicler of Harvard graduates, John Langdon Sibley. He recorded in his diary:

> August 26 [1847] Thursday . . . Yesterday several pieces of plate belonging to the College, having just been marked & polished were exhibited at dinner; one of which, was given by <u>Harris</u>, brother of the wife of President <u>Dunster</u> was given in 1644.[51]

Thaddeus William Harris's interest in Harvard's colonial silver continued throughout the remainder of 1847, culminating in a rather rambling letter written in December of that year to the Honorable Samuel A. Eliot. Although his notes and correspondence indicate he hoped to publish an essay on the topic, no such writings have been located.[52]

From 1847 onward the role played by Harvard's colonial plate changed considerably. During the seventeenth century silver was demanded of fellow commoners and was used in an almost medieval manner at a head table emphasizing the hierarchical class structure which existed among the president and officers of the Corporation, tutors, fellow commoners, senior and junior sophisters, sophomores, and freshmen. Silver was held in regard during this period because it had monetary value, functional usefulness, and class significance. Throughout the eighteenth century the role of silver at Harvard College gradually diminished. Changes in dining styles rendered certain forms, like the great salt, obsolete. The large two-handled covered cups given by Stoughton and Browne were primarily ceremonial in nature and their use appears to have been limited to public occasions such as commencement dinners. Although silver continued to have monetary worth, its function within Harvard was largely commemorative as both corporate and tutorial gifts. Vestiges of the class associations formerly ascribed to the plate can be found in the practice of granting personal use of College silver to officers such as the president, professors, and tutors.

If the records of 1828 and 1847 are to be believed, by the nineteenth century Harvard's silver was largely neglected and forgotten. While the president still retained possession of some of the plate, other objects had been lost or damaged. The reclamation of Harvard's colonial silver in 1847 as potent symbols of the past seems to have been the direct result of the larger historical concerns of an institution celebrating its bicentennial. Although the original function of the great salt was lost, the object was imbued with new status as the oldest relic of the college. Later in the nineteenth century Harvard's silver assumed yet another dimension. In the first book to evaluate the production of American colonial silversmiths, John H. Buck gave Harvard's plate equal footing with the work of craftsmen from England and Europe. His 1888 publication may illustrate the great salt upside-down and suggest that the Stoughton cup was the product of a London silversmith, but his imprimatur upon these objects as works of art is nonetheless significant.[53] Harvard's colonial plate has played a role in almost every major art museum exhibition of American silver from the seminal first presentation in 1906 at the Museum of Fine Arts, Boston, onward. By 1959 the College felt it was necessary to ask the assistance of the leading expert on American colonial silver in discouraging loan requests for the Harvard "State Plate."[54]

Today, key pieces of Harvard's silver are publicly displayed at the University's Fogg Art Museum. At "considerable public occasions," like a fête for Prince Charles in honor of Harvard's 350th anniversary or the installation of a new president, the six surviving colonial vessels are brought out "to be regarded."

Although the functional nature of Harvard's silver has changed dramatically over the centuries, its symbolic role as a signifier of status and continuity endures.

Notes

1. "A Sterling Occasion," editorial, *Harvard Magazine* 94, no. 3 (January/February 1992).

2. This essay is drawn from Janine E. Skerry, "Silver at Harvard College" (Ph.D. diss., Boston University, forthcoming). The author would like to thank Harvard University for permission to cite from its archives and museum files.

3. William C. Lane, "Early Silver Belonging to Harvard College," *Publications of the Colonial Society of Massachusetts* (hereafter cited as *CSM*) 24 (1923): 165–76; Mrs. Yves Henry (Kathryn C.) Buhler, "Harvard College Plate," *Connoisseur Year Book* (1955): 49–57.

4. Each of these three categories of collegiate silver has some precedent in the practices established earlier at Oxford and Cambridge Universities in England. Tutorial silver at those institutions, however, was given directly to the colleges rather than to the instructors. Harvard seems to have been unique among the early colonial American colleges in its extensive use of silver based on English collegiate precedents. Three pieces of American colonial silver associated with Yale College are known today: a teapot dated 1745 made by Jacob Hurd (1702/03–58) of Boston for the Rev. Thomas Clapp, who became rector of Yale College in 1740; a bowl dated 1745 made by Cornelius Kierstede (1657–1757) of New York and New Haven, Connecticut, for Thomas Darling, who served as a tutor at Yale College from 1743–1745; and a tankard dated 1750 made by Samuel Casey (ca. 1724–ca. 1780) of Rhode Island for Ezra Stiles, tutor at Yale from 1749–55. Although each object is engraved with a presentation inscription, there is little evidence to suggest the systematic use of tutorial silver at Yale. See Patricia E. Kane, ed., *Colonial Massachusetts Silversmiths and Jewelers: A Biographical Dictionary* (New Haven, Conn.: Yale University Art Gallery, 1998), 611, and Kathryn C. Buhler and Graham Hood, *American Silver: Garvan and Other Collections in the Yale University Art Gallery*, 2 vols. (New Haven: Yale University Press for the Yale Art Gallery, 1970), 1:231, 289–91.

5. An Account of Grants, Donations, and Bequests to Harvard College: 1636–1776 and 1784–1839, compiled by Andrew Eliot, MS, 2 vols., Harvard University Archives, UAI.15.420. Additionally, six inventories specifically detailing Harvard's silver survive from the colonial period. Taken in 1654, 1656, 1674, 1683, 1736, and 1781, they record from four to fifteen silver or silver-mounted objects with the peak number of items listed in the 1683 accounting.

6. Benjamin Peirce, *A History of Harvard University, from Its Foundation, in the Year 1636, to the Period of the American Revolution* (Cambridge, Mass.: Brown, Shattuck, and Company, 1833), 17.

7. The great salt was previously owned by Harris's sister, Elizabeth, and her first husband, the Rev. Jose Glover; after Glover's death Elizabeth wed Dunster in 1641. With antecedents in the so-called standing salts of the medieval period, a great salt was an extremely fashionable, rare, and elitist table ornament in the American colonies during the 1640s. It would have remained on the table throughout the meal, functioning as much as a symbol of rank as a condiment container. A small circular depression between the three scrolls or knops was the receptacle for the salt; after the main courses the knops on top of great salt would be used to support a dish for fruit.

8. Peirce, *History of Harvard University*, 64–65, 70–71.

9. Samuel Sewall, *The Diary of Samuel Sewall*, ed. M. Halsey Thomas (New York: Farrar, Straus & Giroux, 1973), 1:449–50.

10. *CSM*, 16:846.

11. Philippa Glanville, *Silver in England* (London: Unwin Hyman, Ltd., 1987), 327–28.

12. Samuel Eliot Morison, *The Founding of Harvard College* (Cambridge: Harvard University Press, 1968), 336.

13. Peirce, *History of Harvard University*, appendix XX, 125–26. The sum of money required prior to the acceptance of an individual as a fellow commoner seems to have varied over time. In this same volume Peirce quotes a letter of 1831 from Paine Wingate, class of 1759, who cites the amount as "thirteen pounds six and eight pence" (313).

14. Excerpted from "The Lawes of the Colledge published publiquely before the Students of Harvard Colledge, May 4. 1655," as reprinted in *CSM*, 31: 331. Dating from the seventeenth century, fellow commoners at Cambridge were required to present either a piece of plate or the funds to purchase of such an item; the custom of fellow commoner silver survived at Cambridge until the end of the nineteenth century. See R. A. Crighton, *Cambridge Plate* (Cambridge: Fitzwilliam Museum, 1975), 7–8.

15. See *CSM*, 15:cxxxix–cxl. The addition of George Ball, class of 1734, as a fellow commoner was not noted in this source; he would raise the number such students to thirteen.

16. *CSM*, 31:348, 380. On August 18, 1730, the President and Fellows of Harvard voted to admit George Ball as a fellow commoner. Faculty Records I, 1725–1752, 30, MS Harvard University Archives, UA III 5 5.2.

17. These items are among those noted in the Harvard College silver inventories taken in 1654 and 1656. See College Book III, 40–42, as published in *CSM*, 15:207–9.

18. See College Book I, 85, as published in *CSM*, 15:73.

19. See College Book IV, 192, as published in *CSM*, 16:651.

20. Kathryn C. Buhler has noted that the inscription "Harvard College" is rather exceptional on the school's colonial plate. See Buhler, "Harvard College Plate," 55. Although this is correct with regard to English language designations for the College, variations of its name in Latin are frequently found on tutorial plate of the 1760s and 1770s. See, for example, Buhler, "Harvard College Plate," illus. x and xi; also see Janine E. Skerry, " The Revolutionary Revere: A Critical Assessment of the Silver of Paul Revere," in *Paul Revere — Artisan, Businessman, and Patriot* (Boston: Paul Revere Memorial Association, 1988), 49–50, 164.

21. College Property within the Walls — 1828, 53, MS, Harvard University Archives, UAI 20.828. Due to Professor Hedge's letter, this object has been dubbed the Hedge tankard within some of Harvard's records.

22. The arms, consisting of a cup or *vase* and the sun or *sol*, are a rebus for the name Vassall. The armorial crest also conforms, being a ship or *vessel*. For more on this, see F. B. R[obinson], "The Vassal Tankards," *Harvard Alumni Bulletin* 38, no. 3 (October 11, 1935): 82–84; and Harold T. Bowditch, "The Vassal Tankards — To the Editor of the Bulletin," *Harvard Alumni Bulletin* 38, no. 5 (October 25, 1935): 154–55.

23. The Faculty Records for October 18, 1729, indicate that "Agre'd yt Vassal Sophimore & Vassal

Freshman be admitted Fellow-Commoners." See Lane, "Early Silver," 172.

24. See *CSM*, 31:351, 377; and Peirce, *History of Harvard*, 246–47.

25. As quoted in E. Alfred Jones, *The Old Silver of American Churches* (Letchworth, Eng.: Arden Press for the National Society of the Colonial Dames of America, 1913), 109. Jones states that Brattle was a tutor and fellow at Harvard from 1707 to 1717. This does not appear to be correct.

26. See Richard Walden Hale, *Catalogue of Silver Owned by Nicholas Sever, A.B. 1701, in 1728* (Boston: privately printed, 1931).

27. Edward Thomas Dunn, *Tutor Henry Flynt of Harvard College, 1675–1760* (Ann Arbor, Mich.: University Microfilms, 1968), 380–81.

28. Among the several silversmiths patronized by Henry Flynt, John Coney and Jacob Hurd seem to have been especially favored with Harvard tutorial commissions.

29. Walter M. Whitehill, "Tutor Flynt's Silver Chamber-pot," in *CSM*, 38:360–63.

30. Located conveniently near the Commons Hall, Harvard's Buttery functioned much like a combination storehouse, student commissary, and recording office during the early years of the college. Dining utensils were stored there, and sundry foods, beverages, and supplies were available for sale to the students. In addition to maintaining accounts of student purchases, records of attendance were also kept by the Butler, who was in charge of the Buttery. See *A Collection of College Words and Customs* (Cambridge, Mass.: John Bartlett, 1851), 35–38.

31. College Book I, 49–50, as published in *CSM*, 15:32–34.

32. College Book II, Index by Benjamin Wadsworth, as published in *CSM*, 15:xix, xxii.

33. Diary of Henry Flynt, II, June 25, 1729, as cited in Dunn, *Tutor Henry Flynt*, 308–9.

34. Benjamin Wadsworth's Book Relating to College Affairs, 47, as published in *CSM*, 31:467. The presentation of this beaker to President Wadsworth fulfilled Brown[e]'s obligations as a fellow commoner, for on September 2, 1723, he was admitted to that status by a vote of the Corporation. See College Book IV, 92–93, as published in *CSM*, 16:500–501.

35. An Account of Grants, Donations, and Bequests . . . , vol. 1, 1636–1776, MS, Harvard University Archives, UAI.15.420. Harvard Librarian William C. Lane dated this summary to 1773 for reasons which are unclear to this author. See William C. Lane, "Early Silver Belonging to Harvard College," *CSM*, 24:169.

36. Corporation Records III, 1778–1795, 74–75, MS, Harvard University Archives, UAI 5 30.2.

37. Corporation Records III, 1778–1795, 94–96, MS, Harvard University Archives, UAI 5 30.2.

38. Corporation Records III, 1778–1795, 124, MS, Harvard University Archives, UAI 5 30.2.

39. Corporation Records III, 1778–1795, 128, MS, Harvard University Archives, UAI 5 30.2.

40. Stearns's undated receipt to the Committee for the tankard blazoned its arms in detail and indicated that a portion of the ornament had broken from its cover. When he resigned his appointment as tutor on November 8, 1781, Stearns's letter to Professor Wigglesworth indicated that he would deliver the tankard along with a receipt for books and student records in his possession. No further mention of the tankard has been found beyond this date. See Undated Receipt from Mr. Stearns to Revd. Professor Wigglesworth, Committee Report on College Silver 1781, College Silver, Letters and Manuscripts, MS, Harvard University Archives, HUB 3790.2; and Charles Stearns to [The Revd. Professor Wigglesworth and] the Corporation, November 8, 1781, College Silver, Letters and Manuscripts, MS, Harvard University Archives,

HUB 3790.2. Information on officers of the College, their status, and tenure has been obtained from *Quinquennial Catalogue of the Officers and Graduates of Harvard University, 1636–1905* (Cambridge, Mass.: privately printed, 1905).

41. College Property within the Walls — 1828, 43, MS, Harvard University Archives, UAI 20.828.

42. College Property within the Walls — 1828, 68, MS, Harvard University Archives, UAI 20.828.

43. Harvard constructed a University chapel in the early nineteenth century and began to acquire gifts of ecclesiastical silver for it shortly thereafter. College Property within the Walls — 1828, 67, MS, Harvard University Archives, UAI 20.828.

44. College Book XI, June 18, 1829. See College Silver, Letters and Manuscripts, MS, Harvard University Archives, HUB 3790.2.

45. John Rosario-Pérez, "A Ceremonious Tradition," *Harvard University Gazette*, October 18, 1991, 14–15, 17.

46. Sewall, *Diary*, 1:585.

47. G. W. Stearns to President Everett, March 5, 1847, Harvard College Papers, 2nd series, 1846–47, 14: 271, MS, Harvard University Archives, UAI.5.125.

48. Harvard College Papers, 2nd series, 1846–47, 14, 272, MS, Harvard University Archives, UAI.5.125.

49. T. W. Harris to President Everett, March 5, 1847, Harvard College Papers, 2nd series, 1846–47, 14: 270, MS, Harvard University Archives, UAI.5.125.

50. T. W. Harris to President Everett, August 27, 1847, Harvard College Papers, 2nd series, 1847–48, 15:110–111, MS, Harvard University Archives, UAI.5.125.

51. Private Journal of John Langdon Sibley of Harvard, 1846–1865, 1:132, MS, Harvard University Archives, HUG 1791 72.10.

52. See transcribed notes of Thaddeus W. Harris, 1847, in College Silver, Letters and Manuscripts, MS, Harvard University Archives, HUB 3790. Also, T. W. Harris to Hon. Samuel A. Eliot, December 19, 1847, Harvard College Papers, 2nd series, 1847–48, 15:249–50, MS, Harvard University Archives, UAI.5.125.

53. J. H. Buck, *Old Plate, Ecclesiastical, Decorative, and Domestic: Its Makers and Marks* (New York: Gorham Manufacturing Company, 1888), 97, 108–9.

54. Agnes Mongan, Fogg Museum, to Mrs. Yves Henry Buhler, Museum of Fine Arts, Boston, November 19, 1959, MS, Inventories and Notes on Silver, Registrar's Files, Fogg Art Museum, Harvard University.

Regional Topics

Glistening Reflections of Stability:
The Roles of Silver in Early Maine

EDWIN A. CHURCHILL

IN 1760, two Massachusetts silversmiths, Paul Little of Newbury and John Butler of Boston, made their way northeast to Falmouth (present-day Portland) in the province of Maine.[1] The first silversmiths to settle in this region, they signaled the beginning of a new era. Previously, the area (fig. 1) had been an unpromising site for such urban-oriented, specialized artisans. Throughout the 1600s, Maine towns were tenuous entities stretching along the coast from Kittery to Pemaquid as non-nucleated ribbon settlements of perhaps four to five hundred people each.[2] A society made up largely of farmers, woodsmen, a few basic artisans, and even fewer merchants, it did not provide an economic base sufficient to support workers of fine metals.[3]

Despite the absence of silversmiths, silver was present in a fair number of early Maine homes. Still, evidence suggests that even the best collections were relatively modest; in fact, only a few estate inventories list silver items individually. The earliest items, a silver cup worth £1 10s. and money valued at £6.11.3, appeared in the 1648 estate of Joseph Cross of Wells.[4] Kittery merchant Robert Cutts's 1674 listing included a porringer, a dram cup, a small beaker and nine spoons, whole and broken, valued at £3. The 1681 inventory of Major Brian Pendleton, from Saco and then Portsmouth, included a tankard and three cups, valued at £6.1s.[5] Several inventories included larger but unenumerated silver holdings. Records reveal that in 1663 Kittery entrepreneur Nicholas Frost had £14.13.7 worth of plate, and in 1689 Edward Rishworth of York left behind silver valued at £12.[6] The contrast with a quarter century later is striking. Kittery merchant and public official Elihu Gunnison left an estate of 308 ounces of silver including, among other items, one large and one quart tankard, a punch bowl, two chafing dishes, a large and a small salt, a two-handled cup, a teapot, two candlesticks with snuffer and stand, six porringers, one small and one pint cann, a salver, and three pepper boxes.[7]

Despite the marked humbleness of seventeenth-century holdings, the region underwent a period of significant growth and development that peaked in the early 1670s; had it continued, silversmiths and other specialized craftsmen

213

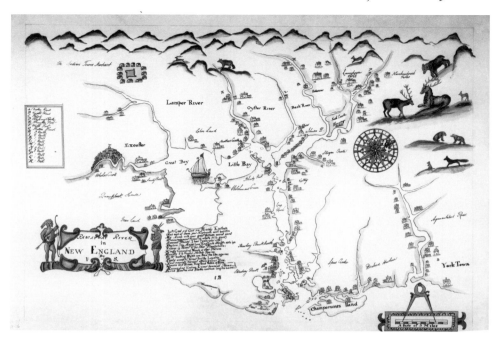

Fig. 1. Unidentified artist "I.S.," *Pascatway River in New England*, ca. 1660. Ink on paper; h. 19 in., w. 29 in. Maine State Archives, Baxter Rare Map Collection.

would have arrived in the area long before Butler and Smith. Such possibilities dissolved in 1675 with the outbreak of warfare between English settlers and local Native Americans, who were soon joined by the French allies. Fighting raged for another half century, and during the most vicious period of conflict, English settlers remained only in the most southerly communities of Kittery, York, and Wells.[8] Not until the late 1720s had warfare diminished to the point that recovery and expansion became possible. Again, the region developed rapidly – a growth evident by midcentury in both the quantity and variety of silver and gold items held by inhabitants. A new sophistication also emerged, embodied in such specialty forms as salvers and spout cups and in the increasingly frequent appearance of jewelry and small gold objects. When Quebec fell to the English in 1759, the Maine frontier became safe from further hostilities.

Silver in Maine, like gold, both symbolized and influenced societal patterns that matched, in many ways, those suggested by English scholar Grahame Clark, who observed that "precious substances contributed most effectively to the functioning of traditional societies by defining roles in the functioning of the hierarchy of authority."[9] In the region, as probably was true in general, the significance of these objects operated in three broad fields. At the most basic level, always present, was the economic worth and solvency of the metal per se.

Building on this foundation, the families that could afford silver tended to use it for different forms of self-presentation: in the community at large, sometimes even internationally, to display and validate their status and power, and in the smaller community of their own families and closer social circles to cement family ties and solidify societal patterns. Of course, these factors overlapped in the seventeenth and eighteenth centuries. Individual pieces often served in two or even all three categories, but here I will discuss them within the contexts that delineate those functions as clearly as possible.

A body of extant items, ranging from major pieces both personal and ecclesiastical to smaller personal objects, suggests a substantial presence of silver in the homes of the wealthier and some of the middling inhabitants of early Maine. The broadest patterns of ownership can be reconstructed from the evidence of these pieces and the archival records that testify to the many pieces that no longer exist. A search through all extant inventories covering the periods 1630–1710, 1725–1735, and 1750–1760 revealed 160 estates that listed silver and gold items.[10] The evidence demonstrates that individual holdings varied dramatically. While most examples, especially larger pieces such as tankards, canns, and porringers, belonged in affluent homes, a fair number of objects were owned by individuals of modest means.[11] For example, the 1752 estate of aforementioned Kittery merchant Elihu Gunnison, worth £1,806.3.10, contained more than three hundred ounces of plate — including tankards, porringers, cups, a cann, and a chafing dish.[12] Conversely, the less affluent 1754 estate (£345.19.4) of York inhabitant Andrew Grover listed but one silver entry, "silver Bows of Spectacles."[13] Spoons, with over three hundred listed examples, appeared in inventories more frequently than any other object. Rings took a distant second — sixty-nine instances — and clothing-related items such as buckles, buttons, and jewelry followed closely behind.

Early Maine probate inventories, like nearly all colonial records, unequivocally tied the value of silver holdings to the weight of the metal. Objects frequently appear in these lists with their value designated by total weight, value per ounce, and total price. In the fairly typical 1752 inventory for Elihu Gunnison, for example, one finds "a large Silver Tankard wt 48 oz; & a punch Bowl wt 28 1/2 oz; one large Salt wt 13 oz," all followed by a tally at the end for "308 ounce a 6/8 pr ounce . . . £102.13.04."[14] The final balancing of the 1756 estate of Thomas Perkins included the sale of a half dozen large silver spoons for £4.6s, the same value given them in the original appraisals.[15] The same estate contained tankards, porringers, and canns that were not sold but probably passed on to heirs.

Silver wares may have been viewed as a buffer in case of economic need, since any piece could, if necessary, be converted into cash or otherwise used against outstanding obligations.[16] Owners, however, rarely embraced this option —

215

Fig. 2a, b. New England sixpence and Spanish colonial two real, 1600s. Silver; diam. (sixpence) ¾ in., diam. (two real) ½ in. Maine Bureau of Parks and Lands.

and certainly not with enthusiasm. When one acquired a new object, the price included not only the value of the metal but about an equal cost for the workmanship. Conversely, when an item went up for sale, potential buyers usually preferred not to pay much over the cost of the metal.[17]

The high commodity value of the metal itself, however, becomes apparent when one examines the economic role accorded fine metal coins.[18] Gold and silver coinage, while more easily used for exchange than fine metal objects, still carried a commodity value that far exceeded its role as a medium of exchange; simply put, coins were worth substantially more than their face value. This meant that a ten shilling coin would be valued at a good deal more than ten shillings worth of cloth, gunpowder, or any other commodity. In a 1666 legal dispute, for example, the court decided that along with "merch. Goods" the defendant was to pay eleven shillings "in money . . . to [be] rated at money price . . . [which] comes to £1,7s,10d" or 27s.10d — a 253 percent increase.[19]

As with other fine metal objects, coins appeared more frequently in the holdings of Maine's wealthier inhabitants, where they clearly functioned as an asset in and of themselves. Their possession generally arose from and indicated an involvement in the world of colonial commerce, where coinage constituted a major commodity in regional and international trade. Because British mercantile policy discouraged the export of gold and silver, colonial merchants sought out other sources of specie, consequently creating a significant cache of non-British coins in colonial coffers (fig. 2), a fact reflected in early probate records.[20] While many documents simply listed "money" or "coins," followed by a value, others noted gold French guineas, Spanish doubloons, and Portuguese moidores along with higher value silver coins such as Spanish pieces of eight, and Dutch "rix" or "lion" dollars.[21] What is clear is the desire by Maine inhabitants, often "of the better sort," to transfer these assets to chosen heirs, thereby bolstering the recipient's economic worth.

•

Despite its fundamental value, silver and gold coinage never carried the status of fine metal presentation and personal items. Objects fashioned from gold and silver, unlike coinage, suggested an individual's distinct stature in his community via the basic fact of a smith's custom workmanship, including such details as engraved initials, inscriptions, and emblems. The value placed on custom pieces suggests the most basic societal aspirations of New England colonials. In their hearts, early Maine settlers were displaced Englishmen and women. They wanted to reconstruct England in the New World, legally, politically, and socially. Every community had a number of outstanding families (by their standards), who sought, as did their Old Country models, income, prestige, power, and the pleasant way of life.[22]

Since Maine's more prosperous inhabitants came largely from England's West Country and Midlands, among other rural communities, they were probably most familiar with the luxuries of the country seat rather than those of the urban home.[23] That model served the colonials well, given their position on a wilderness frontier. Substantial tracts of land, and often the timber that grew on it, served as a key facet of their income and provided the stage for their demonstration of status and power.[24] Mimicking English gentry, Maine's leading citizens built large homes (fig. 3) and adorned them with the finest furnishings.[25] The details of Major Nicholas Shapleigh's Kittery estate depict just such a home. The house "was a full two-story structure of ten rooms plus cellar and garret."[26] In his "Inner rowme," Shapleigh had a bedstead with curtains, valances, and other accessories, and an "ovell Table & Carpet . . . one chest of drawers & Cubbard Cloath . . . 6 Turkey chayres . . . [&] 4 leather Chares" along with other wares, and in "the Major's Lodging Rowme" were "one standing bed & a tumble bed with furniture, a little table & a Carpet . . . a Court Cupboard . . . a iron bound Case . . . [&] one spanish Chest."[27]

Shapleigh's holdings also included "70 ounches of plate," probably displayed on the chest of drawers in the inner room or on the court cupboard in the Major's lodging room.[28] This kind of display, as much as the furniture, was an integral part of the use of material culture to demonstrate one's societal stature. The silver holdings of Sir William Pepperrell, Jr., of South Berwick were probably the most dramatic of those held by any Maine family. The son of prosperous merchant Colonel William Pepperrell, Sir William had an illustrious public service career, capped by his role as the colonial leader in New England's 1745 capture of Louisbourg. For this, he was given a barony and received an extraor-

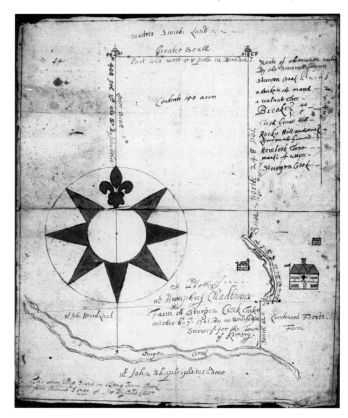

Fig. 3. William Godsoe (1650–ca.1730), *Mr. Humphrey Chadbourne Farm [in Kittery, Maine] . . . , October 6th-7th-1710.* Ink on paper; h. 10 in., w. 12 in. Maine State Archives, Early Court Documents.

dinary silver presentation service (discussed below).[29] Prior to that time, Sir William had acquired other silver objects, such as candlesticks and flatware.[30] Some of the extant pieces exemplify the embodiment of station in silver design. For example, a teapot made by Jacob Hurd of Boston, ca. 1735–45 (fig. 4), has a stylish globular body with splayed foot, curved spout, and wooden scroll handle.[31] Pepperrell also owned a mustard caster by Andrew Tyler of Boston, ca. 1723–30, with a baluster body, high domed cover, and simulated piercing pattern. The initials "P/WM" engraved on it refer to William and his wife, Mary (Hirst) Pepperrell.[32]

When the rapidly growing community of Falmouth, Maine, began attracting new political and commercial figures during the second quarter of the eighteenth century, the newcomers also used silver to declare their status. Samuel Moody (d. 1729) and Edmund Mountford (d. 1739), for example, both left large holdings of silver. Moody, raised in Portsmouth and a graduate of Harvard College, spent a period in the ministry before taking up a career in the military. After serving as commander of Casco Fort (near Falmouth) from 1707 to 1713, he settled in Falmouth and took up an active life as a public official.

Fig. 4. Jacob Hurd (1702/03–1758), teapot, Boston, Massachusetts, 1735–45. Silver, h. 5 ⅛ in. Yale University Art Gallery, Mabel Brady Garvan Collection (1930.1350).

When he died in 1729 he left an estate of ninety-one-and-a-half ounces of silver.[33] Mountford, the son of a successful Boston merchant, purchased a substantial property in Falmouth in 1726 where he later served in a number of offices, including selectman, deputy sheriff, and town agent. Mountford's very "handsome cupboard of plate" comprised two tankards, four porringers, two cups, a pepper box, over a dozen spoons, a pair of tea tongs, gold rings, buttons, necklaces, and miscellaneous other items.[34] Through these acquisitions, "newcomers" such as Moody and Mountford allied themselves with the well-established families, such as the Pepperrells.[35]

The role or roles that a collection or sometimes just a single piece of silver played in its owner's life actually covered a wide range, from the modest expressions of fairly simple homes to the "handsome cupboard of plate"[36] displayed on chests, cupboards, and shelves in halls, parlors, or bedrooms in the great houses.[37] Some objects, such as buttons or buckles worn on the clothes or small objects used mostly within the home, functioned in relatively subtle ways. More prominent objects could be central to social occasions and public perceptions, from a tea set used in the home to a silver-hilted sword worn at a man's side. Several owners ornamented their pieces with family coats of arms in the conscious effort to establish themselves with the status of English gentry,[38]

Fig. 5. Unknown maker, cann, ca. 1750–77. Silver; dimensions unknown. Present location unknown. Photo, courtesy Joseph Frost.

as did the Frosts and Pepperrells of Kittery and the Howards of Fort Western (later Augusta) (fig. 5).[39] Some pieces were actually designed and made specifically for presentation on special occasions, from the domestic rites of birth and marriage to public ceremonies honoring an individual's participation in large historical events (fig. 6).

Among the general population, possessing several small pieces or a larger cache of silver objects must have provided a sense of personal satisfaction, even where ownership was only a distant echo of the resources of the elite. Small objects destined for little more than personal use played similar roles in middling as well as wealthy families. Not surprisingly, records indicate that the most substantial body of silver filled primarily personal and familial roles. Unlike large display pieces, the significance of these smaller objects revolved around their use, either personally or as part of relational activities. They frequently had particular personal significance to the owner, an importance reflected in engraved initials, names, and symbols, markings that many times signaled their societal roles as well. Unlike display items that might be upgraded with better pieces, these pieces were cherished for their strong personal ties.[40]

The most commonly owned pieces, according to the evidence, would have

Fig. 6. Nathaniel Hurd (1730–1778), teapot, Boston, Massachusetts, 1766. Silver, h. 5 ⅞ in. Courtesy, Winterthur Museum (1960.1045).

been the silver spoons. The phenomenon suggests a number of things, including a relatively widespread desire to own silver and the importance of fulfilling that desire in even the most domestic venue. While many silver spoons came as tea service sets — an acquisition that required some wealth — quite a number of homes kept only one or two silver spoons.[41] In those instances where inventories listed "two spoons" or "a pair of spoons," a husband and wife probably held the small treasures for their personal use.[42] In those instances recording one spoon, the head of the house might have reserved it for his or her personal use. Quite often, inventories listing a small number of spoons included one or two small companion hollowware pieces, thereby evoking the image of an individual, a couple, or a small family group sitting down for a snack or meal with favorite personal items. The 1664 estate of John Mitchell of Kittery, for example, noted "Two silver spoones and two cups," and his fellow townsman Thomas Spencer left behind "a silver cupp & spoon" in 1681. The practice still flourished over a half century later: Falmouth resident George Welch owned "1 Silver Spoon [&] . . . 1 Silver Bowl" (1754) and his neighbor Thomas Woodbery held "1 Silver Cup [&] . . . 2 spoons Ditto [silver]" (1758).[43] Domestic intimacy rather than status dynamics seem the heart of such groupings.

221

Fig. 7. Unknown makers, spoons, found at Pemaquid, Maine, ca.1740–70. Silver; various dimensions. Maine Bureau of Parks and Lands.

The combination of the two urges seems evident in the desire to declare personal possession of even the most simple pieces, such as a number of extant spoons that carry individuals' initials. Three apparently unrelated silver spoons (fig. 7), found during the excavations of the various forts at Pemaquid, have the owners' initials engraved on the backs of the handles — a pattern echoed in a number of pewter spoons recovered from the *Defence*, a colonial privateer sunk in Stockton Spring Bay in 1779.[44] In both instances, the initials probably served to distinguish each man's spoon in a military living situation; nonetheless, the practice also suggests a strong sense of personal ownership that would have had a parallel among civilians.

Other small items most easily categorized as "personal gear" may have filled a purpose similar to that served by silver spoons. Objects for personal adornment, including jewelry, and small articles for personal use were apparently more widely accessible and therefore suggest a broader class spectrum of ownership.[45] The jewelry most likely belonged to women as did a small number of articles for personal use. These, interestingly, relate to women's domestic roles.

Fig. 8. Unknown maker, thimble, Pemaquid, Maine, ca. 1660–75. Silver;
h. ¾ in. Maine Bureau of Parks and Lands.

Silver bodkins — needle-shaped tools for pulling tape through hems — were listed in two probate inventories, as were two silver thimbles.[46] One silver thimble was recovered from a Maine archaeological site (fig. 8).[47] These were most likely small treasures to their owners, objects that were passed from generation to generation.

Other small, portable articles belonged primarily to men. Some, such as tobacco and snuff boxes, added elegance to the use of a New World product — the owner would certainly have displayed his silver box when taking its contents. A gentleman could similarly show his silver watch as he checked the time, whether necessary or not. And what better way to express one's status than with a silver-headed cane, several of which appeared among the accoutrements of eighteenth-century Maine's well-to-do.[48]

Like small silver items, objects of personal adornment, such as clothing accessories or jewelry, combined the pleasure of enhanced appearance with a visual statement of status. Although such items eventually became accessible to the middling as well as the upper classes, such finery was initially the province of the elite. Seventeenth-century "sumptuary laws" legislated the distinction; in 1651, the Massachusetts Bay Court expressed its

> Utter detestation & dislike that men or women of Meane condition, educations, & callinges should Take upon them the garbe of gentlemen, by the Wearainge of gold or silver lace, or buttons, or Points at their knees, to walke in great bootes; Or women of the same ranke to weare silke or tiffany hoodes or scarfes, which though allowable to persons of greater estates, or more liberall education. Yet we cannot but judge it intollerable in psons Of such like condition.

The court therefore ordered that

> No person within this jurisdiction . . . whose visible estates, reall & psonall, shall not exceede the . . . value of two hundred pounds, shall weare any gold or silver lace, or gold or silver buttons, or any bone lace above two shillings p[er] yard, or silke hoodes or scarfes, uppon the penalty of ten shillinges for every such offence; & every such delinquent to be psented by the graund jury.[49]

Soon after, the Bay Colony usurped Maine, which then theoretically fell under the same restrictions. In fact, there is little evidence that the 1651 act or other sumptuary laws were ever enforced in early Massachusetts or Maine. Probate records suggest that there was no great need to repress overdressed inhabitants of the lesser sort in Maine — few could afford the cost of fancy dressing.

Nonetheless, small silver pieces fashioned for personal adornment were clearly popular with a relatively broad range of consumers. Of all clothing accessories, buckles were apparently the most popular, judging from the frequency with which they turn up in inventories. Silver buckles appear in fifty-one different inventories and include eighteen instances of shoe buckles, ten of knee buckles, and four of neck buckles.[50] The inventories also mention two gold buckles — one "a golden Buckle for a Girdle" and the second a "gold Brest Buckle."[51] Silver-plated buckles appear nowhere in the records, but two were excavated at Pemaquid, one a seventeenth-century specimen of silver-plated brass with an elaborate floral relief pattern and the second a plain object that still retained its tongue and tongs.[52] Most likely, such items belonged to less affluent individuals who desired the effect of precious metal at less cost.

According to numbers in the inventories, buttons were almost as popular as buckles among Maine inhabitants. Both silver (twenty instances) and gold (thirteen) were mentioned in probate records. The most striking example among these was an entry for "1 Doz. & four Silver twist Buttons" noted alongside a "Silver Cord & Twist." The entries frequently categorized buttons by a specific function or a type of garment, such as "sleeve" buttons, "three silver bottons for a shift," and silver buttons for "one fine broad cloth coat."[53] A number of other silver clothing fasteners identified in the records seem to have fulfilled the same function as buttons. Inventories listed a group of three studs and "1 Holland Jacket [with] Plate Hook & oyes"; excavations at Pemaquid also produced a pair of sleeve or cuff links.[54]

One finds a modest quantity of jewelry, primarily gold or silver, in early Maine probate records. Rings were the most frequently noted items — not surprising, since instances of wedding and mourning bands would have augmented the numbers of those rings owned simply for personal adornment.[55] Necklaces, all of gold, were noted in five estates, and in one case the necklace was listed with gold earrings. Such necklaces were probably, in most instances, simple strings of hollow spherical gold beads.[56] A number of jewelry owners also had silver clasps and gold "lockets" — a contemporary term for clasp.[57] These were generally used to secure necklaces and bracelets. The term "jewelry" could also encompass certain essentially decorative clothing accessories, such as Charles Frost's "best plate hatband" and "my other hatband," noted in his 1724 will; a "Silver Hat lace" listed in a 1753 inventory; and a "read ribbon flowered with Silver" in a February 1727/8 estate.[58] These examples, rare as they are, probably provide only a faint reflection of materials Maine inhabitants used to ornament their clothes and bodies.

◦

While many of the smaller personal or domestic pieces allowed a sense of esteem or luxury across a relatively broad swath of the colonial class structure, the major role of silver (and gold) was highly conservative. In most of its forms, it maintained a highly stratified societal hierarchy. Early on, it symbolized and verified the power and status of the "Great Families" and later signaled the wealth and enhanced stature of a rising merchant class. Thus, in most of its forms, silver belonged almost exclusively to the persons or in the homes of the most powerful families. At its most outspoken, silver took the form of formal presentation pieces — often large, elegantly engraved, and otherwise ornamented — that were designed to signal an individual's importance throughout the community and beyond. The ritualized presentation of these pieces and their later display in the recipients' homes under-scored the significance of the owners' accomplishments, usually war related, and provided enduring symbols of their special status and power.[59]

Several pieces of early Maine presentation silver celebrated local leaders involved in New England's unexpected 1745 capture of hated Louisbourg, the French stronghold on the north shore of Cape Breton. The project had great support in Maine, whose inhabitants were fearful of both nearby Native Americans and French soldiers. William Pepperrell, Jr., already a prominent merchant and politician, led the expedition. His experience with frontier defenses and Maine militias, albeit limited, essentially equaled the credentials that anyone else had to offer. It certainly proved sufficient when he led his colonial forces, with British naval support, to victory over the French at Louisbourg on June 28, 1745.[60]

New Englanders were enormously proud of having captured Louisbourg without the assistance of British ground forces, as were the British who presented Pepperrell with a magnificent group of silver objects. After the success of the siege, Pepperrell sailed to London, where he received a hero's welcome. King George II conferred on him the title of baronet, making him the first native-born American to attain such status. His silver, comprised of many pieces, came from a number of British dignitaries. The Lord Mayor of the City

Fig. 9. John Wirgman (active 1745–1756), two-handled covered grace cup, England, 1749. Silver; h. 13½ in. Portland Museum of Art, Portland, Maine. Museum purchase with gifts from Mr. and Mrs. Joseph William Pepperrell Frost, Estate of William P. Palmer III, and five anonymous donors (1982.123.3).

of London presented him with an elaborately repoussé rococo-style grace cup, engraved with his coat of arms on one side (fig. 9) and his crest on the opposite. British Rear Admiral Peter Warren, who had provided vital naval support during the siege, gave Pepperrell another grace cup and a salver. The cup bore a finely engraved design of flags, fortifications, ships, and other military devices surrounding the Pepperrell coat of arms. On the other side of the cup appeared the inscription:

> In token of their Friendship Harmony
> & Success at the Conquest of the Island of
> Cape Breton PETER WARREN Esq. Rear
> Admiral of the Blue presents this piece of
> Plate to Sr. Wm. Pepperrell Bart, Louisbourg
> Surrendered to his Majesty's forces
> 17 June 1745.

The footed salver was a large piece — fifteen and three-quarters inches in diameter and more than fifty-seven ounces in weight — and just as richly decorated with the same inscription and the Pepperrell arms. Elegant engravings also

Fig. 10. John Burt (1693–1746), tankard, Boston, Massachusetts, ca. 1745. Silver; h. 8 ¼ in. Yale University Art Gallery, Mabel Brady Garvan Collection (1930.1195).

graced a teapot and two small salvers included among the gifts, also from Warren.[61] Pepperrell's presentation pieces became an integral part of the ruling-class role he played in his colonial home. Back in Maine he lived the life of a gentleman with such amenities as a deer park, a retinue of servants, and a luxurious barge manned by a black-liveried crew. Not surprisingly, he entertained lavishly.[62]

Jeremiah Moulton of York received a handsome tankard (fig. 10), presented, according to family tradition, by William Pepperrell. Moulton, who had been captured by Indians as a child, later gained substantial military experience during the English-Native warfare of the 1720s. In the 1745 siege, he distinguished himself in his command of Maine's third regiment. The tankard bears an engraving of the Moulton arms on the front; on a circular handle terminal appears a map with "Lewisburg" above and "Taken by the English / July 17, 1745," below.[63]

Another Louisbourg officer, Colonel Joseph Frye (later major general) also received a tankard for his military service, though his vessel commemorated an event later in his career. Born into a prominent family in Andover, Massachusetts, Frye grew up to pursue an active political and military career. In

1755 Colonel Frye went to Nova Scotia as part of the British and colonial force that deported and dispersed many of the Acadians living in the region.[64] Late in the spring of the following year, his fellow officers from the battalion presented him with a handsome tankard. The piece bore his coat of arms on the front, his ciphered initials on the handle terminations, and a detailed inscription:

> To Joseph Frye, Edq. / Colonel and Commander-in-Chief of / the forces in the services of the / Province of Massachusetts Bay / And late Major of the Sec-/ ond Battalion of General / Shirley's Provincial / Regiment./ This Tankard / From a just sense of his care and conduct / of the Troops while under his command / at Nova Scotia and a proper appre-/ciation of his Paternal Regard / for them since their return / to New England is / presented by / His Most Humble Servants / The Officers of Said Battalion./ Boston, Apr. 2od, 1757.[65]

Reflected in the tankard was a great respect and appreciation for Frye's leadership, service, and prestige, attributes that after further military service in the colonial wars won him a substantial land grant in 1761. The tract of land, in western Maine, became Frye's home in 1771, attracted several more families, and ultimately grew into present-day Fryeburg.

The first known piece of Maine presentation silver honored entrepreneurial rather than military aptitude. A medal struck in 1687 commemorated the achievement of William Phips, one of colonial Maine's most successful inhabitants, who retrieved a substantial treasure from a sunken ship.[66] Born in Woolwich, Maine, Phips became a shipbuilder and merchant, operating in Maine until the Indian Wars drove him to Boston. In 1683 Phips embarked on an audacious scheme: he determined to retrieve the cargo from a Spanish treasure ship that had gone down in shallow waters off the island of Hispaniola in the West Indies forty-four years earlier. Phips's initial effort — backed by King Charles II — ended without the expected retrieval, but he did manage to bring up some silver. His efforts proved more successful on the second try, funded by Christopher, duke of Albermarle, and some friends when King James II proved unwilling to follow his predecessor's example. Diving in forty-three to forty-eight feet of water with equipment largely designed by Phips, the sailors secured £300,000 sterling worth of silver, gold, and jewelry — an enormous haul!

Phips traveled to London to receive the accolades of his grateful backers, and he was an instant sensation. The duke gave Phips a golden cup and the king, who got a share of the booty despite his unwillingness to invest, knighted Phips, had a medal struck in his honor, and made him High Sheriff of New England. Soon after, Phips was appointed Royal Governor of Massachusetts. Unlike the unique pieces described above, the Phips medal, made from dies by Englishman George Bower, was produced in a number of copies in both gold and silver. According to one source, the king presented medals to the ship's

Fig. 11. George Bower (d. 1690), medal, London, 1687. Silver; diam. 2⅛ in. Maine State Museum (96.75.1).

officers, to each of the promoters, and occasionally to his friends and favorites. Most likely, Phips would have done the same. The medal (fig. 11) carried on its face the portraits of James II and his wife with the motto "IACOBVS· II·ET·MARIA·D·G·MAG·BRI·FRAN·ET·HIB·REX·ET·REGINA" (James II and Mary, by the grace of God, King and Queen of Great Britain, France and Ireland). The treasure hunter was rendered on the reverse: a ship, at a distance, with a boat in the foreground over a wreck. Above the image appeared the phrase "·SEMPER TIBI PENDEAT HAMUS·" (Let thy hook always hang [i.e., persevere]), and below, "NAVFRAGA REPERTA / 1687" (Shipwreck recovered / 1687).[67]

The small size of the medals distinguished them categorically from the later presentation pieces, which were large enough to display on top of a cupboard or on a shelf. Judging from the wear on the medal at the Maine State Museum, it seems likely that its owner carried it with him to show as a symbol of an exceptional relation to Phips or even to the king. For Phips, of course, this direct expression of the king's favor must have proven highly useful as he strove for political and social betterment.

For a demonstration of social status and power, nothing could compete with such presentation pieces, which were by definition very limited in distribution. Nonetheless, Maine's leading citizens could express their importance with a variety of smaller silver objects, still limited to those with privilege but much easier to acquire. Personal luxuries, such as seals and seal rings, and social luxu-

Fig. 12a, b. Unknown maker, seal, ca. 1680s. Silver; h. ¾ in. Maine Bureau of Parks and Lands.

ries, such as fine tea sets, could serve the purpose well. The region's elite also indulged in a diminutive form of "presentation," typically presenting one another with small commemorative objects to mark familiar rites of passage.

Those individuals with the privileges of good education and solid wealth could own personal seals and seal rings, often of gold and at times of silver or brass, which they used to impress wax seals on documents. Of the few extant Maine-related seals, the earliest is a gold ring plowed up in 1855, with gold and silver coins, on Richmond Island. It has an elaborately engraved bezel with the initials "CV" centered over a lovers' knot, and inside the band appears the motto "United [conjoined hearts] death only parts." Two seals, one brass and silver, came out of an excavation at early Pemaquid. The silver piece, the more elaborate of the two, has a molded post bored at the top for a string or cord (fig. 12). The initials "DH" over a heart, enhanced by delicate foliate engraving, appear on the face. This seal may have belonged to Dennis Hegeman, a prominent Pemaquid citizen, who was captured by the Indians in 1689 and was still living in Canada in 1693.[68] Among the seals recorded in probate records (six silver items and two gold), one stands out because of the efforts made by the family to pass it through a line of first-born sons. In the will he wrote on January 7, 1690/1, Charles Frost, Sr., bequeathed "My gold seal ring" to his oldest son, Charles. In turn, on September 24, 1724, Charles Frost, Jr., willed "Unto my Eldest Son Charles Frost . . . my Seal ring." The ring still resides in family hands.[69]

Beginning early in the eighteenth century, some gentlemen had the opportunity to demonstrate their status and power with a most select article, the silver-hilted sword, which symbolized the leadership, wealth, and gentility of their possessors. The men who owned them usually carried military titles as well, ranging from captain to colonel, and they also usually had substantial holdings of silver. For example, William Whipple of Kittery owned overall 117 ounces of silver; Thomas Perkins of Arundel owned a distant but still impressive 42 ounces. In general, the list of the owners' surnames — Pepperrell, Frost, Hammond, Gerrish, Whipple, Lithgow — reads like a "Who's Who" for early Maine.[70]

The small, relatively poor population of the seventeenth century and the region's limited military preparedness probably explains the rarity of such swords during the early years. Finally, in the eighteenth century after the most devastating wars had passed, Maine gradually recovered and even began to experience some growth and prosperity. Local militia forces were reestablished and upgraded and new military leaders emphasized their stations with fine silver-hilted swords. Major Charles Frost owned the earliest silver-mounted Maine swords on record. These appear in his 1724 will as "my best Plate Hilted Sword, . . . my other Plated hilted Sword, . . . and my Silver Hilted Seymater." Then records are silent about such swords until the 1750s, at which point eight turn up: four from Kittery, three from Berwick, and one from Arundel.[71] Two swords, still extant, testify to the period in between. Sir William Pepperrell wore one (fig. 13) at the siege of Louisbourg.[72] Another descended through the Lithgow family. Stamped twice on the handguard with "AT," the piece has been attributed to the Boston silversmith Andrew Tyler (1692/93–1741). However, it is also marked "1701" thereby casting doubt on the attribution. The name "CAPT. WM. LITH-GOW," engraved on one side of the counterguard, identifies the owner as the William Lithgow who served as commander of St. Georges Fort (Thomaston, Maine) in the 1730s and later at one of several Kennebec River forts.[73]

Somewhere between the presentation items, which bespoke the recipient's importance so broadly, and the more democratic domestic pieces, such as silver spoons, are the larger and much more elaborate silver objects that served as social ritual centerpieces in well-to-do homes. The tea set epitomized this role in the daily lives of Maine's middle and upper classes. The expense of the tea, the costly equipage, and the leisure time needed to enjoy the tea ritual and to learn the associated etiquette eliminated the less affluent from participation. In the genteel families that could afford it, the tea ceremony served to cement family ties and maintain social networks, with regular reinforcement through frequent reciprocal visits. From such gatherings evolved advantageous marriages, profitable business deals, and useful political agreements. Furthermore, for the participants, they were a lot of fun.[74]

Probably due to Maine's long years of military conflicts, tea drinking reached the region a bit late. Probate records dated as late as the mid-1730s reveal no tea-

Fig. 13. Unknown maker, sword with silver hilt and scabbard, ca. 1720–25. Silver, steel, leather, wood; l. 38 ½ in. Massachusetts Historical Society, Gift of Usher Parsons (0308.01–02).

related articles. Over the next decade and a half, though, tea consumption became well established.[75] Teaspoons, often in sets of six and probably intended for entertaining, appeared in nineteen Maine inventories; frequently, the same list included other tea paraphernalia. For example, Thomas Perkins, Jr.'s 1756 inventory noted "1 Tea Pot [probably ceramic] & 1/2 Doz. Tea Spoons & Tongs . . . [and] 1/2 Doz. Tea Cups . . . & 1/2 Doz. Large Silver Spoons." This collection pales in comparison to the 1750 holdings of Josiah Cocks, late of Falmouth, which included "1 Dutch Tea Table . . . , 1 Mahogany Tea Chest with Canisters . . . , 1 Brass Ditto with Ditto . . . , 3 large Silver Spoons, 4 Tea Do . . . , Cheny [China] war . . . , 1 Block Tin Teapot . . . , 1 Tea Kettle . . . [and] 1 Coffee pot." The tea service ritual had reached colonial Maine.[76]

Despite this obvious surge in the desirability of tea accoutrements, few Maine-related silver hollowware pieces previous to 1765 seem to have survived. Only one reference, to an ambiguous tea "strainer," appears anywhere in the inventories, and only one extant piece, Sir William Pepperrell's silver teapot by Jacob Hurd, ca. 1735–1745, precedes the 1760s.[77] Until that time, according to the evidence, few people in the region could afford silver tea service pieces; most probably settled for more humble wares, as did the two individuals who owned teapots of "block tin," one of the base metal substitutes for silver.[78] The sudden rise in hollowware pieces in 1760s included a silver creamer and a pair of sugar tongs, made by Paul Revere in 1762 for Stephen and Deborah (Ellis) Smith of Machias; a teapot by Benjamin Burt, signed S / P*E / 1765, for Peter and Elizabeth (Wendell) Smith of Falmouth; and a service with a teapot and creamer by Nathaniel Hurd and a sugar bowl by his father Jacob, all with the Howard family coat of arms. The creamer dates from 1766, the year that Samuel Howard of Fort Western (present-day Augusta) married Sarah Lithgow.[79]

Major acquisitions of silver pieces, both domestic and display, often coincided with major family events. Birth, love, marriage, and death were all observed with gifts of silver, which also served to integrate the recipient into the social network of major families. In his 1724 will, for example, Major Charles Frost made gifts to each of his daughters that clearly linked the young women to their prestigious birth family: he bequeathed each daughter a silver porringer, which he probably acquired soon after each birth, "marked with her Name" if unmarried or "with her Maiden Name" if married. Two other items listed in early-eighteenth-century estate inventories, "a childs whyrl" and an "old whisel piece," were probably gifts for new infants.[80]

Marriage, an event that illustrates most explicitly the web of societal connections among families, frequently merited gifts of silver. Wedding bands, certainly the most visible emblems of one's wedded status, undoubtedly comprised a fair number of the nearly seventy rings, invariably gold, located in pre-1760 Maine probate records.[81] One anonymous testament to love, a seventeenth-century silver thimble (see fig. 8) excavated at Pemaquid, displays two entwined hearts bearing the initials "S H," flanked by two cupids.[82] Later pieces, ranging from spoons to tea services, often had a triangular set of initials with that of the surname surmounting those of each partner's given name. Examples of this sort include a pair of canns marked "W / WM" for William and Mary (Cutts) Whipple of Kittery, apparently acquired about the time of their marriage in 1762, and two tankards with "S / I*S" engraved on the handle for Jonathan and Sarah Sayward of York, married in 1760.[83] Families would often use silver to honor a marriage some years after the wedding ceremony. For example, a teaspoon marked "S / M*M / 1764" belonged to Moses and Miriam (Stone) Sewell of York, who were married seven years earlier, and a pair of sugar tongs marked "F / E*M" for Enoch and Mary (Wright) Freeman of Portland were probably acquired some time after their marriage in 1742.[84]

The tradition of the mourning ring, once as well known as the wedding band, typically graced the funeral rites of Maine's leading citizens. Unlike those of lesser inhabitants, the funerals of the region's elite involved a level of solemn ostentation appropriate to their rank. At the funeral, select individuals often received gold mourning rings, which provided a comforting link to departed and reminded the recipients of their own mortality and the promise of eternity.[85] One 1768 example by Nathaniel Hurd, memorializing the demise of Falmouth merchant Alexander Ross, features a skull and wings on an otherwise plain gold band.[86] Sir William Pepperrell fulfilled the expectations of his position when he provided mourning rings for the 1751 funeral of his son Andrew Pepperrell. On the other hand, Dorcus Cutts of York, declaring herself "sensible of ye Vanity of Splendid & pompous Funerals," willed that no rings should be given at her funeral, which took place in 1758; she further bequeathed anything left in the estate to the poor.[87]

Mourning rings in particular also reified the bond between the elite and the ministry of a region. Although often less affluent than their well-to-do parishioners, due to their station the local clergy were part of the elite circle and, like their secular friends, often had holdings of silver.[88] Ministers frequently received rings — the 1733 will of Nathan Lord of Berwick bequeathed "to my Minister a Gold Ring to Remembr me after my Decease" — and had rings distributed at their funerals. For instance, when Rev. Jeremiah Wise of Berwick died in January 1756, "the freeholders and other inhabitants of the First Parish of Berwick" ordered "all things necessary to the funeral" including "six rings for the bearers, [and] gloves for the bearers and their wives." These rings, one of which still exists, bore the skull and wings and the inscription "Revd. Mr. J. Wise OC / 22 Jan 1756 A 76."[89]

◦

Domestic silver displays and presentation pieces, both familial and broadly political, demonstrated the owner's prestige and power at that moment in time. Many citizens with the necessary wealth also sought to establish personal and family legacies via silver, which they achieved both through simple inheritance and through the grand gesture of bequests of silver wares to the community church.

Given the importance of the acquisition of silver and gold items among colonial gentry, it is not surprising that each family would also put a great deal of effort into the details of generational descent. The wills of the two Pepperrell patriarchs, which demonstrate the usual patterns of bequest albeit in a particularly exaggerated form, also show the association between the distribution of the family silver and the preservation of the family name. In his 1733 will, Colonel William Pepperrell left all his plate to his wife but instructed that upon her death one half would go to son William (the future baronet) and the other half would be divided among five daughters and the children of a sixth who had died. In 1759, Sir William, who had no direct male heir, willed that his daughter's son William Pepperrell Sparhawk could, upon legally dropping his surname, inherit the title and, among other things, "all my Set of Plate which I received of Sir Peter Warren," all family paintings, and the first Sir William's sword and gold watch. Even that, however, by no means depleted the silver holding of Sir William, for when his widow May died in 1790, she left in "old & new Silver plate" over 340 ounces valued at £102.5.5.[90]

Inheritance patterns also mirrored the dual economic structure, in which men participated in specific occupations such as yeoman, merchant, artisan, or mariner, and women provided the domestic support structure — which included food, clothing, and childcare — and in large part fulfilled major social roles. According to the patterns in probate records, male heirs received land and tools and women received the personal goods that enabled their domestic roles.[91] Berwick widow Mary Hill, for example, willed her daughter May Leighton "one silver Salver along with wearing apparel and household goods" and at the same time saw to it that the real estate would go to her son. Mary Wise, widow of Berwick minister Jeremiah Wise, divided her substantial silver holdings, including a "Salt Seller," a cann, and two porringers, among her two daughters and three granddaughters. Among the specific objects handed down the male line were silver-hilted swords, objects that Captain Moses Butler of Berwick and Captain William Whipple of Kittery directed specifically to sons.[92]

Major Charles Frost's 1724 will exemplifies the patterns noted above. Although all but one child received his or her individual piece of silver, the daughters were to divide "all the plate of his first wife," except specific pieces given to the sons — and given according to a very clear hierarchy. Charles, the eldest son, received a silver-headed leading staff, the "best plate handled sword, a silver tobacco box," the "best" plate hatband, a seal ring, and a porringer. The next son, John, was to have the second silver-hilted sword, the "other" plate hatband, and a porringer. Third son, Simon, was in line for a watch, a silver seal, a silver-hilted "seymater," and two silver spoons. Finally, youngest son Eliot inherited all his father's "money in Silver and Gold," all his father's gold rings (excepting the seal ring), and a steel-hilted sword.[93]

While inheritance patterns maintained or attempted to maintain wealth within a family, which could then of course contribute to a continued status in the community, gifts of plate to the church, where they were used for the sacred communion ritual, made a much more direct statement. As expressed by Gerald Ward, "one of [the donors'] . . . reasons for giving pieces of suitably engraved, durable silver was to demonstrate their exalted role in the social hierarchy through their benevolence to grateful, yet suitably subservient congregations." Generations of parishioners, using the same pieces, would remember the family's generosity and status.[94]

The two major groups of pre-1760 church silver in Maine, one belonging to the South Berwick First Congregational Church and the other to the First Congregational Church of Kittery, include significant representations of two of the region's most powerful families. The South Berwick church has six early pieces, at least two of which came directly from the Frost family. Major Charles Frost bequeathed a small English tankard in 1724. A simple piece with a plain cylindrical body and molded lip and base, it stands five and a quarter inches high and sports a flat-topped cover with pointed front, a double cupped thumbpiece, and a large scrolled handle. It has a London date-letter for 1674–75 and a "WC" maker's mark.[95] The major's sister, Mary Hill, also gave the church a beaker. Three unrelated members of the local elite donated the remaining pieces, four beakers and a basin. Elder Nathan Lord, a well-to-do yeoman, left a £20 bequest with which the church purchased two of the beakers. In 1703, Ichabod Plaisted, a merchant and militia colonel, gave "Two silver Cupps, a Table cloth & Napkins . . . to the Chh. To furnish the Communion Table." The "Crisening basin," given in 1763, came from Elder Humphrey Chadebourne, a wealthy Berwick gentleman.[96]

The Pepperrell family appears to be responsible for nearly all of the seven early pieces, dating from 1733 to about 1765, at the First Congregational Church of Kittery. Three are cups acquired with funds from the bequest of William Pepperrell, Sr.; his daughter Jane Turell left money for a fourth cup, similar in style, that the church acquired in about 1765. Sir William Pepperrell, the elder Pepperrell's son, left funds that were used for the purchase of a baptismal basin. A large, two-handled cup, with the inscription "This piece of / plate is presented to the / first Church in / Kittery by an / Unknown / Hand," is attributed in local tradition to Lady Mary Pepperrell, wife of Sir William. Identified as a "sprinkling font" by one author, it may have been a companion piece with the baptismal basin provided by her husband.[97]

The final piece, a two-handled cup, duplicated the first three Pepperrell cups. William Whipple, a relative newcomer to the region — he arrived from Ipswich in 1722 — gave the cup in 1728 as an outright gift rather than a bequest. This donation, along with several other factors, suggests that Whipple wanted to establish his position among the local gentry. His elegantly furnished home included a fine cupboard of plate that consisted of a tankard, one small and four large porringers, a spout cup, two cans, twelve large spoons, eleven teaspoons, tongs, a pepper box, a mustard pot, and a strainer. He also owned a silver-hilted sword and carried about a fine silver watch.[98]

Extant pieces from churches in York and Falmouth (now Portland) probably came from a series of new acquisitions that took place as towns expanded in the late colonial and post-Revolutionary periods. In many cases, the growth prompted communities to found new churches and to upgrade the wares of their older churches. During this time, the First Congregational Church of York acquired a number of pieces (fig. 14) from the bequests of Alexander Maxwell and Deacon Jeremiah Bragdon. An ambitious farmer, Maxwell instructed in his will that, after his wife's demise, half of his land and marsh should go to Rev. Samuel Moody and half to the church. Using these funds, the church had four matching tankards made in 1760 and a set of six beakers in 1785; Boston smith Daniel Parker filled both commissions. Parker also made a two-handled cup bought with Bragdon's bequest in 1767.[99] The Falmouth pieces,

Fig. 14. Daniel Parker (1726–1785), silverwares, Boston, Massachusetts, 1760–1785. Silver; h. (tankards) 9 in. Old York Historical Society.

from the First Parish Church, include two tankards and a cann. The tankards, dating ca. 1760–1770 and made by Daniel Boyer of Boston (1725–1779), are simply inscribed "The first / Church of Christ / IN / FALMOUTH." The pint cann was a gift to Rev. Samuel Deane from twenty-one young men in the parish.[100]

Looking at all of these collections chronologically, one can trace subtle shifts in the conventions that shaped the relationship between the town church and the town elite. The South Berwick holdings, which represent the earliest period and came mostly through direct donations or bequests from unrelated individuals, show the most variation in style. The Kittery church, from a slightly later period overall, purchased its silver using monetary bequests. The consistency among the five smaller cups and the one large one reflects a stylistic lineage.[101] An evolution in inscriptions suggests an increasing proclivity to use church silver in the definition of status. South Berwick's 1703 beakers carried the simple inscription "'X. dono I / a / c Plaisted / 1702." The engraving on the Frost tankard donated two decades later read "Ex Dono / Charles Frost / to the Church / of Berwick." In 1734, the Kittery church acquired three of its two-handled cups as "The Gift of Honble Wm. Pepperell Esqr / to the First Church of Christ In Kittery / 1733." He was thoroughly outdone by the baptismal basin from his son, which had the family arms on the rim and a very detailed inscription: "The Gift of the Honble. Sir WILLIAM PEPPERRELL Baronet, Lieut. General of His Majesty's Forces, & of the Province of the Massachusetts &c. &c. to the First Church in KITTERY."[102]

The shimmer of precious metals probably was a major presence in the lives of a limited number of early Maine inhabitants. However, the effect of these items extended far into the local communities and across the region as a whole. The major role of silver (and gold) was highly conservative — maintaining the societal structure. Early on, it symbolized and verified the power and status of the "Great Families" and later signaled the wealth and enhanced stature of the rising merchant class. A powerful emblem of marriage and family, it was also part of social networking epitomized in the colonial tea ritual. A comfort in its actual metallic value per se, it could, in currency form, serve a role in keeping all in their proper places and seriously chastising those who deviated. Many of the society's patterns would still have been similar without the presence of silver and gold; however, there is little doubt that precious metals strengthened extant cultural structures. Without these wares, early Maine would not have been quite the same.

Notes

1. Henry N. Flynt and Martha Gandy Fales, *The Heritage Foundation Collection of Silver, with Biographical Sketches of New England Silversmiths, 1625–1825* (Old Deerfield, Mass.: Heritage Foundation, 1968), 174, 267.

2. Edwin A. Churchill, "Mid-Seventeenth Century Maine: A World on the Edge," in *American Beginnings: Exploration, Culture and Cartography in the Land of Norumbega*, ed. Emerson W. Baker, Edwin A. Churchill, Richard S. D'Abate, Kristine L. Jones, Victor A. Konrad, and Harold E. L. Prins (Lincoln: University of Nebraska Press, 1994), 240–41; William Hubbard, *The History of the Indian Wars in New England*, 2 vols., ed. Samuel G. Drake (Roxbury, Mass.: W. Elliot Woodward, 1865), 2:76; Samuel Maverick, "A Brief Description of New England and the Several Towns Therein, Together with the Present Government Thereof," *Proceedings of the Massachusetts Historical Society*, 2d ser., 1 (1884–1885): 231–32.

3. Churchill, "Mid-Seventeenth Century Maine," 251–57; Edwin A. Churchill, "Too Great the Challenge: The Birth and Death of Falmouth, Maine, 1624–1676" (Ph.D. diss., University of Maine, 1979), 273–78.

4. *York Deeds*, 18 vols., various eds. (Portland: [Vols. 1–9], and Bethel: [Vols. 10–18]: various publishers, 1887–1910) (hereafter cited as *YD*) 5 (1): 29.

5. Charles T. Libby, Robert E. Moody, and Neal W. Allen, eds., *Provincial and Court Records of Maine, 1636–1727*, 6 vols. (Portland: Maine Historical Society, 1928–1975) (hereafter cited as *PCRM*), 2: 292–95; *YD*, 5 (1): 6.

6. *PCRM*, 2: 380–83; *YD*, 5 (1): 56.

7. York County Registry of Probate, vols. 1–20 (hereafter cited as YCRP), 8:209–11.

8. In order to understand any piece of silver, extant or otherwise, as it functioned in Maine during this period, it is vital to keep in mind the effects of war on the general development of the region and on the available sources for research today. The availability of inventories in state

records clearly reflect the impact of the warfare. The town of Kittery, the furthest from the fighting, had the highest rate of silver ownership in the state, and the estates of Kittery inhabitants were the most frequently recorded in Maine files. To the east, the situation deteriorated rapidly. Although the communities of Berwick, Wells, and York managed to survive the wars, their populations dropped; correspondingly, so did the number of inventories. East of Wells, the region was essentially deserted, except for a couple of brief periods, until the 1730s and 1740s; not surprisingly, there were few inventories from the region during the war years.

9. Grahame Clark, *Symbols of Excellence* (Cambridge: Cambridge University Press, 1986), 93; Churchill, "Too Great the Challenge," 138–39, 410–20.

10. *PCRM*, vol. 1–2; *YD*; YCRP.

11. This and the next paragraph were developed from an analysis of 160 Maine estates dating from 1648 to 1760 with listed silver and gold items.

12. YCRP, 8:209–11.

13. YCRP, 9:4–5.

14. YCRP, 8:209–11. For other examples see *YD*, 5 (1):16–17, and YCRP, 9:154.

15. YCRP, 9:86–87, 146–47. See also YCRP, 8:137–39, 176–77.

16. Gerald W. R. Ward, "'An Handsome Cupboard of Plate': The Role of Silver in American Life," in *Silver in American Life: Selections from the Mabel Brady Garvan and Other Collections at Yale University*, ed. Barbara McLean Ward and Gerald W. R. Ward (New York: American Federation of Arts, 1979), 33.

17. Communication with Robert B. Barker, April 18, 1996.

18. Coins appeared with relative frequency in Maine court and probate records and are continually coming to light in archaeological excavations in the region. It is important to note that there were two very distinct types of coins — those of precious metals (gold and silver) and those of base materials (most often copper). The base metal coins, by and large, served for local exchange, the stuff of normal day-to-day transactions. Yet, even though they were a vital component in daily life, they were viewed not as real money but as a convenient substitute. Philip L. Mossman, *Money of the American Colonies and Confederation: A Numismatic, Economic and Historical Correlation* (New York: American Numismatic Society, 1993), 112–13.

19. *PCRM*, 1:276.

20. Mossman, *Money of the American Colonies*, 30–32, 36–37.

21. YCRP, 1:45, 81; 3:186, 257; 9:218–19; Mossman, *Money of the American Colonies*, 52, 64–72.

22. Mark Girouard, "The Power House," in *The Treasure Houses of Britain: Five Hundred Years of Private Patronage and Art Collecting*, ed. Gervase Jackson-Stops (Washington D.C. and New Haven, Conn.: National Gallery of Art and Yale University Press, 1985), 22; Churchill, "Mid-Seventeenth Century Maine," 249–50; David Grayson Allen, "Vacuum Domicilium: The Social and Cultural Landscape of Seventeenth-Century New England," in *New England Begins: The Seventeenth Century*, ed. Jonathan L. Fairbanks and Robert F. Trent, 3 vols. (Boston: Museum of Fine Arts, Boston, 1982), 1:1–2, 49.

23. "Early Maine leadership — demographic and economic profiles," Maine Silver Files, Maine State Museum (hereafter MSM). A major source of information on this topic is Sybil Noyes, Charles T. Libby, and Walter G. Davis, *Genealogical Dictionary of Maine and New Hampshire* (Baltimore: Genealogical Publishing Co., 1972) (hereafter cited as NLD).

24. "Early Maine Leadership," Maine Silver Files, MSM. Major sources of information on Maine's sawmills and millers include Richard Candee, "Merchant and Millwright: The Water Powered Sawmills of Piscataqua," *Old-Time New England* 40 (Spring 1970): 131–49, and *YD*, vols. 1–5, along with selected references in YCRP, vols. 1–10, and *PCRM*, vols. 1 and 2.

25. Richard M. Candee, "The Architecture of Maine's Settlements: Vernacular Architecture to About 1720," in *Maine Forms of American Architecture*, ed. Deborah Thompson (Camden, Me.: *Downeast Magazine*, 1976), 37; Richard M. Candee, "Wooden Buildings in Early Maine and New Hampshire: A Technological and Cultural History, 1600–1720" (Ph.D. diss., University of Pennsylvania, 1976), chapter 2. Examples of finely furnished best spaces include the Kittery estates of Captain John Mitchell (1664), William Leighton (1667), and Robert Cutts (1674), and the York estate of Major John Davis (1691). *PCRM*, 1:227–29, 301–4; 2:292–94; *YD*, 5 (1):65.

26. Candee, "The Architecture of Maine Settlement," 38.

27. *YD*, 5 (1):15–17.

28. *YD*, 5 (1):15–17.

29. NLD, 540–41.

30. Personal communication with Joseph W. P. Frost, March 29, 1996.

31. Kathryn C. Buhler and Graham Hood, *American Silver: Garvan and Other Collections in the Yale University Art Gallery*, 2 vols. (New Haven: Yale University Press for the Yale University Art Gallery, 1970), 1:121–22.

32. Communication with Michael K. Brown, May 3, 1985. The caster is part of the Bayou Bend Collection, the Museum of Fine Arts, Houston. Buhler and Hood, *American Silver*, 1:59, 61, illustrates a caster by Tyler similar to that held at Bayou Bend.

33. NLD, 487; YCRP, 4:49.

34. William Willis, *The History of Portland, from 1632 to 1864*, 2d ed. (Portland, Me.: Bailey and Noyes, 1865), 824–26; YCRP, 8:130–32.

35. Some extant family objects not covered in the body of the paper are still worth recording. A piece of Frost family silver still extant is known only from a photograph. A mid-eighteenth-century baluster-shaped cann, according to a note on the back, was apparently "purchased by some movie actor or actress from Hollywood for their collection" (photo of Frost cann, privately held). A modest number of other documented major pieces have been identified. For example, a pair of tankards were made about 1760 by Boston silversmith Benjamin Burt for York merchant Jonathan Sayward and his wife Sarah (Mitchell) (no. 1958.001, tankard, Old York Historical Society-Collections Database Report; Penny J. Sander, *Elegant Embellishments: Furnishings from New England Homes, 1660–1860* [Boston: Society for the Preservation of New England Antiquities, 1982], 35; Richard C. Nylander, "The Jonathan Sayward House, York, Maine," *Antiques* 116, no. 4 [September 1979]: 567–77; NLD, 610–11). Also, two keyhole-handled porringers, dating from about the same period, were the property of Maine's early elite. One created by Stephen Emery of Boston, was made for Thomas and Elizabeth Cutts of Saco. The other descended through the Freeman family of Falmouth. Quite likely created for Enoch Freeman, it apparently passed to his son Samuel and then Samuel's daughter Dorcus (Freeman) Homes (*American Silver Collected by Philip H. Hammerslough* [Hartford, Conn.: privately printed, 1965], 3:41; NLD, 177–79; no. 1841, porringer, Maine Historical Society Curatorial Files; Willis, *Portland*, 746–47, 805–7).

36. Ward, "Handsome Cupboard of Plate," 33, 102–3.

37. YCRP, 1:18, 79; 2:1–2, 27–29; 3:147–49.

38. Martha Gandy Fales, *Early American Silver for the Cautious Collector* (New York: Funk & Wagnells, 1970), 238–40.

39. Buhler and Hood, *American Silver*, 1:121–22; John Eldridge Frost, *The Nicholas Frost Family* (Milford, N.H.: The Cabinet Press, 1943), frontispiece, I, 15; photo of Frost cann, privately held; Ian M.G. Quimby, *American Silver at Winterthur* (Winterthur: Henry Francis du Pont Winterthur Museum, 1995), 133–34.

40. The significance of personal objects is clearly reflected in the 1724 will of Major Charles Frost, YCRP, 3:145–47. Even with small objects, only a minority of the inhabitants owned silver and gold objects, and despite some exceptions, most owners were of the upper-middle and upper classes. "Probate Records, 1648–1760," Maine Silver Files, MSM; Churchill, "Mid-Seventeenth Century Maine," 241; James S. Leamon, *Revolution Downeast: The War for American Independence in Maine* (Amherst: University of Massachusetts Press, 1993), 6. Barbara McLean Ward makes the same point for New England in "Metalwares" in *The Great River: Art and Society of the Connecticut Valley, 1635–1820*, ed. Gerald W. R. Ward and William N. Hosley, Jr. (Hartford, Conn.: Wadsworth Atheneum, 1985), 274.

41. "Forms of Silver — Early Maine," Silver Files, MSM.

42. "Forms of Silver — Early Maine," Silver Files, MSM.

43. *PCRM*, 1:227–29; *YD*, 5 (1):13; YCRP, 9:261–62; 10:16.

44. Pemaquid spoons: Robert L. Bradley and Helen B. Camp, *The Forts of Pemaquid, Maine: An Archaeological and Historical Study* (Augusta: Maine Historic Preservation Commission, The Maine Archaeological Society, and the Maine Bureau of Parks and Lands, 1994), 184–85, 187. The *Defence* spoons, part of the *Defence* collections, are at the MSM. Excepting one with raised cast letters, all had initials engraved or scratched into the back of the handles.

45. "Forms of Silver — Early Maine," Silver Files, MSM.

46. *YD*, 5 (1):9; YCRP, 4:75; 8:57, 140–41.

47. Helen B. Camp, *Archaeological Excavation at Pemaquid, Maine, 1965–1974* (Augusta: Maine State Museum, 1975), 44–45; Emerson W. Baker, *The Clark and Lake Company: The Historical Archaeology of a Seventeenth-Century Maine Settlement* (Augusta: Maine Historical Preservation Commission, 1985), 21.

48. "Forms of Silver — Early Maine," Silver Files, MSM.

49. Nathaniel Shurtleff, ed., *Records of the Governor and Company of the Massachusetts Bay* (Boston: William White, 1854), 3:243.

50. "Forms of Silver — Early Maine," Silver Files, MSM.

51. YCRP, 8:140–41, 160–61.

52. Camp, *Pemaquid*, 44–45. The "close plating" process is described in Frederick Bradbury, *History of Old Sheffield Plate* (London: Macmillan and Co., 1912), 5–6, and Diana Cramer, "Philadelphia Silverplaters, 1778 to 1840: Part II, The Methods and Hints at the Answer," *Silver* 23, no. 4 (July-August 1990): 19.

53. "Forms of Silver — Early Maine," Silver Files, MSM; *PCRM*, 2: 295–97; *YD*, 5 (1):33; YCRP, 8:244–45.

54. YCRP, 4:49; 8:48–9; Camp, *Pemaquid*, 48.

55. "Forms of Silver — Early Maine," Silver Files, MSM. See also YCRP, 2:27–29; 8:130–32.

56. YCRP, 8: 130–32, 140–41, 236; 9: 133; 10: 130; Martha Gandy Fales, *Jewelry in America, 1600–1900* (Woodbridge, Eng.: Antique Collectors' Club, 1995), 58. One inventory listed an amber necklace and a second noted "20 amber beads" (YCRP, 8:118, 140–41; Fales, *Jewelry in America*, 21, 121–22).

57. "Forms of Silver — Early Maine," Silver Files, MSM; Fales, *Jewelry in America*, 58, 60. The silver clasps appeared in five inventories and the gold in three.

58. YCRP, 3:145–47, 262; 9:150–51. It is not wholly clear that the "Silver Hat lace" and "read ribbon" actually refer to silver material (e.g., silver thread) or simply some type of silvery colored element of the pieces. Only two other mentions of jewelry, one a 1678 notice of "one gould pine 28s" and the other an ambiguous listing of "Jewells," appear in the probate records (*YD*, 5 [1]: 31–32; YCRP, 9:89).

59. Gerald W. R. Ward, introduction to David B. Warren, Katherine S. Howe, and Michael K. Brown, *Marks of Achievement: Four Centuries of American Presentation Silver* (Houston: Museum of Fine Arts, 1987), 21.

60. Extensive coverage of the Louisbourg Expedition is provided in George A. Rawlyk, *Yankees at Louisbourg* (Orono: University of Maine Press, 1967), and Henry S. Burrage, *Maine at Louisburg* (Augusta, Me.: Burleigh & Flynt, 1910). A succinct account is provided in Howard H. Peckham, *The Colonial Wars, 1689–1762* (Chicago: University of Chicago Press, 1964), 97–106, and a detailed account of Pepperrell's role is given in Bryon Fairchild, *Messrs. William Pepperrell: Merchants at Piscataqua* (Ithaca, N.Y.: Cornell University Press, 1954), 172–77.

61. Information on the Pepperrell silver came from files at the Portland Museum of Art; Burton W. F. Trafton, Jr., "Louisbourg and the Pepperrell Silver," *Antiques* 89, no. 3 (March 1966): 366–68; Michael K. Brown, "The Colonial Period," in Warren, *Marks of Achievement*, 29–30; communication with Joseph W. P. Frost, March 29, 1996.

62. Trafton, "Louisbourg and Pepperrell Silver," 366; Joseph W. P. Frost, "Living with Antiques: Pepperrell Mansion, Kittery Point, Maine," *Antiques* 89, no. 3 (March 1966): 368–69.

63. Buhler and Hood, *American Silver*, 1:100–102; NLD, 499; Charles E. Banks, *History of York, Maine*, 2 vols. (Boston: The Calkins Press, 1931), 1:295–97, 322–30, 332–33.

64. Allen Johnson and Duman Malone, eds., *Dictionary of American Biography* (New York: Charles Scribner's Sons, 1931), 7:50–51; Peckham, *Colonial Wars*, 162–63; John Stuart Barrows, *Fryeburg, Maine: An Historical Sketch* (Fryeburg: Pequawkit Press, 1938), 28–36, 50, 170–87.

65. No. 666, tankard, Maine Historical Society curatorial files.

66. The information on Phips and his activities was found in Alice Lounsberry, *Sir William Phips: Treasure Fisherman and Governor of the Massachusetts Bay Colony* (New York: Charles Scribner's Sons, 1941). The recovery of the Spanish treasure is covered in chapters 4 and 5.

67. Edward Hawkins, comp., and Augustus W. Frankes and Herbert A. Grueber, eds., *Medallic Illustrations of the History of Great Britain and Ireland to the Death of George II* (London: Trustees of the British Museum, 1885), 1:619; C. Wyllys Betts, William T. R. Marvin, and Lyman Haynes Low, eds., *American Colonial History Illustrated by Contemporary Medals* (Glendale, N.Y.: Benchmark Publishing Co., 1970), 35.

68. Fales, *Jewelry in America*, 20; William Willis, "Remarks on Coins Found at Portland in 1849, and Richmond's Island in 1855," *Collections of the Maine Historical Society*, 1st ser., 6 (1859):143; Camp, *Pemaquid*, 48; NLD, 324.

69. YCRP, 1:45, 118–19; 3:145–47; 8:130–32, 140–41; personal communication with Joseph W. P. Frost, March 29, 1996; NLD, 324.

70. Same sources as footnote 45 plus NLD, 246, 257, 303, 444, 540, 543; Leola G. Bushman, "Peter Grant: Scotch Exile: Kittery and Berwick, Maine," typescript, 1971, 37–38, Maine State Library, Augusta, Me.; Charles N. Sinnett, comp., "The Gerrish Genealogy," typescript, ca. 1920, 4–5, Maine State Library; Everett S. Stackpole, *Old Kittery and Her Families* (Lewiston, Me.: Press of Lewiston Journal Company, 1903), 255–56.

71. YCRP, 3:145–47; 8:137–39, 176–77, 228; 9:39–40, 86–87, 154, 164, 200–201.

72. No. 0308.01, Massachusetts Historical Society; "Donation from Usher Parsons," *Proceedings of the Massachusetts Historical Society* 1 (1862): 373.

73. *Maine Antique Digest* (April 1994), 11-C; Flynt and Fales, *Heritage Foundation Collection*, 345; James W. North, *The History of Augusta from the Earliest Settlement to the Present Time* (Augusta, Me.: Clapp and North, 1817), 225, 901.

74. Rodris Roth, "Tea-Drinking in Eighteenth-Century America: Its Etiquette and Equipage," in *Material Life in America, 1600–1860*, ed. Robert Blair St. George (Boston: Northeastern University Press, 1988), 439–46.

75. A clear shift eastward also appears in the ownership of tea-related wares by the 1750s. Probate records only indicate two estates in Kittery with teaspoons. York, which enjoyed some commercial success during the mid-eighteenth century, had five such listings. Nearby Wells had three estates with silver tea equipage, including one with a teapot and one with "tea dishes." In Falmouth, the rising mercantile center in the region, six estates listed silver tea wares including three teapots. "Tea Service – Early Maine," Silver Files, MSM.

76. "Tea Service – Early Maine," Silver Files, MSM; YCRP, 8:73–74; 9:107, 146–47.

77. Buhler and Hood, *American Silver*, 1:121–22; YCRP, 8:137–39.

78. "Block Tin" was a high grade pewter in which antimony replaced most or all of the lead, creating a harder, shinier surface than lead-containing pewter. When kept well polished, it served as a reasonable alternative to silver wares. See Edwin A. Churchill, *Hail Britannia: Maine Pewter and Silverplate* (Augusta, Me.: Maine State Museum, 1992), 59–60; "Pewter," in E. Chambers, *Cyclopaedia, Or an Universal Dictionary of Arts and Sciences*, vol. 2 (London: numerous sponsors, 1738); and Malachy Postlethwayt, *The Universal Dictionary of Trade and Commerce*, vol. 2 (London: John and Paul Knapton, 1755).

79. Excerpts from the account books of Paul Revere provided by Michael K. Brown, December 7, 1984; Francis Hill Bigelow, *Historic Silver of the Colonies and Its Makers* (New York: Macmillan, 1917), 344, 410; Quimby, *American Silver at Winterthur*, 133–34; *Antiques* 138, no. 1 (July 1990): 92. The two Revere pieces and to a lesser degree the Howard example demonstrate the midcentury expansion of silver ownership eastward.

80. YCRP, 1:98–99; 2:13–14; 3:145–47.

81. Fales, *Jewelry in America*, 30; "Forms of Silver – Early Maine," Silver Files, MSM.

82. Camp, *Pemaquid*, 44–45.

83. *The New England Silversmith: An Exhibition of New England Silver from the Mid-Seventeenth Century to the Present* (Providence: Museum of Art, Rhode Island School of Design, 1975), no. 68; No. 1958.001, accession files, Old York Historical Society.

84. No. 1969.003, accession files, Old York Historical Society; communication with Michael K. Brown, May 24, 1985; No. 318, Bayou Bend Curatorial Files.

85. An excellent discussion of mourning rings and other jewelry is presented in Fales, *Jewelry in America*, 23–28.

86. John D. Kernan, "Gold Funeral Rings," *Antiques* 89, no. 4 (April 1966): 568–69; Willis, *Portland*, 455.

87. Fales, *Jewelry in America*, 25–27.

88. The estate of Reverend Shubael Dummer of York (1692), valued at £70.15.4, included a tankard, a wine cup, and a spoon (*YD*, 5 [1]: 72). That of Reverend John Wade of Berwick (1705), valued at £218.16s., listed a tankard and six spoons (YCRP, 1:115). The March 1, 1747/8, will of Mary, wife of Berwick pastor Reverend Jeremiah Wise, noted a salt cellar, a cann, two porringers, two gold rings, and other gold and silver (YCRP, 8:27–29).

89. Fales, *Jewelry in America*, 24–25; William Sargent, comp., *Maine Wills, 1640–1760* (Portland: Brown, Thurston, & Co., 1887), 345; file notes, South Berwick First Parish Federated Church.

90. YCRP, 4:177–80; 10:63–69; 15:545.

91. Churchill, "Mid-Seventeenth Century Maine," 252–55; Laurel T. Ulrich, *Good Wives: Image and Reality in the Lives of Women in Northern New England, 1650–1750* (New York: Oxford University Press, 1980), 20–24, 27–32, 35–50; Barbara McLean Ward, "Women's Property and Family Continuity in Eighteenth-Century Connecticut," in *Early American Probate Inventories*, ed. Peter Benes (Boston: Boston University, 1989), 77–78.

92. YCRP, 8:27–29, 147, 223–24; 9:200–201.

93. YCRP, 3:145–47.

94. Ward, introduction, in Warren, *Marks of Achievement*, 21. Similar points are made in Barbara McLean Ward, "'In a Feasting Posture': Communion Vessels and Community Values in Seventeenth- and Eighteenth-Century New England," *Winterthur Portfolio* 23, no. 1 (Spring 1988): 18–19.

95. E. Alfred Jones, *The Old Silver of American Churches* (Letchworth, Eng.: Arden Press for the National Society of the Colonial Dames of America, 1913), 451–52, plate CXXX; YCRP, 3:145–47. The tankard is presently held by the First Parish Federated Church in Berwick. It also bears the pounced date and letters "1647 / F / IE," perhaps the initials of yet-unidentified Frost relatives.

96. Jones, *Old Silver of American Churches*, 451–54; "Records of the First Church of Berwick (South Berwick), Me.," *New England Historical and Genealogical Register* 82 (January 1928): 74; (April 1928): 204; (July 1928): 331; Sargent, *Maine Wills*, 341–42; NLD, 134, 443–44, 559.

97. Jones, *Old Silver of American Churches*, 236–38; Stephen Decatur, "The Early Church Silver of Kittery, Maine," *American Collector* (November 1936): 3, 15; NLD, 540.

98. Jones, *Old Silver of American Churches*, 237–38; Decatur, "Church Silver of Kittery," 3; NLD, 540; YCRP, 8:137–39; 9:86–87.

99. Jones, *Old Silver of American Churches*, 510; NLD, 470–71; YCRP, 7:87; 11:270–72; Banks, *York*, 2:78, 224.

100. Jones, *Old Silver of American Churches*, 377–78; Willis, *Portland*, 399, 650–52, 655–56.

101. Ward, "Feasting Posture," 5. In 1828 all of the South Berwick beakers acquired matching molded bases (communication with the Reverend James Christianson, 1994).

102. Jones, *Old Silver of American Churches*, 236, 451–52. The elaboration of inscriptions over time and the increased emphasis on status is considered in Ward, "Feasting Posture," 15–16. On the other hand, elements of social leveling were also present. In both churches, the drinking vessels were generally of the same form thereby eliminating the opportunity to delineate rank in terms of who got what vessel. Similarly, the practice of passing the cup from hand to hand enhanced the idea of community and equality. For further discussion on these issues, see Ward, "Feasting Posture," 4, 12, 14, and Ward and Ward, *Silver in American Life*, 91.

"An influential and useful man": Samuel Bartlett of Concord, Massachusetts

DAVID F. WOOD

THE PHRASE HISTORIAN LEMUEL SHATTUCK used to describe silversmith Samuel Bartlett (1752–1821) — "he was an influential and useful man" — would not apply to one who was a craftsman solely.[1] In addition to being a silversmith, Samuel Bartlett was a good citizen; in addition to being a clerk, he was literate, professional, and provident. Born in the largest city in colonial New England, Bartlett grew up in a period of contracting economic opportunity and political change.[2] A youth in occupied Boston, he came of age in Revolutionary Massachusetts, provided for a large family during a period of constitutional crisis, and abandoned his craft in the same period that saw the beginning of New England's industrial revolution. The record of Bartlett's life includes examples of some of the new challenges and opportunities that were changing the nature of craft, civil service, and citizenship in this region in the Revolutionary era.[3]

Samuel Bartlett was born, probably in Boston, in 1752. He was the son of Roger Bartlett of Branscombe, England, and of Anna Hurd of Charlestown, Massachusetts, who married in 1749. Roger Bartlett was a mariner, a captain of merchant ships engaged in the Bristol-to-Boston trade; Anna Hurd was the daughter of Benjamin and Elizabeth Hurd.[4] Samuel grew up in Boston's industrial North End, where he attended Christ Church on North Street. The only son in the family, Bartlett initially wanted to be a mariner like his father. His mother, however, persuaded him to become "a pupil of the famous master Tileston"[5] — an education that would provide him with the skills for a career in commerce or to augment the training of a craft trade. Silversmithing, apparently, had not yet emerged as his profession of choice.

John Tileston, "one of the noted school-masters of the past, 'the father of good writing in Boston,'"[6] devoted seventy years to teaching at the North Writing School, where he had started as an apprentice at the age of fourteen. The school, located on Bennett Street, taught the practical aspects of reading, arithmetic, and writing mostly to students anticipating careers in business, rather than the classical education that grammar schools provided as preparation for college — that is, Harvard. The North Writing School was one of three public writing schools in Boston, all of which admitted students as young as seven. The only public school in the North End, Tileston's was particularly large, with as many as 150 students present at times in the 1760s. Tileston's journal records the purchase of slates by the dozen, paper by the ream, and quills by the thousand. His students included sons of the North End's many craftsmen and tradesmen, and some boys did serve craft apprenticeships while attending classes. Among them were the carver Simeon Skillin, Jr., whose father and brothers were also carvers; Gawen Brown, Jr., the son of a London-trained clockmaker; silversmith Henry Loring, the son of silversmith Joseph Loring; and Paul Revere III, the son of the Patriot and a third-generation silversmith.[7]

The celebrated orator Edward Everett, perhaps best known for delivering a two-hour address at Gettysburg that was upstaged by Lincoln's two minutes, went on to college after attending the Writing School. Recollecting his early education some years later, Everett provided a colorful picture of life at the school:

> Master Tileston was advanced in years, and had found a qualification for his calling as a writing-master in what might have seemed, at first, to threaten to be an obstruction. The fingers of his right hand had been contracted and stiffened in early life by a burn, but were fixed in just the position to hold a pen and a penknife, and nothing else. As they were also considerably indurated, they served as a convenient instrument of discipline. A copy badly written, or a blotted page, was sometimes visited with an infliction which would have done no discredit to the beak of a bald eagle.

Everett went on to say: "I desire, however to speak of him with gratitude; for he put me on the track of an acquisition which has been extremely useful to me in after life — that of a plain, legible hand."[8] An account book kept by brassfounder and coppersmith John Andrews, who also appears in Tileston's lists of students, exemplifies that hand.[9]

Although Samuel would have found himself among a number of future artisans in this environment, he probably did not undertake his education at Tileston's school with that goal in mind. Rather, according to his biographer, Concord physician Josiah Bartlett (no relation), circumstances forced Samuel to abandon his studies in order to pursue a trade.[10] The biographer records that Samuel was partially deafened at the Boston Massacre on March 5, 1770 — the only hint of any political activity on Samuel's part.[11] That handicap, together with the "disturbed state of the country," turned the young man toward his future as a silversmith. Josiah Bartlett could be in error over this event: eighteen is a late age to initiate a craft apprenticeship, which typically began at age fourteen and lasted about eight years.[12] If Samuel's training in fact followed this more traditional path, he could have started his apprenticeship with Samuel Minott, a leading Boston silversmith, during his schooling: apprenticeships often provided for schooling as well as clothing and housing.

Samuel Minott ran his shop in Boston for at least forty years and, according to Patricia E. Kane, ranked with Paul Revere, Jr., and Benjamin Burt as "one of the principal retailers of silver in Boston in the late colonial period."[13] Samuel Bartlett, however, is the only apprentice known to have received his training at Minott's shop — an anomaly for a shop so active for so long; evidence suggests that Benjamin Burt's shop trained at least eight young men.[14] Of course, Minott probably did train others, including possibly Joseph Lasinby Brown (1753–1804), who later became a business colleague of Bartlett's. The only son of Boston housewright Ebenezer Brown and Elizabeth Lasinby, whose family were shipwrights, Joseph was also a native of the North End. Like Bartlett, he attended Christ Church and Tileston's school. Referred to as a goldsmith or jeweller in legal documents, Brown seems to have carried on this trade in the North End from the late 1770s until 1785.[15]

The dearth of known apprentices from Minott's shop may also reflect the particular spin that Minott put on his business: he favored a high retail volume and may have kept production at a relatively low level. He focused instead on selling merchandise, domestic and imported, produced elsewhere. According to an advertisement placed in Boston in 1772, Minott's goldsmith shop remained a shop separate from his retail shop, in which he sold various goods, including teas, spices, and groceries; creamware, delft, and stoneware; and silver, coral beads, and jewelry.[16] He also bought silver from Paul Revere's shop, and his mark occurs together with those of six other silversmiths who were providing him goods for resale.[17] In the shop Bartlett later set up in Concord, he made use of many of these same marketing strategies.

By 1775, as the war for American independence began, Samuel Bartlett had achieved his professional and personal independence. Josiah Bartlett and Lemuel Shattuck, however, disagree about the exact time at which the young man became autonomous. Bartlett wrote that "before he got through his time [apprenticeship], the war of the Revolution began." Shattuck believed that Bartlett removed to Concord in 1775, "soon after commencing business."[18] Both nonetheless recognized the beginning of the Revolution as the cause of Bartlett's next change of circumstance, and it seems certain that Bartlett had attained his majority — that is, turned twenty-one — in 1773, the year of the Boston Tea Party. When the war began, catching his father at sea, Samuel first relocated to Woburn, about ten miles from Boston, with his mother and his two sisters and their families. He married Polly Barrett, the daughter of Boston merchant Isaiah Barrett, in September 1776. Soon after, the newlyweds moved to Concord.

Bartlett may have moved to Concord simply because it was one of the towns that provided refuge for people fleeing Boston. In addition to the faculty and students of Harvard College, who removed there for the duration of the siege, some eighty of Boston and Charlestown's poor escaped to Concord at the beginning of the war.[19] Among the other tradesmen who chose Concord at around the same time were Emerson Cogswell (1744–1808), who established himself as a hatter on the Mill Dam, and Bartlett's fellow silversmith Joseph Lasinby Brown; all three men would eventually work themselves into the fabric of the town's social and economic life.[20]

Bartlett's reasons for leaving besieged Boston are easy to imagine, but any professional appeal Concord would have held is harder to see.[21] Silversmith John Ball had been working in Concord for ten years without conspicuous success; his silver is rare and he seems to have had to recapitalize periodically by mortgaging inherited land.[22] Concord probate records from the end of the eighteenth century, reflecting midcentury households, portray a limited market for silver. The inventories note silver teaspoons and buckles but little else. Tankards are rare, only five or six recorded, and predictably occur in households with the other reliable markers of wealth, eight-day clocks and looking glasses. The most extensive assemblage of silver in eighteenth-century Concord belonged to physician and moneylender Abel Prescott. Prescott owned three tankards, six canns, a large pair and a small pair of porringers, a small porringer, a sugar box, a creampot, pepper caster and sugar tongs, two sets of pepper casters, a silver teapot, and seven large spoons and twelve small. He also owned three pairs of gold sleeve buttons made by John Ball — the one instance of local patronage documented in his inventory.[23]

Bartlett accommodated himself to Concord's limited market, choosing not to set up immediately as a silversmith. "On coming to Concord," Josiah Bartlett wrote, "Mr. Bartlett opened a small store, vending the usual merchandise of a country trader."[24] He may have modeled his operation on Minott's retail shop in Boston, with its sundry goods and mix of silver by various smiths.[25] At the same time he commenced trade, Bartlett began to integrate himself into the civic life of the town. As early as 1777, for example, Bartlett, along with Cogswell, participated in the founding of a remarkable institution that continues to the present, the Social Circle; Joseph Brown joined them in 1785. An unofficial parliament of twenty-five townsmen, the Social Circle met on Tuesdays during the winter to discuss town or other matters, including many suggestions for town improvements and celebrations that later won adoption.[26]

Bartlett completed four public commissions during his career, all for communion silver. The first two were filled prior to his acquiring a shop separate from his house, and the first commission may in fact have preceded his move to

Concord altogether. All four commissions resulted from bequests, the two earliest made during the Revolutionary War. In the second instance, the work was not paid for until the 1780s; this piece is nevertheless the earliest securely dated piece of Bartlett's silver. In the first case, it is not clear when Bartlett did the work as no record of payment survives and the evidence of the silver itself is somewhat equivocal.

The first of the early commissions originated in the will of Deacon Thomas Waite of the First Church, Boston. When proved on May 19, 1775, a month after the North Bridge fight, the will revealed a bequest for church silver: "I give to the First Church of Christ in Boston a Silver Flaggon for the use of the Communion Table equal in value and size to that given to the said Church by the Honl William Dummer."[27] The flagon made with Waite's bequest carries Samuel Bartlett's full surname mark ("S·BARTLETT"), but it has not proved possible to date it with precision. If it was indeed made near the date of the bequest, this flagon would be among Bartlett's earliest independent work; historical circumstance, however, would argue for a later date (fig. 1).[28]

Most likely, since the conditions of war hardly favored the production of fine metal objects, the First Church deacons waited for the end of hostilities to fulfill Waite's instructions. The occupation and closing of Boston's port, the beginning of the Revolutionary War on April 19, and the subsequent siege of the city affected every aspect of Boston life. Shattuck estimated that the city's population dropped from over 15,000 to under 3,000 as a result of a massive exodus.[29] Consequently, Boston silversmiths turned out very little church silver in 1775. Some of the manufacturers, such as Revere, were otherwise engaged. At least one church put its silver, which represented a substantial portion of the church assets, into hiding; the First Parish in Charlestown removed the communion silver to Reading, Massachusetts, on April 22, 1775, three days after the North Bridge fight, and didn't bring it back until 1783.[30]

An examination of the First Church flagon reveals a few details of manufacture that might be seen to support Josiah Bartlett's suggestion that Samuel's apprenticeship was interrupted by the Revolution. The products of Boston's late colonial silversmiths are fairly consistent in conception and execution, and both are generally very competent. Bartlett's flagon falls a little short on both counts. The bodies of eighteenth-century hollowware forms such as canns, tankards, and flagons were shaped by raising, the process of hammering a sheet of silver on a series of specialized anvils (stakes) held in a vise. The hammering both shapes and stretches the silver. As part of the process, the metal has to be periodically annealed — that is, heated red hot and quenched in liquid, which makes the metal ductile and readily worked. The hammering rearranges the crystalline structure of the alloy and makes the metal hard; if worked too long

Fig. 1. Samuel Bartlett (1752–1821), flagon, probably Concord, Massachusetts, about 1775–95. Silver, h. 14 3/16 in. First and Second Church, Boston, on loan to the Museum of Fine Arts, Boston. Photo, courtesy Museum Fine Arts, Boston.

after annealing, the metal will crack. Some stress cracks present in the bottom of the Waite flagon are the result of the metal being worked too long after annealing, suggesting an inexperienced craftsman. In addition, the base on a hollowware form is often cast and the casting finished by turning on a lathe. The marks of this process are usually visible on the underside. The base of the Waite flagon, however, was raised from a sheet, then finished with files and soldered to the body, an unusual working method for Boston-area craftsmen. As a result, the base seems hesitant and fussy in composition, compared to the usually sure handling evident in Boston silver.

Contrary to these details of execution, which suggest an early date, is the engraving on the flagon, which suggests a date a decade or even two after 1775. The inscription is in an oval surround composed of a double border of scalloping and bright cutting, all elements of neoclassical design. The effect of the border resembles the engraved surround on a 1786 tankard by Benjamin Burt.[31] Although the engraving may have been added later, this detail together with the historical circumstances favor the argument that the First Church delayed executing Waite's bequest until after the war ended.

251

Fig. 2. Sidney L. Smith, replica of Amos Doolittle's "A View of the Town of Concord (1775)," Boston, Massachusetts, 1903. Hand-colored engraving on paper; h. approx. 15 in., w. approx. 20 in. Concord Museum (P1403).

Since the war undoubtedly dampened Bartlett's silversmithing prospects in Concord, he apparently waited until its conclusion to pursue his craft there.[32] Although even the postwar local market was limited, Concord nevertheless offered an advantageous location because it was a half-shire town for Middlesex County. The minor courts met there regularly throughout the eighteenth century, bringing in as many as 500 people from all over the county twice a year. At this time Bartlett apparently lived in a house with a shop attached across the street from the Wright tavern, near the courthouse in the center of Concord (fig. 2). By the end of the war, in the mid-1780s, Bartlett had a good enough reputation to attract a commission from the First Church in Weston, a town in eastern Middlesex County. With this commission, Samuel Bartlett resumed silversmithing after his venture as a dry-goods merchant.

In his will, proved in 1777, Weston, Massachusetts, merchant Isaac Bigelow bequeathed "To the Church of Christ in Weston a silver Tankard, to be made the value of all the silver and gold in my possession, exclusive of the making unless my executors judge it more than necessary."[33] Unlike the piece for the

Fig. 3. Samuel Bartlett (1752–1821), tankard, Concord, Massachusetts, 1775–95. Silver; h. 9⅛ in. Unitarian Church of First Parish, Weston, on loan to the Museum of Fine Arts, Boston. Photo, courtesy Museum of Fine Arts, Boston.

First Church of Boston, with its surrounding ambiguity, the Weston tankard can be dated confidently to 1785, which makes it clear that the Revolution interfered with the execution of the bequest. The account for Bigelow's estate records on September 14, 1785, the cost of the tankard: £20.6.7.[34]

This tankard is typical of Boston work of the third quarter of the eighteenth century (fig. 3). It resembles in form a tankard made by Samuel Minott in 1765 now in the Museum of Fine Arts, Boston.[35] The tapering body of the Weston tankard rests on a cast molded foot, and it has a reinforcing midband and a domed, hinged top with a cast urn-and-flame finial. The inscription is surrounded by a meandering floral swag that is still quite rococo in spirit, resembling, for instance, the flowers engraved on a pair of canns made by Revere in the 1760s.[36] The marks of a cloth-covered stake on the inside of this tankard (evidence of the later removal of a substantial dent) obscure the original workmanship to a certain extent, but this tankard seems to be competently made in all aspects.

In 1788, three years after the Weston commission, Bartlett bought the old jail in Concord to use as a shop and home. Although Concord business never reached the dimension of the Boston trade, Bartlett nonetheless established himself with the local market and as a local citizen. He provided his neighbors with spoons and other small items of his own manufacture along with other dry goods, probably including Boston-made silver along with English buckles, while at the same time making small items for other Boston silversmiths to retail. Josiah Bartlett wrote that "here he plied his trade, and in many families are still shown the silver spoons of his manufacture."[37]

The most numerous surviving form by Bartlett is indeed the spoon, particularly teaspoons displaying the "bright-cut" style of engraving favored by silversmiths for neoclassical forms (figs. 4, 5). His other domestic silver, now relatively rare, is also small scale. Among the forms with Bartlett's mark are tablespoons, creampots, salts, porringers, canns, a strainer, plated shoe buckles, and a miniature teapot (some are illustrated in fig. 6).[38] All compare in workmanship to the products of any of several contemporary Boston shops. Also, similar to the pattern seen in Minott's work, a relatively large proportion of the surviving Bartlett silver pairs his mark with those of other makers. A strainer bears Minott's mark along with Bartlett's, and Bartlett's mark occurs with Joseph Loring's on a pair of porringers, a ladle, and a cann. In all such cases, the presence of two marks raises the question of authorship: Were these smiths warranting the quality of Bartlett's silver for their customers or was he selling theirs? The porringers present a particularly interesting example, since they appear to have been Loring's personal possessions; engraved with the initials of Joseph and Mary Loring, they probably descended in the Loring family. Had Loring both made and owned them, what would account for the presence of Bartlett's mark? In this case it is logical to credit Bartlett with their manufacture.

Bartlett probably numbered among the silversmiths who provided Samuel Minott with finished goods for resale in his Boston shop, and perhaps he did the same for Loring as well. If Bartlett was providing Boston makers such as Minott with finished goods, the shoe buckles with his mark on them suggest trade in the opposite direction, since these items were likely English imports. Joseph Loring provided Zachariah Brigden with shoe buckles and chapes for buckles, almost certainly English imports, and may very well have supplied Bartlett with the same products.[39]

For the church silver commissions, which were large and relatively complicated, and perhaps for the smaller goods as well, Bartlett seems to have had the assistance of Joseph Brown. In 1785, the same year as the Weston tankard commission, Brown moved to Concord, where he lived and worked for the next ten years. He returned to Boston about the same time that Samuel Bartlett moved to Cambridge. Grindall Reynolds speculated in 1888, probably correctly, that Brown came to Concord to work with his erstwhile neighbor and schoolmate.[40] No silver bearing Brown's mark is known.

Fig. 4. Samuel Bartlett (1752–1821), tablespoon, Concord, Massachusetts, 1775–97. Silver; l. 7 ¾ in. Concord Museum (SI).

Fig. 5. Samuel Bartlett (1752–1821), three teaspoons, Concord, Massachusetts, 1775–97. Silver; l. (middle spoon) 5 in. Concord Museum (S27; 1992.14–1,2).

Fig. 6. Samuel Bartlett (1752–1821), cann, creampot, pair of salts, strainer, and porringer, Concord, Massachusetts, 1785–95. Silver; h. (cann) 5½ in. Concord Museum (1991.31; S150; 1990.28-29; S151; 1991.7).

Early in the last decade of the century, Bartlett had clearly established himself as an important Concord citizen and as a reliable tradesman. His largest silver commission and the largest grouping of his silver to survive in its original context dates from this period; it stems from the bequest made to the First Parish in Concord by Dr. John Cuming, who died in 1788 (fig. 7; see also figs. 8, 9). Cuming was a successful physician and veteran of both the French and Indian and Revolutionary Wars, and he served the town as a selectman. He also accumulated a considerable estate through inheritance, his work as a physician, money lending, and land speculation, particularly in the pasture lands of southern New Hampshire around Mason and New Ipswich. He had no children; his bequests included £25 for poor communicants in Concord as well as other money for the poor and a famous bequest to Harvard University that ultimately was used to found the medical school. "I give and bequeath," reads his will, "to the Church in the town of Concord, Fifty Pounds Sterling, to be as soon as may be laid out in silver vessels to furnish the Communion Table." The commission, probably executed in 1792, shows up in church records as a payment made early in 1793 for £66.13.4 to Samuel Bartlett, Esq., "Artificer." In 1792 Bartlett also made five cups for the church in Groton, a Middlesex County town about twelve miles west of Concord. The cups for the Cuming bequest (fig. 8) are similar to a pair of the Groton cups and nearly identical to the other three.[41]

Fig. 7. Communion silver by Samuel Bartlett (1752–1821), ca. 1792, for the First Church, Concord. From E. Alfred Jones, *The Old Silver of American Churches* (Letchworth, Eng.: Arden Press for the National Society of the Colonial Dames of America, 1913), plate LII, no. 1. Photo, courtesy Museum of Fine Arts, Boston.

Fig. 8. Samuel Bartlett (1752–1821), cup, Concord, Massachusetts, ca. 1792. Silver; h. 6 ¼ in. First Parish Church, Concord, Massachusetts. Photo, courtesy Concord Museum.

Fig. 9. Samuel Bartlett (1752–1821), pair of flagons, Concord, Massachusetts, ca. 1792. Silver; h. (each) 15 in. First Parish Church, Concord.
Photo, courtesy Concord Museum.

Formally, the flagons for the Cuming bequest are the most magnificent surviving Bartlett product (fig. 9). The workmanship is excellent and includes nice
details such as high, domed tops and large, scrolled thumb grips. Prior to the
Cuming bequest, the Concord church silver consisted of a suite of six caudle
cups made by John Coney, two of them before 1690 and four of them in 1714.
The silver Bartlett made represents something of a departure for the Concord
church; for the first time since their gathering they were using ecclesiastical
forms (flagons and footed cups) in their communion service.[42]

Samuel Bartlett's careers as a citizen and as a silversmith converge somewhat
on the First Parish silver. The decades following the end of the Revolutionary
War were a time of significant change for the Congregational churches of New
England, and Concord's First Parish was no exception. Externally, the process
of disestablishment from the state had begun, and internally Minister Ezra
Ripley (who served in Concord's pulpit from 1776 until his death in 1844) was
struggling to keep his Concord congregation together.[43] Beginning in the early
1790s, the First Parish changed the image of their meetinghouse, built in 1711.
In 1791, the town appointed a committee, which included Samuel Bartlett, for

Fig. 10. John Warner Barber (1798–1885), *Central Part of Concord, Massachusetts*, 1839. Wood engraving on paper, h. 3 ¼ in., w. 6 ½ in. From *Massachusetts Historical Collections* (Worcester, Mass.: Dorr, Howland & Co., 1839), 378. Concord Museum.

"repairing and altering the Meeting house in said Concord." Their recommendations included the addition of a steeple to the building (fig. 10).[44]

There are many factors that may account for this apparent relaxation of the earlier, Puritan strictures against the palpably ecclesiastical forms, but it can be seen at least to be coincident with other changes within the church.[45] The deacons of the church in 1792, who were responsible for awarding the John Cuming commission, were Joseph Chandler, George Minott, John White, and William Parkman. William Parkman was a tavernkeeper in the south part of Concord and later a storekeeper in the center of town. Minister Grindall Reynolds referred to Parkman in a biographical sketch as "an old Puritan." Parkman disapproved of dancing, and as a justice of the peace, he was in the habit of trying and fining sabbath breakers for Sunday travel until one of his defendants had the law overturned on appeal.[46] He remained a faithful member of Dr. Ripley's flock. John White was involved in both decisions, the communion silver and the renovations of the church building. A merchant like William Parkman, John White was a dissident with regard to church matters. He led the faction that refused to accept Unitarianism and split off from the First Parish to form the Trinity Congregational Church in 1826, the great grief of Ezra Ripley's long ministry.[47]

Samuel Bartlett had embarked on the second career that brought him into the heart of these matters — that of citizen — soon after coming to Concord. He first appears in the town records in relation to a 1781–82 school money apportionment, which may mean that he schooled some students that year.

Subsequently, he began to hold the small offices required of all but the indigent. His first appointment to office came in 1785, when he was named one of the ten surveyors of highways and one of the two clerks of the market. Over the next ten years, Bartlett held seven town offices including sealer of weights and measures and clerk of the market, and he served on twelve town committees.[48] Bartlett did not belong either to a Masonic lodge (Concord had no lodge until 1797) or to the militia, but he has received credit for reviving the Social Circle after internal dispute briefly ended its meetings. Given the composition of the Social Circle, drawn as it was from the merchants, artisans, and professional men in the center of town, membership must have provided contacts and opportunities.

In 1786, just one year after Bartlett's first appointment to town office, Concord became embroiled in the uprising known as Shays's Rebellion, and Bartlett served on committees central to the town's role in the event. Stirred by economic hardship based primarily in spiraling inflation, an angry mob formed and began roaming from town to town in central Massachusetts; the men focused on disrupting the work of the courts, particularly the Court of Common Pleas, which handed down rulings on credit disputes and bankruptcy. Bartlett joined in the efforts at mediation — town-and-county based committees that hoped to communicate the need for calmer measures to both the mobs and the courts. The documents drawn up by these committees suggest the contemporary view of the source of the trouble.

The economic problems underlying the unrest, in the words of the instructions given delegates to a state convention by the town committees — instructions Bartlett may have helped compose — were due to the war debt; a decay of public faith and credit; want of public and private virtue; neglect of economy, frugality, and industry; and a fondness for foreign luxuries, fashions, and manners. The county appealed to the General Court for relief from the burdensome expense of the Court of Common Pleas, from the exorbitant fees of lawyers, and from the high salaries of public officers. Concord's records reflect the general view that inflationary paper currency bore responsibility for much of the trouble. The stagnation of business was attributed to the want of a circulating medium, by which they meant specie or hard currency rather than paper, and to the unsettled accounts of the United States both domestically and abroad. The instructions from the town to the delegates (among them Samuel Bartlett) to the County Convention in Concord in August 1786 included the admonition to "adhere to the rules prescribed in the Constitution of this Commonwealth . . . in Peticular to oppose any Instruction in favor of paper money being emitted in this Commonwealth."

By mid-September the riots in Hampshire and Worcester counties were moving east, and a hundred armed men from Groton assembled in Concord on September 13. By taking possession of the ground in front of the courthouse they hoped to disrupt the proceedings of the Court of General Sessions of the Peace and Court of Common Pleas for Middlesex County. Bartlett and four others had drafted an appeal to surrounding towns to gather in Concord in order to calm those who had come to disrupt the courts. While the Groton men assembled in front of the courthouse, the convention from surrounding towns met at the meetinghouse, chaired by Isaac Stearns of Billerica and with Samuel Bartlett as secretary. This convention attempted unsuccessfully to act as mediators between the armed men and the justices, and the courts did not sit.[49]

Soon after his involvement in the committee that oversaw the changes to the First Parish Church, Bartlett relocated his home one last time. In his almost twenty years in Concord, he had established himself in the business and society of the town; his wife bore and raised twelve of their thirteen children in Concord with the help of apprentice housewife Hannah Ross.[50] Nonetheless, in 1794 a new opportunity opened up for Bartlett in Cambridge. That year, William Winslow resigned as Register of Deeds for Middlesex County, and after a series of votes, Bartlett was elected his successor.[51]

Bartlett had not, however, won the seat unopposed. His early education in John Tileston's school provided him with one of the most significant qualifications for the job — the ability to write — but it was a skill his competitor could claim as well if not better. Abiel Heywood, a 1781 graduate of Harvard College, was known for his excellent writing and had spent thirty-five years as town clerk in Concord.[52] By leaving the silversmith's bench and challenging a college man for office, Bartlett boldly crossed a class line. As late as 1833 the question of whether a common school education was sufficient to qualify a mechanic to hold public office still constituted a matter of debate at the Boston Apprentices' Library. Students at the University of Vermont in the 1840s argued the related question, "Ought Farmers and Mechanics Go to College?"[53] Nevertheless, in 1794 Samuel Bartlett with his public school education won the office.

Bartlett moved to Cambridge in 1795; he would spend the rest of his life there in his new profession. His first entries in the probate court records are dated 1795, after which he kept them without interruption until 1821. During those years he filled 110 volumes, each containing 550 pages — 60,000 pages all told — with the careful Boston hand he had learned from John Tileston in the 1760s. The silver he produced for the churches in Groton and Concord is the latest datable Bartlett silver; it is unlikely that he made much more silver, if any, after moving to Cambridge.

In the quarter century that Bartlett lived in Cambridge, his wife bore the last of their thirteen children and Bartlett built up a comfortable estate for his family. An inventory taken at his house in Cambridge after his death in 1821 gives some indication of the life he made there. In the parlor were a dozen chairs, a settee, a rocking chair, a pair of card tables, a four-foot mahogany table, a looking glass, a pier glass, a pair of chimney lamps, a Franklin stove and brass fire set, a pembroke table, two pictures, a fire screen, an old hearth rug, a thermometer, a floor cloth, a writing desk, and a lolling chair. The itemized list from a closet recorded four dozen plates, a brown dining set and two tea sets, three dozen glasses and six decanters, one silver soup ladle, one silver cup, a half dozen tablespoons, four salt spoons, twenty-three teaspoons, and a pair of sugar tongs. He had six chambers in all, furnished on a declining scale. The first chamber had an old carpet, a desk and bookcase, a bureau, light stand, night cabinet, and looking glass; a high-post bedstead with bed bolster, pillows, counterpane, and curtains; a half dozen mahogany chairs, a roundabout chair, an armchair, a small round table, two pictures, and an old hearth rug; a brass fire set, fire board, and cricket; a small table, two trunks, and four baskets; and another thermometer and several other small things including a silver watch.[54]

His assets also included about 150 books. These encompassed a number of law books, some general such as Blackstone's *Commentary*, some specialized such as Sullivan's *Land Titles* and a directory to probate court records; histories of America, Massachusetts, and Boston, as well as books on the French Revolution and the Court of Bonaparte; geography books and travel books; essays on comets and essays by Goldsmith; novels by Laurence Sterne; and religious volumes such as books of sermons, Unitarian treatises, and of course the Bible and *Pilgrim's Progress*. Among Bartlett's contemporaries in Concord only Caleb Bates, a ship captain and shipowner engaged in the China trade, furnished his home in a comparable fashion. Bartlett's cash flow also suggested a level of prosperity. He had $900 to lend his son in 1812 and more surplus to lend others; in all, his inventory lists thirteen different debtors who had borrowed money between 1808 and 1821. The estate reached a total value of about $3,500.[55]

The comfortable circumstances of Bartlett's life documented in his inventory attest in one regard to the wisdom of the choices he had made. On a material level, the value of his household goods exceeded that left by Joseph Loring, who continued his silversmithing career in Boston after the Revolution.[56] In addition, Bartlett raised a large family and made provision for them, including putting a son through college. Benjamin D. Bartlett "attended the common schools at Cambridge, where he was prepared for college, and entered Harvard University at the age of seventeen, in 1806." He studied medicine, moved to Concord to practice in 1814, and moved on to Bath, Maine, in 1817.[57]

It may seem, from the vantage of the present, undesirable for an individual to lay down the ability to fashion objects of beauty and utility to pick up a clerk's pen.[58] The evidence leaves little doubt, however, that he fared better as an employee of the county than he would have as a mechanic. His decision to abandon the workman's bench has numerous parallels among New England craftsmen of the period, and his success is evidence of his ability. It was not opportunity alone that determined Bartlett's course; Joseph Lasinby Brown, for example, whose life matched Bartlett's in so many ways, made little of similar circumstances. "With apparently more than usual opportunity," Grindall Reynolds wrote of Brown, "either from ill health or want of energy, or some other unknown reason, he certainly amassed nothing."[59] A testament to Bartlett's fit conduct of his life is found in the judgement of his historians; Lemuel Shattuck in 1835 called Samuel Bartlett "an influential and useful man," and Josiah Bartlett echoed that appraisal in 1858, deeming Bartlett "a quiet, unobtrusive, kind-hearted Christian gentleman, who . . . exerted his influence for the good of all around him."[60]

Notes

1. Lemuel Shattuck, *A History of the Town of Concord* (Boston: Russell, Odiorne, and Company, 1835), 142. "Useful" seems now like a pale encomium but in nineteenth-century parlance referred to a certain level of civic virtue, including an unambitious willingness to serve. Shattuck similarly referred to cabinetmaker Joseph Hosmer, after detailing his role as a patriot and his service in the Revolutionary war and in the State congress, as "eminently a useful man" (*History of Concord*, 376).

2. For a discussion of the changing economic opportunities for Boston craftsmen in the early eighteenth century, see Barbara McLean Ward, "Boston Goldsmiths, 1690–1730," in *The Craftsman in Early America*, ed. Ian M. G. Quimby (New York and London: W. W. Norton, 1984), 126–57. Patricia E. Kane writes of the later eighteenth century: "The final three decades of goldsmithing in colonial Boston were marked by another period of stagnation in the growth of the trade" (Patricia E. Kane, ed., *Colonial Massachusetts Silversmiths and Jewelers: A Biographical Dictionary* [New Haven: Yale University Art Gallery, 1998], 85). Over the same period, Boston's population remained constant, at around 15,000, and the port's activity declined relative to other New England ports and to Philadelphia (John J. McCusker and Russell R. Menard, *The Economy of British America, 1607–1789* [Chapel Hill: University of North Carolina Press, 1985], 109, 196).

3. The artisanal and political careers of Bartlett's more influential North End neighbor Paul Revere are extensively documented and analyzed. See *Paul Revere — Artisan, Businessman and Patriot* (Boston: Paul Revere Memorial Association, 1988); and David Hackett Fischer, *Paul Revere's Ride* (New York: Oxford University Press, 1994). For discussion of a humbler craftsman who bridged this period, see Alfred E. Young, "George Robert Twelves Hewes (1742–1840): A Boston Shoemaker and the Memory of the American Revolution," *William and Mary Quarterly*, 3d ser., 38, no. 4 (October 1981): 561–623.

4. Josiah Bartlett, "Samuel Bartlett," in *The Centennial of the Social Circle in Concord* (Cambridge: Riverside Press, 1882), 68; Kane, *Colonial Massachusetts Silversmiths*, 179.

5. Bartlett, "Samuel Bartlett," 69. The list of North Writing School pupils from 1761–65 does not include Samuel Bartlett's name. However, in his journal, John Tileston recorded a number of gifts from parents of pupils, like the present of £3.10s., old tenor, from John Allen's father, the half dozen oranges sent him by Captain Vernon, whose son Thomas was a student, or the two dozen pickle-limes from the same source. An entry in 1765, written in the same format as other recorded gifts from parents, reads "Mr. Bartlett sent me a Dozen of Bristol Beer," possibly referring to Roger Bartlett (D. C. Colesworthy, *John Tileston's School* [Boston: Antiquarian Book Store, 1887], 77).

6. Grindall Reynolds, "Joseph Lasinby Brown," in *Memoirs of Members of the Social Circle in Concord*, 2d ser. (Cambridge, Mass.: Riverside Press, 1888), 5. Concord minister Grindall Reynolds (1822–1894) attended Boston public schools and Harvard Divinity School.

7. Colesworthy, *John Tileston's School*, 49–67. An example of Skillin's handwriting appears in Leroy L. Thwing, "The Four Carving Skillins," *Antiques* 33, no. 6 (June 1938): 327.

8. Colesworthy, *John Tileston's School*, 45–46.

9. The Andrews account book is in the collection of the Constitution Museum, Charlestown, Mass.

10. Bartlett, "Samuel Bartlett," 69.

11. His name does not appear on the lists of Boston voluntary groups associated with the patriot cause; see Fischer, *Paul Revere's Ride*, 302–7.

12. Kane, *Colonial Massachusetts Silversmiths*, 47, 102–3, n. 6.

13. Kane, *Colonial Massachusetts Silversmiths*, 689.

14. Kane, *Colonial Massachusetts Silversmiths*, 225.

15. Reynolds, "Joseph Lasinby Brown," 6.

16. Kathryn C. Buhler, *American Silver, 1655–1825, in the Museum of Fine Arts, Boston*, 2 vols. (Boston: Museum of Fine Arts, Boston, 1972), 1:363.

17. Kane, *Colonial Massachusetts Silversmiths*, 687–89.

18. Bartlett, "Samuel Bartlett," 69; Shattuck, *History of Concord*, 142.

19. Robert A. Gross, *The Minutemen and Their World* (New York: Hill and Wang, 1976), 134.

20. William S. Robinson, "Emerson Cogswell," in *Centennial of the Social Circle in Concord* (Cambridge: Riverside Press, 1882), 99–106.

21. A tablespoon by Samuel Bartlett in the Concord Museum collection has a traditional history of having been thrown down a well by the British soldiers on April 19, 1775, thus suggesting some connection between Bartlett and Concord prior to the beginning of the Revolution, but this somewhat implausible story is not supported by any other evidence and is in fact undermined by the initials engraved on it, which do not agree with those of the principals cited in the story.

22. Kane, *Colonial Massachusetts Silversmiths*, 166–69; David F. Wood, ed., *The Concord Museum: Decorative Arts from a New England Collection* (Concord, Mass.: Concord Museum, 1996), 134–35. N. Bartlet (no relation) was long believed to have worked in Concord, but there is no evidence he ever did (Kane, *Colonial Massachusetts Silversmiths*, 177). Samuel Bartlett knew John Ball (he witnessed a deed for him in 1781), but there is no indication he knew him before coming to Concord in 1776 (Kane, *Colonial Massachusetts Silversmiths*, 167).

23. Middlesex County, Massachusetts, Probate Court, docket 429.

24. Bartlett, "Samuel Bartlett," 70.

25. Buhler, *American Silver, 1655–1825*, 1:363.

26. Robert A. Gross discusses the Social Circle and the development of Concord's elite in an unpublished paper, "The Metropolitan Connection: Elites and Community in Concord and Boston." Their great contribution to history has been the biographies of deceased members; Samuel Bartlett's was written in 1858.

27. E. Alfred Jones, *The Old Silver of American Churches* (Letchworth, Eng.: Arden Press for the National Society of Colonial Dames of America, 1913), 31, plate XIII. William Dummer, the son of goldsmith Jeremiah Dummer, had given the First Parish in 1726 a flagon made by John Edwards. The flagon is similar to one made by Edwards for the Church in Brattle Street in 1712, which is illustrated in Buhler, *American Silver, 1685–1825*, 1:101.

28. The First Parish deacons must have had confidence in Samuel Bartlett's ability to undertake the job, perhaps because of his connection to Minott's shop. Samuel Minott had supplied his share or more of communion silver in the 1760s, much of it in collaboration with another maker, either Josiah Austin or William Simpkins. Minott himself was probably not available, since he was a Tory; his arrest was ordered early in 1776 (Kane, *Colonial Massachusetts Silversmiths*, 687).

29. *A Report of the Record Commissioners of the City of Boston* (Boston: Rockwell and Churchill, 1890), iv.

30. Jones, *Old Silver of American Churches*, 124.

31. Buhler, *American Silver, 1685–1825*, 1:348–49.

32. Josiah Bartlett writes of Samuel Bartlett's failing in business, though the nature of the failure is not clear ("Samuel Bartlett," 70). Grindall Reynolds does not specifically mention a failure, but writes of Bartlett that he, "having tried his hand at shop-keeping in Concord, resumed the practice of his trade there" (Reynolds, "Joseph Lasinby Brown," 9).

33. Jones, *Old Silver of American Churches*, 486, plate CXXXVII.

34. Jones, *Old Silver of American Churches*, 486.

35. Buhler, *American Silver, 1685–1825*, 1:365–67.

36. Buhler, *American Silver, 1685–1825*, 1:404.

37. Bartlett, "Samuel Bartlett," 70.

38. Kane, *Colonial Massachusetts Silversmiths*, 180–82, lists all the known pieces by Bartlett; cf. Wood, *Concord Museum*, 136–38.

39. Kane, *Colonial Massachusetts Silversmiths*, 667.

40. In 1888, Grindall Reynolds speculated that Joseph Brown attended Tileston's school, and in fact his name appears on the list of Tileston's students from 1761–65 ("Joseph Lasinby Brown," 5; Colesworthy, *John Tileston's School*, 50).

41. Jones, *Old Silver of American Churches*, 134–35, plate LII, 1; 191–92, plate XLIX.

42. It is also possible the flagons and cups are products of a Boston shop, like Loring's, Minott's, or Revere's.

43. Robert Gross, *The Transcendentalists and Their World* (forthcoming). I would like to thank Dr.

Gross for generously sharing manuscript material and discussing the topic with me on several occasions.

44. Concord Town Records Volume D3-1 (1790–1808), 1791, Concord Free Public Library.

45. For a discussion of this topic see Barbara McLean Ward, "'In a Feasting Posture': Communion Vessels and Community Values in Seventeenth- and Eighteenth-Century New England," *Winterthur Portfolio* 23, no. 1 (Spring 1988): 1–24.

46. Grindall Reynolds, "William Parkman," in *Memoirs of Members of the Social Circle*, 22–27.

47. Daniel Shattuck, "John White," in *Centennial of the Social Circle in Concord*, 143–51.

48. Concord Town Records Volume D1-8 (1777–1790), Concord Free Public Library.

49. Shattuck, *History of Concord*, 129–42; Concord Town Records Volume D1-8 (1777–1790), 1786, Concord Free Public Library.

50. Lawrence W. Towner, "Indentures of Boston," in *Colonial Society of Massachusetts Publications* 43 (1966): 445.

51. Concord Town Records Volume D3-1 (1790–1808), 1794, Concord Free Public Library.

52. Francis R. Gourgas, "Abiel Heywood," in *Memoirs of Members of the Social Circle*, 228–33.

53. Ellen B. Ballou, *The Building of the House* (Boston: Houghton Mifflin Company, 1970), 30. Provision for future generations as a factor in decision making in colonial America is discussed in James Henretta, "Families and Farms, Mentalité in Pre-Industrial America" *William and Mary Quarterly*, 3d ser., 35, no. 1 (January 1978): 3–32.

54. Middlesex County Probate Court, docket 1360.

55. Middlesex County Probate Court, docket 1360.

56. Kane, *Colonial Massachusetts Silversmiths*, 666.

57. Josiah Bartlett, "Benjamin D. Bartlett," in *Memoirs of Members of the Social Circle*, 141–42.

58. Samuel Bartlett is certainly not alone among New England craftsmen in seeking to escape the bench for his own and his family's benefit. Cabinetmaker Joseph Hosmer, who was Bartlett's neighbor and a fellow Social Circle member, did the same when he became sheriff of Middlesex County and a state representative.

59. Reynolds, "Joseph Lasinby Brown," 14.

60. Shattuck, *History of Concord*, 142; Bartlett, "Samuel Bartlett," 73.

Index

Page numbers in *italics* refer to illustrations.

Notes on Contributors

RICHARD LYMAN BUSHMAN is Gouverneur Morris Professor of History at Columbia University, New York City.

EDWIN A. CHURCHILL is the chief curator of the Maine State Museum, Augusta.

MADELINE SIEFKE ESTILL is an independent scholar in Ithaca, New York.

JONATHAN L. FAIRBANKS is the Katharine Lane Weems Curator of American Decorative Arts and Sculpture Emeritus, Museum of Fine Arts, Boston.

JEANNINE FALINO is the Carolyn and Peter Lynch Curator of Decorative Arts and Sculpture, Art of the Americas, Museum of Fine Arts, Boston.

PATRICIA E. KANE is the curator of American decorative arts at the Yale University Art Gallery, New Haven, Connecticut.

KAREN PARSONS teaches history and material culture at the Loomis Chaffee School, Windsor, Connecticut.

JANINE E. SKERRY is the curator of ceramics and glass at Colonial Williamsburg, Williamsburg, Virginia.

JOHN W. TYLER is editor of publications for the Colonial Society of Massachusetts.

BARBARA MCLEAN WARD is the director/curator of the Moffatt-Ladd House and Garden, Portsmouth, New Hampshire, and a member of the faculty for the Museum Studies Program at Tufts University, Medford, Massachusetts.

GERALD W. R. WARD is the Katharine Lane Weems Curator of Decorative Arts and Sculpture, Art of the Americas, Museum of Fine Arts, Boston.

DAVID F. WOOD is the curator of the Concord Museum, Concord, Massachusetts.

HAEC OLIM

MEMINISSE JUVABIT

Designed by Roderick Stinehour
with Avanda Peters
of Stinehour Design
and printed at
The Stinehour Press
Bound by
Acme Bookbinding